ENERGY, ECONOMIC GROWTH, AND THE ENVIRONMENT

ENERGY, ECONOMIC GROWTH, AND THE ENVIRONMENT

Papers presented at a Forum conducted by Resources for the Future, Inc. in Washington, D.C., 20–21 April 1971

Edited by Sam H. Schurr

Published for Resources for the Future, Inc.
By The Johns Hopkins University Press, Baltimore and London

RESOURCES FOR THE FUTURE, INC.
1755 Massachusetts Avenue, N.W., Washington, D.C. 20036

Resources for the Future is a nonprofit corporation for research and education in the development, conservation, and use of natural resources and the improvement of the quality of the environment. It was established in 1952 with the cooperation of the Ford Foundation. Part of the work of Resources for the Future is carried out by its resident staff; part is supported by grants to universities and other nonprofit organizations. Unless otherwise stated, interpretations and conclusions in RFF publications are those of the authors; the organization takes responsibility for the selection of significant subjects for study, the competence of the researchers, and their freedom of inquiry.

Charts were drawn by Clare and Frank J. Ford.
The index was prepared by Helen Eisenhart.

RFF editors: Henry Jarrett, Vera W. Dodds, Nora E. Roots, Tadd Fisher.

Contents

v

Editor's Introduction

The plans for the Resources for the Future public forum at which these papers were originally presented were guided by an acute awareness of the apparent conflict that has been emerging between two societal objectives that are both of prime importance: providing energy to meet the needs of future economic growth and protecting the quality of the natural environment. The papers were intended as a basis for informed discussion of the issues by the several hundred persons who attended the meetings on April 20-21, 1971, in Washington, D.C. They are presented in this book in the belief that they may contribute useful factual background and analytical insights to the continuing debate on this vital area of public policy.

The approach to the subject is apparent in the specific topics dealt with and the sequence in which they were taken up at the forum. The bedrock issue of economic growth was addressed first because one area of public debate of ever-growing importance has been concerned with growth, as such. The rate and pattern of economic growth have been called into question by many who believe that the kind of growth that the United States has experienced is a grossly misleading proxy for an increase in the welfare of the American people. The close interrelationship among the historical growth in energy consumption, the growth and composition of the nation's total output of goods and services, the efficiency with which these goods and services have been produced and the environmental dangers resulting from the levels of energy consumption experienced make the growth question central to the energy-environment debate.

The second broad topic involves the interaction between energy and the environment. A general awareness that detrimental environmental consequences

attend practically all aspects of energy production, conversion, and use, and that, conversely, environmental restrictions may carry serious implications for energy availability and costs is insufficient for informed public discussions. What is needed is a basis for assessing, and if possible, measuring, the consequences that flow in both directions—the effects of energy use on the quality of the natural environment and the effects of environmental restrictions on energy costs and availability. The three papers on this theme were intended as efforts in the direction of quantification of these effects. They serve also to highlight the insufficiencies of existing information on the subject and the urgent need for improved data as a basis for public discussion leading to sound decisions on matters involving energy and the environment.

Even with perfect knowledge of the matrix by which energy use and environmental quality are interrelated, informed public debate would still be lacking an essential dimension, if, as seems probable, the continued growth of energy consumption by existing means and the achievement of desirable environmental objectives are basically incompatible. If worthy goals are in conflict, what means are available for their reconciliation or, at least, for avoiding confrontations that will result in the polarization of public attitudes with its attendant dangers? Two main avenues received attention: institutional devices designed to resolve conflict and technological changes that could lead to a reduction in the adverse environmental consequences that now accompany the production and consumption of energy. Inventions, both in the political and technical realm, are sure to play a part in the resolution of the energy-environment conflict, and the three papers in the final session were meant to open windows on the possibilities that they offer.

The debt that Resources for the Future owes to the distinguished authors who presented papers at the forum and who participated in the general discussion is obvious. Thanks are due also to members of the RFF staff who were important to the enterprise, particularly Joel Darmstadter whose background paper, which appears as an appendix to this book, was made available to the other authors in advance of the forum. The assistance of Tadd Fisher in preparing the volume for publication is gratefully acknowledged. At an earlier stage, the efforts of Sally Nishiyama and Helen-Marie Streich in helping with the mechanics of planning and running the public forum were vital to its success.

Sam H. Schurr
Director
Energy and Minerals Program
Resources for the Future, Inc.

I.
ON ECONOMIC GROWTH

Coming to Terms with Growth and the Environment

WALTER W. HELLER

A conference of ecologists and environmentalists, economists and technologists—convened to illuminate the complex interplay of energy, economic growth, and the environment—should open, not with a declaration of war or of conflicting faiths, but with a declaration of humility. Conceptually, to be sure, we know quite a lot about this interplay—about the *processes* of resource use and disposal that overload and degrade our natural environment; about the chilling *possibility* that untrammeled growth and uncontrolled technology could eventually destroy the ecosystem that sustains us; about the *methods*, both economic and technological, by which man can arrest or reverse the march to environmental ruin; and about the *directions of changes* in priorities and institutions needed to put these methods to work.

But empirically, we really know very little. In trying to determine the causal relationship, assess the trade-offs, and strike a reasoned cost-benefit balance between economic growth and environmental integrity, we constantly run into the unknown or unknowable (or even the unthinkable), into the unmeasured or

Walter W. Heller is Regents' Professor of Economics at the University of Minnesota and has been a member of the university faculty since 1946. He also is Chairman of the National Bureau of Economic Research. He has served as Consultant to the Executive Office of the President (1965–69); Chairman of the Council of Economic Advisers (1961–64); and Chief of Internal Finance, U.S. Military Government, Germany (1947–48). At various times he has been a consultant to the United Nations, the Committee for Economic Development, the Brookings Institution, and the U.S. Bureau of the Census. He was Chairman of the Group of Fiscal Experts, Organization for Economic Cooperation and Development, 1966–68; and Tax Adviser to King Hussein and the Royal Commission of Jordan, 1960. Dr. Heller was born in Buffalo, N.Y. in 1915. He received his B.A. degree from Oberlin College and his M.S. and Ph.D. from the University of Wisconsin.

3

unmeasurable (or even the infinite). Not surprisingly, then, much of what we "know," much of the evidence, is fragmentary and inconclusive. More disconcertingly, the findings are often contradictory. A case in point: qualified and concerned analysts of the energy-growth-environment linkage have arrived at radically different assessments of future shock to the environment—almost a "no-big-deal" versus a "crime-against-humanity" split on the projected impact of energy growth on the environment by the year 2000.

Humility should lead us, then, to acknowledge and define our collective ignorance, as well as our sparse knowledge, with two purposes in mind:

1. Identifying our joint research needs and priorities.
2. Shaping our responses to clear and present environmental dangers in light of that ignorance, i.e., pursuing courses of action that permit flexible and automatic adjustment to new information, new techniques, new values, and new resource parameters.[1]

But humility in the context of this forum calls for more. It demands a sensitivity in one discipline to the concepts, concerns, and convictions in another. Lest anyone fear, however, that I am about to submerge controversy in a sea of humility, let me reassure you. Let me set the framework for my further discussion in terms of the apparent differences in perception between ecologists and economists that have to be narrowed or reconciled if we are to make a productive joint attack on the growth-energy-environment problem. At many points, as you will see, I humbly beg to differ.

First, in starkest terms, the ecologist lays down an environmental imperative that requires an end to economic growth—or sharp curtailment of it—as the price of biological survival.[2] The economist counters with a socioeconomic imperative that requires the continuation of growth as the price of social survival. Some ecologists see the arresting of growth as a necessary, though not sufficient, condition for saving the ecosystem. The economist sees growth as a necessary, though not sufficient, condition for social progress and stability. To focus differences even more sharply, the economist tends to regard the *structure* rather than the *fact* of growth as the root of environmental evil and indeed views growth itself as one of the prerequisites to success in restoring the environment.

---

[1] After writing this, I encountered something in much the same vein in the introductory comments in the October 1970 *Bulletin of the Atomic Scientists* concerning the summary of the Massachusetts Institute of Technology Study of Critical Environmental Problems (SCEP): "One of the striking aspects of SCEP is its humility. It does not attempt to ring the doomsday bell. Rather, it stands as a sober, reflective, and careful statement of what man knows about the effects of these pollutants [carbon dioxide, sulfur dioxide, oxides of nitrogen, chlorinated hydrocarbons, other hydrocarbons, heavy metals, and oil] on the environment and what he has yet to learn. . . . It goes on to suggest what man can do about the problems he does understand and how he can acquire essential information about those he doesn't." The SCEP approach commends itself to this forum.

[2] I use the term "ecologist" here, not in the technical sense of a natural-systems biologist, but as a proxy for "noneconomist environmentalists."

Second, the ecologist counters that the Great God Growth has feet of clay. In his view, if we counted the full costs of water, air, land, visual, and noise pollution—i.e., the drawing down of our environmental capital—the advance of measured gross national product (GNP) in the past quarter-century might well turn out to be an illusion. In responding, the economist is at pains to make clear that he is anything but Mecca-nistic about GNP. He is under no illusion that GNP is an index of social welfare (or, for that matter, that it is even feasible to construct a single index of welfare, or that greater material welfare is a guarantee of greater happiness). But he does believe that a careful reading of economic and social data yields persuasive evidence that real GNP per capita *has* advanced even after adjusting for increases in population, prices, and pollution; and that a rise in social welfare has accompanied the rise in output of goods and services.

Third, in a very real sense, the most vexing difference between ecologists and economists may not be in their conflicting interpretations of the evidence but in their divergent modes of thinking. At the risk of exaggerating a bit for emphasis, I perceive the dedicated environmentalist as thinking in terms of exponential rates of deterioration, thresholds, flash points, and of absolute limits to be dealt with by absolute bans. (And I confess to a bit of absolutism myself when it comes to roads in the North Cascades, oil exploration in Puget Sound, and 70,000 tons a day of taconite tailings dumped into Lake Superior.)

In basic approach, the economist could hardly agree less. He thinks in terms of marginalism, trade-offs, and a careful cost-benefit calculus—not marginalism in the sense of minor adjustments but in the sense of balancing costs and benefits at the margin. As he sees it, the right solution in striking a balance between nature and man, between environment and growth, and between technology and ecology, would be the one that pushes depollution to, but not beyond, the point where the costs—the forgone satisfactions of a greater supply of additional goods and services—just equal the benefits—the gained satisfactions of clear air, water, landscape, and sound waves. What the economist regards as rational is to seek, not total or *maximum* cleansing of the environment—prohibitions tend to be prohibitively expensive—but an *optimum* arising out of a careful matching of the "bads" that we overcome and the "goods" that we forgo in the process.

Fourth, when economists and ecologists turn to the search for solutions, they find a considerable area of agreement. They would agree, for example, that where the trade-off is between today's "goods" and tomorrow's "bads," government has to step in to enforce a rational calculus. Indeed, many environmental problems can be handled only by government prohibitions and regulations (mercury and DDT come to mind) and by public expenditures for collective sewage disposal, land reclamation, and environmental clean-up. They can also join in identifying the essentially costless changes that serve growth and the environment simultaneously, thus requiring no trade-offs. One thinks, for example, of technological advances that have substituted coal and oil for wood as energy sources (the per capita consumption of timber in the United States was no

higher in 1968 than thirty years earlier) and have enabled us to reduce both costs and diesel engine pollution by moving oil and coal by pipeline rather than rail. And one looks forward to the day when thermal byproducts of energy production can be converted from pollutants to a productive source of space heating and cooling for industrial, commercial, and apartment buildings.

But where hard choices will have to be made, the economist wants to put as much of the load on the price system as it can efficiently carry. His main device would be to put price tags—for example, in the form of effluent fees or pollution permits or refundable materials fees—on the now largely free use of air, water, and land areas as dumping grounds for industrial and commercial wastes. The environmentalist's instinct is to recoil against this "license to pollute." By the same reasoning, perhaps, he feels way down deep that to let mineral resources and fossil fuels be managed through the pricing system constitutes a "license to exploit" the biosphere, a license that should be revoked or subjected to tighter regulation. But the economist wants to spread the net of the pricing mechanism widely to capitalize on its automaticity in digesting information and responding to it, its ability to integrate a vast range of decisions, its stimulus to natural resource conservation, and its lowering of demands on the government bureaucracy. His goal, of course, is not to collect fees or taxes but to build enough economic incentives into the market system to bring pollution to bay.

THE ROLE OF ECONOMIC GROWTH

Turning to the first of these four issues, one should keep in mind that the growth-versus-environment contest is in one sense a mismatch: economic growth is a means, an instrumental goal, while environmental quality is an end in itself, an important component of the quality of existence. In assessing the instrumental goal of growth, we need to inquire:

1. Whether it is growth itself, or its particular forms, that lead to environmental trouble (and if the latter, how production and technology can be redirected into environmentally more tolerable channels).
2. What social costs the nation would incur in giving up growth.
3. Whether the war on pollution could, as a practical matter, be pressed and won without growth.

Can Growth Be Stopped?

To discuss the benefits of growth in the context of environmental quality implies, first, that a realistic option exists—one that is conceptually and institutionally possible—of stopping growth or slowing it to a crawl and, second, that there is a trade-off, an inverse relation, between the rate of economic growth and the quality of the natural environment.

Whether no-growth is a conceivable alternative depends first on the nature of the growth process and the sources of growth.[3] Growth of the U.S. economy in the basic sense of growth of output per capita is anchored in (1) increases in the stock of human capital through investments in education, training, and experience; (2) increases in the stock of nonhuman capital through investment in equipment, machinery, and plant; and (3) improvements in the state of U.S. scientific and managerial technology through investments in research and development, better management and organization, and more efficient production techniques. The deepest wellspring—the "major permissive source," as Simon Kuznets puts it—of modern economic growth is the advance of technology in its broadest economic sense, that is, the advance of knowledge.

Considering man's unquenchable thirst for understanding through better education and his enduring quest for increased knowledge and easier ways of doing things—through research and development, large-scale experimentation, and small-scale tinkering—one can only conclude that growth in output per man-hour cannot be stopped. Conceivably, total output could be held in check by highly restrictive taxes and tight monetary policy or by direct controls. Since output per man-hour would continue to rise, stopping total growth would require a rapid decline in the average workweek—one calculation puts it at twenty-six hours by 1980—and a corresponding increase in leisure and non-market activity. (My secretary asks, "What's so bad about *that*?") This appraisal recognizes also that the labor force would continue to grow. Even with a zero population growth policy, it would take several decades to stabilize the population.[4]

[3]For an authoritative and detailed examination of this subject, see Edward F. Denison, *The Sources of Economic Growth in the United States and the Alternatives before Us* (Committee for Economic Development, 1962), and Denison's *Why Growth Rates Differ* (Brookings Institution, 1967).

[4]In *Economic Report of the President, February 1970*, p. 110, the Council of Economic Advisers reported that because of the high proportion of young people in the population, cutting the fertility rate to a level consistent with zero population growth would not stabilize the U.S. population until 2037 (at 276 million). Recent studies and new fertility data strongly suggest that, barring a reversal of present trends, the United States is already well on its way toward the desired slowdown or even stabilization of population growth. In a recent analysis, Glen G. Cain concluded that "the widely-discussed issue of the threat of the U.S. population bomb is . . . a non-issue." ("Issues in the Economics of a Population Policy for the United States," a discussion paper of the Institute for Research on Poverty, University of Wisconsin, 1971.) In the context of the RFF forum, it should also be noted that other new studies warn us that a slowdown or cessation of population growth won't solve as much of the environmental problem as we might hope. Ansley J. Coale, for example, stated, "There is no doubt that slower population growth would make it easier to improve our environment, but not much easier." ("Man and His Environment," *Science*, vol. 170, no. 3954 [October 9, 1970]). Herman B. Miller, Chief of the Population Division of the Bureau of the Census, is more specific: "Two-thirds of the rise in expenditure for goods and services would take place even if our population stopped growing tomorrow but continued to increase its income and spend its money in the same old way." (*New York Times*, February 19, 1971.)

The point of a no-growth policy would be to check and reverse the erosion of the environment. But there is nothing inherent in a no-growth economy that would change our polluting ways. So one has to posit active and costly steps to restore and protect the environment. This would require an absolute reduction in material living standards, as conventionally measured, in exchange for a more livable natural environment.

Just to sketch this picture is to raise serious questions of its social, political, and economic feasibility. Short of a believable threat of human extinction, it is hard to imagine that the public would accept the tight controls, lowered material living standards, and large income transfers required to create and manage a stationary state. Whether the necessary shifts could be accomplished without vast unemployment and economic dislocation is another question. The shift to a no-growth state of being might even throw the fragile ecology of our economic system so out of kilter as to threaten its breakdown. Having said this, let me quickly add that if the human race were to discover that it would be committing suicide unless it reduced its standard of living (at least for its affluent people), I dare say it would develop ways of managing the economic system to accommodate this necessity. Short of dire threats, however, economic growth seems destined to continue. To cope with growing contamination of the environment, the United States is thus driven to a redirection of growth and technology and to a reordering of priorities in the uses of growth.

The Growth-Ecology Trade-Off

But this still does not resolve the question of whether national policymakers should continue to stimulate growth or should seek consciously to retard it. That depends not just on the benefits of growth, which I will discuss in a moment, but on its environmental costs, on the growth-ecology trade-off. To the question of how much growth may have to be given up to protect the natural environment and maintain a habitable planet, both ecologists and economists offer a wide range of answers.

Among those who focus on global environmental problems, the spectrum runs from those who are persuaded that global pollution puts life on this planet in jeopardy to those who conclude that no one knows enough to answer the question. So far as I know, the category of ecologists (or economists, for that matter) who hold a "no-problem" view of this matter is an empty box. In its significant but selective survey, the group for the Study of Critical Environmental Problems (SCEP) offered some reassurance on the climatic effects of growth in output and fossil fuel energy but called for prompt counteraction to the ravages of toxic pesticides and heavy metals and excessive nutrient run-offs.[5]

---

[5] The SCEP group concluded, for example, that "the probability of direct climate change in this century resulting from CO_2 is small," though its long-term consequences

Among economists there are those who accept the "spaceship earth" concept of finite limits to the assimilative capacity of the environment and who believe that growth will test those limits within relevant time horizons and must therefore be retarded. But a majority of the economics profession lean toward the findings of a recent econometric probe of this problem by William Nordhaus and James Tobin.

1. With respect to appropriable resources like minerals and fossil fuels, which the market already treats as economic goods, the Nordhaus-Tobin estimates show "little reason to worry about the exhaustion of resources." As in the past, rising prices of fossil fuels are expected to provide strong incentives for conserving supplies and developing substitute materials and processes.

2. For nonappropriable resources, for "public goods" like air and water, they see the problem of abuse as much more serious. But the environmental disturbance and misdirection of resources that result from treating public natural resources as if they were free goods could, they believe, be corrected by charging for them. "The misdirection is due to a defect in the pricing system—a serious but by no means irreparable defect and one which would in any case be present in a stationary economy."

3. With respect to global ecological collapse, they appropriately conclude that "there is probably very little that economists can say."[6]

The issue is far from resolved. But the evidence to date supports the view that it is less the *fact* of growth than the *manner* of growth and the *uses* made of growth that lie at the bottom of U.S. environmental troubles. And elusive as a consensus on the basic growth-environment trade-offs may be, it appears that a

---

might be large. With respect to particulate matter, SCEP found that "the area of greatest uncertainty in connection with the effects of particles on the heat balance of the atmosphere is our current lack of knowledge of their optical properties in scattering or absorbing radiation from the sun or the earth." On thermal pollution: "Although by the year 2000 global thermal power output may be as much as six times the present level, we do not expect it to affect global climate," but they noted that the problem of "heat islands" may become severe. They concluded that atmospheric oxygen is practically constant, having stood very close to 20.946 percent since 1910, and that "calculations show that depletion of oxygen by burning all the recoverable fossil fuels in the world would reduce it only to 20.800%." They recommended drastic curtailment of the use of DDT and mercury as well as the control of nutrient discharges, together with early development of technology to reclaim and recycle nutrients in areas of high concentration. (*Man's Impact on the Global Environment: Assessment and Recommendations for Action*, Report of the Study of Critical Environmental Problems sponsored by the Massachusetts Institute of Technology [MIT Press, 1970], pp. 12, 13, 19, 75, 136, 138, 149.)

[6] William Nordhaus and James Tobin, "Is Growth Obsolete?" (paper presented at the National Bureau of Economic Research Colloquium on Economic Growth, San Francisco, December 10, 1970, to be published by the NBER in the proceedings, 1972).

consensus on the urgency of changing the forms and uses of growth is already materializing. As a consequence, the nation already is being confronted with hard choices and the need for painful institutional changes. I submit that both the hard choices and the painful changes required to restore the environment will come much easier in an atmosphere of growth than of stagnation.

Benefits of Growth

Turning to the benefits side of the picture, we are well advised, first of all, to take growth out of the one-dimensional context of the natural environment. In a broader context, the environmental claims against the bounties of growth must include shares not only for cleansing the physical environment of air, water, and land pollution and of urban congestion and sprawl, but also for:

1. Cleansing the social environment of the cancers of poverty, ignorance, malnutrition, and disease.
2. Cleansing the human environment of the degradation and blight of the urban ghetto and the rural slum.
3. Cleansing our personal environment of the fear of crime and violence.

Even with the aid of a rise of 55 percent in GNP and 34 percent in real per capita personal income from 1959 to 1969, we have found in the United States that our inroads on these problems have not kept pace with our rising expectations and aspirations. Imagine the tensions between rich and poor, between black and white, between blue-collar and white-collar workers, between old and young, if we had been forced to finance even the minimal demands of the disadvantaged out of a no-growth national income instead of a one-third increase in that income.

A specific example may be instructive. Between 1959 and 1969 the number of persons below the poverty line fell from 39 million to 24 million, from 22.4 percent to 12.2 percent of a rising population. The improvement came from a 3 percent increase in productivity per year, a drop in unemployment from 6 percent to 4 percent, shifts of the poor from lower to higher income occupations and regions, and an extraordinary growth in government cash transfers, from $26 billion in 1960 to over $50 billion in 1970. Every one of these factors was in some way the direct outgrowth of, or was associated with or facilitated by, per capita economic growth.[7] Given their huge stake in growth as a source of the wherewithal and much of the will to improve their lot, the poor could be pardoned for saying, "Damn the externalities, full speed ahead."

---

[7]Testimony of Robert J. Lampman in *Economic Opportunity Amendments of 1971*, pt. 1, Hearings before the Subcommittee on Employment, Manpower, and Poverty of the Senate Committee on Labor and Public Welfare, 92 Cong. 1 sess. (March 23, 1971).

Looking ahead, the Council of Economic Advisers projected a rise in real GNP (in 1969 dollars) of roughly $325 billion, or 35 percent, from 1970 to 1976. In the face of claims on these increases that are already staked out or clearly in the making—claims that leave only a small net "fiscal dividend" by 1976—it will be hard enough to finance the wars on poverty, discrimination, and pollution even with vigorous economic growth.[8] Consider the problem in a no-growth setting: to wrench resources away from one use to transplant them in another, to wrest incomes from one group for transfer to another, to redeploy federal revenues from current to new channels (even assuming that we could pry loose a substantial part of the $70 billion devoted annually to military expenditures)—and to do all this on a sufficient scale to meet the urgent social problems that face us—might well involve us in unbearable social and political tensions.[9] In this context, one rightly views growth as a necessary condition for social advance, for improving the quality of the *total* environment.

Apart from the tangible bounties that growth can bestow, we should keep in mind some of its intangible dividends. Change, innovation, and risk thrive in an atmosphere of growth. It fosters a social mobility and opens up options that no stationary state can provide. This is not to deny that a no-growth economy, with its large rations of leisure, would appeal to those in the upcoming generation who lay less store by the work ethic and material goods than their forebears. But if they associate this with tranquility—in the face of the intensified struggle for shares of a fixed income on the part of their more numerous and more competitive contemporaries—I believe they are mistaken.

Let me return now to the context of the natural environment, to the growing consensus that we have to stop and reverse the ugly and destructive waste

[8]For the underlying numbers on GNP increases and the claims against them, see the *Economic Report of the President, February 1971*, p. 95. See also chap. 7 of Charles L. Schultze and others, *Setting National Priorities: The 1972 Budget* (Brookings Institution, 1971). Schultze and his colleagues projected a rise in real GNP (1970 dollars) of $353 billion. In current dollars (i.e., allowing for inflation), they foresee a rise from $977 billion in 1970 to $1,585 billion in 1976, a rise of $608 billion. Even with the resulting automatic growth of federal revenues from a full-employment-equivalent level of some $230 billion in fiscal 1972 to $312 billion in fiscal 1976, the "built-in" growth of federal expenditures would leave only a $17 billion net "fiscal dividend" in 1976 to utilize for new programs or expansion of existing programs (pp. 321–33).

[9]For example, in Robert S. Benson and Harold Wolman, eds., *Counterbudget: A Blueprint for Changing National Priorities, 1971–1976* (Praeger, 1971), the National Urban Coalition converted the easy rhetoric of "reordering priorities" into a chart of specific needs. Putting most of its emphasis on "human development programs," the coalition called for a $52 billion rise in federal expenditures on health care in the next five years, $29 billion for income support, $11 billion for education, and $16 billion for aid to state and local governments. Even with its judgment that $24 billion could be cut from military spending over the next five years, this adds up to increased federal spending of nearly $100 billion—apart from the outlays on the battle against pollution!

disposal practices of our modern society. To accomplish this, the taxpaper must foot huge bills to overcome past neglect as well as to finance future collective waste treatment and preserve open space and wilderness. Producers and consumers will have to bear the brunt of outright bans on ecologically dangerous materials and to pay rent for the use of the environment's waste assimilation services that they have been enjoying largely free of charge.

A modest estimate of the demands on the federal budget for an adequate environmental program would raise the present outlay of $5 billion a year to about $15 billion, an increase of some $50 billion over the next five years. Without growth, and given the limits to the congressional will to tax, how could we hope to raise the required revenues?

Or take the case of agricultural and industrial pollution. Imagine the resistance of producers to the internalizing of external costs in a society without expansion and the profit opportunities that go with it. How could consumers be induced to accept the necessary price increases in a world of fixed incomes? Again, if the only alternative, if the ultimate cost, were biological self-destruction, the answers would be different. But in the absence of that fate, or because of its extreme remoteness, growth enters as a vital social lubricant and is the best bet for getting people to give up private "goods" to overcome public "bads."

GNP AND SOCIAL WELFARE

To some of what I just said, the ecologist may reply, "Not so fast, not so fast—when you count all the costs, especially when you subtract the costs of chewing up the environment, you'll find that what you call growth in output and income since World War II is really a case of living off our environmental capital." Or he may say, "The composition of production has changed in such a way that we are no better off than twenty-five years ago." True, he may say these things, but the evidence does not bear him out. But if he adds, "GNP is a mighty sorry index of welfare; you'll have to show me something better than that in rebuttal," the economist says, "Right on!"

Granting that rising GNP is a poor index of human betterment is not to deny that one is generally associated with the other. It should require no lengthy demonstration to show that, while a significant part of GNP is illusory in a welfare sense,[10] wide differences and large advances in per capita GNP are asso-

[10]In the Godkin Lectures, five years ago, I put this point as follows: "If, as *byproducts* in our quest for growth, we destroy the purity of our air and water, generate ugliness and social disorder, displace workers and their skills, gobble up our natural resources, and chew up the amenities in and around our cities, the repair of that damage should have first call on the proceeds of growth. If the damage is essentially a private cost forced on society, as in the case of industrial effluents and smoke discharge, it should be forced back on those private units. But much of the problem and the cost can be met only by government. (If we

ciated with significant differences and advances in well-being. In a careful appraisal of the growth-welfare correlation, Robert Lampman found that a 26 percent gain in real GNP per capita from 1947 to 1962 brought with it a 26 percent gain in per capita private consumption, a distinct improvement in income security, and a significant reduction in poverty. He concluded: "All things considered, the pattern of growth in the United States in the post-war years yielded benefits to individuals far in excess of the costs it required of them. To that extent, our material progress has had humane content.[11]

A question that has more recently intrigued students of GNP is whether it is possible within the framework of a national accounts system to develop a better approximation of welfare. (Noneconomists may be pleased to hear that four observers who have written on this problem in the past four months have come up with four different positions on the subject.)

Economists labor under no illusion that GNP is a satisfactory measure of welfare or that it can be turned into one. They would agree with J. Petit-Senn that "not what we have, but what we enjoy, constitutes our abundance." What makes people think that GNP has become the economist's Holy Grail is the indispensable role it plays in measuring the economy's output potential and its performance in using that potential. It is highly useful and constantly used by economists (1) as a guide to fiscal and monetary policy for management of aggregate demand, and (2) as a measure of the availability of output to meet changing national priorities.

For these purposes, the emphasis of the national accounts must be primarily on market, and secondarily on governmental, demand and output since these are central to national stabilization policies and priority-setting.[12] And for these purposes, the national income and product accounts—with a bit of tinkering here and there—are generally respected and defended by economists.

But when the scene of battle moves to measurement of *social* performance, there is a sharp division of opinion over the possibility and advisability of modifying the GNP—or more properly, the net national product (NNP)—accounts to make them more useful in gauging social performance. Arthur Okun flatly rejected any such thought in his communication to the Office of Business Eco-

could isolate that part of it which is a direct cost or byproduct of growth . . . we should probably make a subtraction each year from our total output, an adjustment of our GNP figures, to take account of it.)" Walter Heller, *New Dimensions of Political Economy* (Harvard University Press, 1966), p. 111.

[11] Robert J. Lampman, "Recent U.S. Economic Growth and the Gain in Human Welfare," in Walter W. Heller, ed., *Perspectives on Economic Growth* (Random House, 1968), pp. 143–62.

[12] To be precise, net national product is the appropriate measure for gauging the quantity of output available to meet our needs—provided, of course, that the depreciation that represents the differences between GNP and NNP is calculated in a rational and consistent way.

nomics: "I urge that you not try to 'fix it'—to convert GNP into a purported measure of social welfare. . . . Resist at all costs, because . . . nobody can do that job." Edward Denison, writing in a somewhat similar vein, noted that to convert NNP into a welfare measure would require such unattainable measures as an index of real, rather than money, costs incurred in production; a measure of changes in needs that U.S. output must satisfy; measures of the quality of both the human and the physical environment; and a measure of the "goodness" of the size-distribution of income.[13]

Denison also weighed the possibility of getting a better measure of net gains from production by subtracting from the value of greater output the value of the environmental damage caused by producing it. But he concluded (1) that the impossibility of measuring the "goodness" of the environment and the portion of its deterioration traceable to production rules out such an attempt; and (2) that to deduct, as a proxy for that deterioration, outlays made to improve the environment is totally undesirable, since it would mean that the more resources we diverted from other uses to improve the environment, the more we would reduce measured NNP.

But F. Thomas Juster and the Nordhaus-Tobin team take quite a different tack. Juster proposed a comprehensive alternative framework for the national accounts, with emphasis on "extension and refinement of the existing accounts to make them more useful for the analysis of trends in social and economic welfare, while at the same time insuring that a market subsector is retained to facilitate cyclical analysis."[14]

Going beyond the Juster proposals, Nordhaus and Tobin have boldly undertaken to appraise the rough quantitative significance of some of the deficiencies of GNP and, more particularly, of NNP as measures of economic welfare. The flavor of their pioneering probe is suggested by some of the adjustments they make in the NNP numbers (all in 1958 prices):

1. According to their estimates, putting dollar tags on the value of leisure and do-it-yourself work adds a huge $925 billion to the recorded NNP of

[13] See the comments contributed by Arthur M. Okun to the 50th Anniversary Edition of the Department of Commerce *Survey of Current Business*, January 1972, preprinted in *Brookings Bulletin*, vol. 8, no. 3 (Summer 1971); and Edward F. Denison, "Welfare Measurement and the GNP," *Survey of Current Business*, January 1971.

[14] His ambitious proposals are developed and explained in detail in "On the Measurement of Economic and Social Performance," *51st Annual Report of the National Bureau of Economic Research* (New York: September 1971), pp. 43–52. See also F. Thomas Juster, "A Framework for the Measurement of Economic and Social Performance"; Wassily Leontief, "National Income, Economic Structure, and Environmental Externalities"; and Orris C. Herfindahl and Allen V. Kneese, "Measuring Social and Economic Change" (papers delivered at the National Bureau of Economic Research Conference on Measurement of Economic and Social Performance, Princeton University, November 4–6, 1971, mimeo.).

$560 billion in 1965 (as against an add-on, for example, of $627 billion to the NNP of $292 billion in 1947).

2. They also add in almost $80 billion to represent the stream of services of private and public capital goods (against $37 billion in 1947).

3. Their subtractions from NNP include (a) $95 billion in 1965 (and $32 billion in 1947) representing "regrettables" like police services and national defense, that is, intermediate expenditures that are really costs, not enjoyments, of an advanced industrial society; (b) $91 billion of capital consumption allowances in 1965 (versus $51 billion in 1946) and $101 billion for the capital-widening requirements of growth in 1965 (and a negative $5 billion in 1947); and (c) an allowance of $31 billion in 1965 (as against $11 billion in 1947) for "disamenities" or "negative externalities" representing deterioration of the environment.

Having made these heroic adjustments, they concluded:

> There is no evidence to support the claim that welfare has grown less rapidly than NNP. Rather, NNP seems to underestimate the gain in welfare, chiefly because of its omission of leisure from consumption. Subject to the limitations of the estimates, we conclude that the economic welfare of the average American has been growing at a rate that doubles every 30 years.[15]

All observers agree that no amount of adjustment of the national accounts can capture the myriad values and subtleties that are required to measure social welfare. Indeed, no single index of social welfare can be calculated, because we have nothing like the pricing system to solve the impossible problem of attaching weights to the various components, be they pollution, crime, health, discrimination, or whatever. But to conclude that no *single* index can be constructed is not to undermine or discourage the efforts to develop a set of social indicators, not anchored in the GNP accounts, that will permit us to make better judgments on advances as well as failures in social performance.

DIVERGENT MODES OF THOUGHT

Part of the difficulty in achieving a meeting of the minds between economists and ecologists is that the economist tends to seek optimality by selecting the right procedures—for example, forcing the producer to bear the cost and the consumer to pay the price for waste-disposal access to the environment, thereby creating incentives to abate pollution—rather than prescribing the right outcome, namely, ending or drastically curtailing pollution. He is dedicated to that outcome but prefers to have the market system, rather than a government regulator, do as much of the work for him as possible. Whether a meeting of minds will

[15] Nordhaus and Tobin, "Is Growth Obsolete?"

evolve remains to be seen. Moderates in both camps are moving toward a middle ground, but given existing attitudes, I doubt that full accommodation will be easy.

For his part, the ecologist will have to overcome his natural impatience with concepts of fine balancing of costs and benefits, an impatience that probably grows out of his feelings that cost-benefit analyses lack ethical content and moral inputs and that the more or less infinite benefits of environmental preservation make refined cost calculations more or less irrelevant. And he rightly stresses the nonlinearity of the cost curves of waste disposal as output rises: no-cost or low-cost in the early stages when discharges stay well within the absorptive capacity of the environment, then rising fairly sharply when accumulation and concentration begin to exceed that capacity, and exponentially when they saturate it.

For his part, the economist will have to break out of the web of marginal cost-benefit balance in cases where the relevant costs and benefits can't be captured in that web.[16] Irreparable damage—whether to human health by arsenic and lead poisoning, or to bald eagles by DDT, or to the Alaskan tundra by hot oil, or to the beauty of a canyon by a hydroelectric dam—cannot be handled by the fine tuning of marginalism. Nor is this approach applicable where the benefits are short-run and calculable while costs are long-run and incalculable. So the economist should beware of forcing onto the pricing mechanism jobs that it will almost surely do badly. But he rightly insists that, despite these limitations, the cost-benefit principle is applicable to a very broad range of pollution problems where measurements or reasonable approximations *are* possible.

The question of nonlinearity is a tougher one, in application if not in concept. Few would dispute that there is an initial zone where discharges are not pollutants, because they are well within the regenerative ability of land and water ecosystems that eliminate waste by cycling it through plants and animals and decomposers. Nor is it difficult to agree that, at the opposite end, costs can

---

[16] The combination of high-intensity feed-grain farming with a high concentration of feedlots for livestock near urban centers may be a case in point. The feed-grain farmer—using chemical fertilizers, pesticides, and herbicides that increase both feed-grain yields and the nutrient runoff that ruins surrounding waters—has been able to bring feed-grain prices down to a level that makes the concentrated feedlots profitable. They, in turn, discharge staggering quantities of animal wastes into urban sewage systems or onto the surrounding land and water. If some way is found of forcing the cost of this discharge back onto these "animal factories," the marginalist's reaction may be to invest in expensive equipment to recycle the wastes back to the land as substitutes for the present chemical fertilizers. But it is quite possible that the high-technology approach that is likely to result from marginal cost-marginal benefit thinking will be the more costly one. The optimal solution may be to decentralize, to go back to the more primitive recycling process of putting the cattle back on grazing land where they can turn forage into waste available as substitutes for chemical fertilizers. (On the other hand, if some agricultural economists are right in their belief that the animal factories are "economic" only because they do not have to absorb the costs of waste disposal, even the marginal approach may do the trick.)

rise exponentially and ecocycles can be destroyed by overloading waters with nutrients, the atmosphere with noxious gases and particulate matter, and so on.

It is in the middle zone that things get sticky. An economist tends to believe that the zone of gradual and roughly linear rise in environmental damage is broad and that it widens—that the cost curve moves to the right—especially when the impetus of full-cost pricing moves science and technology to devise and put in place new techniques of waste disposal and recycling. Where the zone of tolerance or reasonable cost is very limited, as in the case of mercury, marginalism obviously won't do. The total or near-total ban is the only remedy. Whether mercury is a proxy for just a handful of cases or the forerunner of an exponential rise in contamination of the earth, land surface, air mass, and waterways, will determine in good part our relative reliance on total-ban versus marginal-adjustment approaches to environmental action.

The economist is inclined to doubt that such cases will multiply rapidly. Past demonstrations of the capacity of our economy, our technology, and our institutions to adapt and adjust to changing circumstances and shocks are impressive. We are still in the early stages of identifying, quantifying, and reacting to the multiple threats to our environment. It may be that we are too quick in accepting the concept of finite limits and closing physical frontiers implicit in the concept of spaceship earth (dramatized by Kenneth Boulding).[17] At least two previous episodes in U.S. history come to mind to suggest that we may yet escape (or push into the remote future) the ultimate biophysical limits, may yet be able to turn the ecological dials back from the "self-destruct" position without stopping growth in output, energy, technology, and living standards.

The first was the closing of America's geographical frontiers, which allegedly robbed this country of much of its mobility and dynamism. But other frontiers—scientific, technological, economic—soon opened up new vistas and opportunities, new frontiers that far surpassed any physical frontiers.

The second episode is much more recent. We do not need to stretch our memories very far to recall the great furor some twenty or twenty-five years ago about "running out of resources," especially energy, mineral, and other natural resources. We were being told by presidential commissions that we were about to exhaust our supplies of mineral resources and the productive potential of our agricultural land. But as we now know, intensive scientific research and technological development—responding partly to the alarums that were sounded but mostly to the signals sent out by the pricing system—resulted in the upgrading of old resources, the discovery of new ones, the development of substitutes, and the application of more efficient ways of utilizing available resources and adjusting to changes in relative availabilities.

[17]Kenneth Boulding, "The Economics of the Coming Spaceship Earth," in Henry Jarrett, ed., *Environmental Quality in a Growing Economy* (Johns Hopkins Press for Resources for the Future, 1966).

Today, the problem is less one of limited resource availability and more one of growing threats to environmental quality and the metabolism of the biosphere. Concentrations of toxic and nondegradable wastes pose a mounting problem. But at this relatively early stage of our environmental experience and awareness, it seems premature to conclude that mounting problems are insurmountable. As our new knowledge and concern are translated into changes in our institutional arrangements and cost-price structure, strong incentives will be generated to redirect production and technology into less destructive channels.

Letting imagination soar a bit, one can conceive of scientific and technological discoveries enabling us to exploit solar energy, at least for purposes of photosynthesis, and perhaps even to build a proxy for the sun in the form of fusion power sometime in the next half century or so. Such developments might well provide the key to unlock the doors that the ecologist tells us are closing all around us. One gallon of water would give us the energy we now get from seven barrels of crude oil. Electricity would be penny cheap but no longer pound foolish. The recycling of wastes would be routine. The reconstituting of natural resources would come into the realm of the possible. I do not assert that this will happen, only that it may.

Coming back to our own era and moving from the global to the local impact of our environmental debauchery, one can also base some hope on the benign examples of what determination plus the application of fairly modest resources can do in reclaiming resources that once seemed beyond redemption. Striking examples are provided by the reclaiming of San Diego Bay, Lake Washington in Seattle, and the Thames near London (where dolphins again frolic). These examples are hardly decisive, but they offer a significant demonstration, in microcosm, that the process of ecological destruction can be halted and reversed once the volume of pollutants is reduced below the level of natural regeneration or dispersal. One should add that no rounded judgment is possible without taking into account whether pollution was curbed by recycling and changing waste into harmless forms or simply by redirecting the flows and discharging wastes into some other harmful form. The economist who lives by cost-benefit analysis must occasionally die by it.

Implicit in the foregoing discussion is that much of the difference between economists and ecologists on the speed and certainty of our descent into environmental hell rests in their divergent views on the role of technology. The ecologist sees pollution-intensive technology at the core of a mindless pursuit of economic growth. The economist points to the frequency of an inverse relationship between technological advance and pollution, as in materials-conserving and waste-recycling technology. And by institutional changes—such as creating property rights in, and charging for the use of, our collectively owned air, water, and landscape—he believes that technology will become ever more mindful of the environment.

What is important to note here is that the dichotomy runs much deeper than a disagreement on facts. For even if we accept Barry Commoner's verdict that the technology accompanying U.S. growth is the Frankenstein that is destroying our environment, there remains the critical operational question: Is this technology autonomous and out of control, an inevitable concomitant of growth?[18] Or does progress in science and technology respond to social and economic forces? If so, can it be bent to our will?

An affirmative answer to the last two questions is gaining support in recent investigations. The direction of technical changes in the private sector as well as the emphasis of research in the public sector are shown to respond to differences in the relative prices of resource endowments and other factors of production.[19] For decades the pattern of technical change has been biased in the direction of excessive production of residuals by zero-pricing or underpricing the use of the environment into which they are dumped. It follows that assessing the appropriate charges for waste disposal (and putting the right prices on resource amenities) will not only improve the pattern of production to the benefit of the environment but will also stimulate pollution-abating technology. Indeed, as relative prices are changed to reflect real economic and social costs, the longer-run impact on the direction of technological effort may be considerably more important than the short-run resource allocation effects.[20]

As the biases in the cost and pricing system that make pollution profitable are diminished or eliminated, we may well find more technical complementarities than our limited experience leads us to think. Making pollution abatement mandatory by regulation or making continued pollution painfully costly by waste disposal charges will create a sharp spur to pollution-abatement technology. The relevant technology will no longer be treated on a corrective, band-aid, and after-thought basis, an approach that is likely to be inefficient and costly. Instead, it will be done on a preventive, built-in, and advanced-planning basis. Heartening examples of making virtue out of necessity in the form of profitable recycling already abound. And as economic growth leads to the re-

[18] One economist who answers in the affirmative is E. J. Mishan, who says: "As a collective enterprise, science has no more social conscience than the problem-solving computers it employs. Indeed, like some ponderous multi-purpose robot that is powered by its own insatiable curiosity, science lurches onward. . . . " (*Technology and Growth: The Price We Pay* [Praeger, 1970], p. 129).

[19] See, for example, Jacob Schmookler, *Invention and Economic Growth* (Harvard University Press, 1966), a searching study of inventive activity in which Schmookler concluded that the greater part of technical change in the United States has been a response to technical problems or opportunities perceived in economic terms.

[20] I am indebted to my colleague, Vernon W. Ruttan, for this line of thought. He develops and documents his thesis at length in "Technology and the Environment," the Presidential Address delivered before the American Agricultural Economics Association, August 16, 1971, to be published in a forthcoming issue of the *American Journal of Agricultural Economics*.

placement of old processes, equipment, and plants with new ones, it will hasten the change to cleaner and healthier methods of production.

This brings me back to an earlier theme. In the past, the market mechanism (with some assistance from government inducements, incentives, and research and development investments) altered the technical coefficients for traditional natural resources like coal, iron, and oil in response to the signals sent out by the pricing mechanism. Those resources were conserved, while the ones that were largely left out of the pricing mechanism suffered. If prices are put on them now by internalizing the external costs of air, water, quiet, and landscape, it seems reasonable to assume that the market mechanism will cause new shifts in resource use and technology leading us to conserve *these* resources and let Spaceship Earth cruise on a good deal longer.

THE SEARCH FOR SOLUTIONS

Although ecologists and economists are not likely to agree on precisely how far the battle against pollution should be pushed—on how many social and material goods should be given up to overcome environmental "bads"—one perceives some early signs of convergence on the policy approaches and instruments that should be used in that battle. When Barry Commoner traces much of our trouble to the fact that "pollution pays" (or at least that pollution-intensive technology pays) and seven environmental organizations form the Coalition to Tax Pollution, economists and environmentalists are beginning to get on the same policy wave-length.[21]

A greater measure of agreement on the direction of environmental policy action need not and indeed does not imply agreement on ultimate goals, i.e., what level of pollution is tolerable. First, the ecologist is more conscious of, and gives more credence and weight to, pollution's hazards to health, life, and ecosystems. Second, the working environmentalist places a very high value on the aesthetics and amenities of the environment—he is willing to pay a higher price and a higher percentage of his income for a high-quality environment than is the population as a whole.

However strongly the economist may be committed personally to the environmental cause, he tends, first, to put relatively more weight on dangers arising from the social environment. He puts more emphasis on the trade-offs between environmental and social progress, perhaps regarding environmental deterioration as more reversible than social deterioration. Second, as an economist, he feels more bound by society's, than by his own, value judgment as to the desirable level of environmental quality, i.e., the permissible level of pollution.

[21] In July 1971, the Coalition to Tax Pollution was formed by Environmental Action, Inc., The Federation of American Scientists, Friends of the Earth, Metropolitan Washington Coalition for Clean Air, the Sierra Club, The Wilderness Society, and Zero Population Growth. Their first target is the enactment of an effective tax on sulfur oxide emissions.

A third kind of difference in objectives or focus arises out of the conflicting roles of economic growth as both a generator of pollution and a source of weapons to fight it. The ecologist tends to concentrate on the scarcity of physical and natural resources in the earth's skin and its limited supply of fossil fuels, metals, clean air, and water. The economist focuses on the scarcity of total resources, of the total supply of goods and services available in consumable form. Not surprisingly, then, the ecologist sees growth and the technology underlying it mainly as a part of the *problem*. The economist, viewing the huge costs and difficulties of redirecting resources to rescue the environment, regards the bounties of growth as a vital part of the *solution*.

I cannot attempt here anything like a thorough appraisal of the various components of a program to overcome pollution. But neither can I resist making some selected observations on the approaches the nation needs to take. For if we are indeed to make economic growth our environmental servant, not our master, we have to translate general principles and values into operational specifics without delay.

Government Expenditures

There is little disagreement among students of the environmental problem, of whatever discipline, that government has a vital direct role to play in (1) providing public sewage disposal facilities; (2) cleaning up the no-man's land of past pollution whose costs can no longer be internalized; (3) preserving park, forest, and wilderness space; (4) relieving congestion; (5) developing pollution-monitoring devices; and (6) financing research in the techniques of pollution abatement and environmental protection.

Research in specific anti-pollution techniques and, more broadly, in pollution-averting technology is a particularly appropriate object of public sector support. Such research tends to be very costly. Since its benefits are largely external—much of the gain spills over to the benefit of other productive units and to future generations—private units are often unwilling or unable to incur its costs. In the energy field, the development of controlled thermonuclear fusion and of new methods to exploit solar energy fit into this category. Only government has the resources and the perspective to determine whether and how we can harness such energy sources.

In programming its own resource-using expenditures, government should also set an example by plugging in the implicit environmental costs. Military and space efforts, for example, are voracious consumers of energy and materials. This heavy draught on our physical environment should be given full weight in the cost-benefit calculations. We would find, I believe, that redirecting technical efforts and resources away from military and related space enterprises would have a high environmental payoff.

One should also underscore the need for sophisticated monitoring devices, both to measure waste and heat discharges and to measure the damage they do.

Emissions of noxious gases, particulate matter, heat, and other effluents must be measured as a basis for administering either regulations or effluent charges. Yet the *amount* of any given discharge into the air, for example, tells us little about its actual *cost*. Even if we can measure the total load of gas and smog carried by the ambient air in a region, this does not tell us what costs are inflicted on things and people. To the extent possible, then, costs of corrosion of metal surfaces, deteriorated property values, damage to painted surfaces, impairment of health, and so on must be measured.

Even then, we have only begun to measure the costs of pollution and the benefits we will enjoy from curtailing it. What about cleaning and air conditioning bills, smarting eyes, loss of wildlife and recreational space, not to mention the subtle inroads on ecocycles? Even if we could measure these, we can at best only approximate, perhaps by polling techniques, the subjective values attached to clean water and air and quiet surroundings.

Balanced against the benefits must be an appraisal of the costs of installing anti-pollution machinery and processes or altering production techniques to overcome pollution. On these, we are getting more quantitative data and experience every day as we intensify anti-pollution efforts. In devising specific programs to restore the environment, we must be keenly aware of (1) the need for improved cost and benefit information, and (2) the importance of designing programs that take realistic account of our limited knowledge of actual costs and benefits.

Regulations and Charges

As already mentioned, direct regulation and prohibition are instruments for environmental protection that must be used where intolerable dangers to health and life are involved or where irreversible and infinite damage to the environment is threatened. Also, a combination of regulations and user charges[22] may be the best way to go about certain pollution control problems, especially during a transitional period. For example, an absolute limit on emissions might be established by regulation to prevent really dangerous abuses of air or water at the same time that a uniform tax per unit of discharge is imposed as the main anti-pollution instrument. By and large, however, economists strongly prefer taxes and user charges to direct regulation on at least four grounds.

First, the regulatory power is often slow and cumbersome. By the time regulations are designed and applied, and then enforced through prolonged and costly court proceedings, much of the battle is lost.

Second, under the unrelenting pressure of producing units to internalize benefits and externalize costs, regulators bend more readily than tax collectors.

[22] Robert M. Solow has been particularly instructive on the subject of regulations and subsidies versus taxes in "The Economists' Approach to Pollution," his vice-presidential

Since the large and powerful can exercise far greater pressure than the small and weak, the impersonal and objective approach implicit in a tax per unit of discharge provides a fairer competitive environment. And for both large and small producers, it is a far healthier incentive atmosphere when energies are devoted, not to out-maneuvering the regulators, but to reducing pollution taxes by reducing pollution.

Third, fees or taxes accomplish any desired level of pollution abatement more cheaply than regulation. Reduce sulfur oxide pollution by a ban on emissions in excess of a certain amount, and all emitters have to conform to the regulation, even though the cost per unit of reduction will be far higher for some producers than for others. But put a tax on the emissions—a proportional or progressive penalty on discharges of sulfur oxide—and the factories that use processes conducive to low-cost cutbacks of pollution will reduce emissions more than those for whom it is a high-cost undertaking. Any prescribed quality of ambient air can be achieved at a lower cost through the proportional charge approach than through an arbitrary limit. And the incentive to depollute does not stop at some arbitrary cutoff point—the more pollution is cut, the lower the tax.

Fourth, by decentralizing some of the decision making and leaving discretion in the hands of the individual polluter to decide how far to go and what methods to use in minimizing his payments to the government, the tax or charge approach does not require as much centralized information. Also, the process of collecting the tax or charge will itself yield additional information—and the level of the tax or charge can be fairly readily adjusted in the light of the new information. In a field beset by large factual gaps and uncertainties, this economizing of information is no small advantage.

The tax or charge is also far superior to the subsidy approach, which has two damning flaws. First, in its usual form—fast tax write-offs or direct subsidies for installation of pollution control equipment—it is a very costly way to stop pollution. In effect, it prescribes a particular way of doing the job, i.e., through waste treatment facilities, when there might be considerably cheaper ways of doing it, e.g., modifying production techniques, substituting less toxic for more toxic materials, recycling wastes, relocating production, and so on. Moreover, since the alternative is free use of the air and water for waste disposal, the subsidy may have to cover the full cost of abatement before the producer will accept it. The second flaw is found in the very nature of the subsidy. The subsidy does not internalize the costs, but simply shifts them from one segment of the public—the users of foul air and water—to another segment, the general taxpayer.

address to Section K of the American Association for the Advancement of Science, at the annual meeting in Chicago, December 1970. An adaptation of the address was published in *Science*, August 6, 1971.

What kind of a system of taxes or user charges would be most effective? Fortunately, this question is engaging the energies and ingenuity of many economists today. Effluent charges, taxes, auctioning of pollution rights, materials-use fees—these are a few of the entries. The effluent fee, charge, or tax would simply charge so-and-so-much per unit of pollutant. The Coalition to Tax Pollution, for example, would tax sulfur emissions at 20 cents a pound by 1975, arriving at this level via four annual 5-cent steps.[23]

Another approach is to determine the permissible level of air or water pollution, issue certificates to pollute in this amount, and auction them off to the highest bidders. Competitive bidding for the certificates would raise the cost of pollution so high as to create a strong incentive to depollute.[24]

An intriguing proposal to impose a comprehensive materials-use fee has recently been made by Edwin Mills. He would charge a materials-use fee to the original producer or importer of specified materials removed from the environment. The level of the fee would be set high enough to cover the social cost of the most harmful way in which the material would normally be discharged into the environment. To the degree that the actual waste disposal was less harmful than the maximum, the fee would be refunded. Mills's proposal, though hardly operational in its present form, has the advantage of focusing on the total problem of materials disposal and making a comprehensive correction for the divergence between social costs and private costs.[25]

As a guide to thinking, the Mills proposal is particularly helpful because it underscores the fact that not just the level of output but the form of our technology and the nature of our disposal processes are important in determining the environmental impact of economic growth. True, as Allen Kneese notes, the physical law of the conservation of mass means that we don't really consume things in any ultimate sense. We simply change them from usables to residuals.[26] But even a growing mass of residuals can leave less and less pollution in its wake if we succeed in changing the form, the degree of recycling, the location, and the durability of those residuals in a constructive way. Under present institutional arrangements, the price system is rigged against constructive

[23] In its release on the subject (Washington, D.C., July 22, 1971) the Coalition said: "We believe that pollution taxes are a much-needed tactic to combat pollution. It will be necessary to make the economic self-interest of polluters consistent with the goal of a clean environment if we are to achieve this objective. Pollution taxes, unique among pollution control strategies, accomplish this."

[24] See J. H. Dales, *Pollution, Property, and Prices* (University of Toronto Press, 1968); and the discussion in *Economic Report of the President, February 1971*, pp. 114–22.

[25] Edwin S. Mills, "User Fees and the Quality of the Environment," an essay to be published in a volume honoring Richard A. Musgrave, which will be edited by Warren Smith, Department of Economics, University of Michigan.

[26] Allen V. Kneese, "Environmental Pollution: Economics and Policy," in American Economic Association, *Papers and Proceedings* (May 1971).

disposal. Once we redress the balance, it will be financially advantageous to minimize the burden of residuals on the environment.[27]

Before leaving the subject of charges and taxes, I should record several caveats and reminders. Even after we have devised workable techniques of internalizing the external costs of pollution, we still have to resolve a very difficult problem of choice. It is one in which the obvious and reasonably measurable costs of overcoming pollution are set against benefits that are in large part intangible and unmeasurable. The social cost of upgrading the quality of air or water is, if not yet known, at least knowable. The social benefit of an additional unit of water or air quality is in large part in the realm of values and hence unknowable. That does not, however, make the choice in any sense unique. Like many other social choices, it has to be made through the political process. Science can develop solutions and inform the political process, but it cannot dictate the answers.

Further, in setting up any system of charges, we should not overlook the potential for large-scale economies through collective methods of industrial waste disposal and recycling. We already do it in the treatment of municipal sewage. Perhaps there are opportunities for gathering liquid effluents, and possibly even smoke emissions, into central depollution and recycling facilities that would cost materially less per unit of output than handling them on a plant-by-plant basis. (The use of a Rhine tributary in this way is one case in point.) If it is kept in mind that the objective is to get the full costs of environmental use into the prices that consumers pay—and at the same time to cut those costs—rather than to force costs on individual producers, the net cost of pollution control may be reduced substantially.

The potential of other forms of institutional change should also be explored. For example, in seeking to minimize the intrusion on the environment associated with the production of energy, we should look not just at cleaner sources but at more efficient uses. Electricity is one of the most rapidly increasing uses of energy, yet we dump about two-thirds of the heat into the environment, using only one-third in constructive application. If we can develop complementarities through the joint production of steam and electricity for space heating and water heating and air conditioning, we could reduce both the energy costs and the related capital costs. The problem is institutional. The way the relevant industries are regulated and the products are priced, joint production is not

[27]For illuminating discussions of the role of the pricing system and means of putting it to work in preserving the environment, see the papers by Solow, Ruttan, and Mills already cited, as well as the article by Larry E. Ruff, "The Economic Common Sense of Pollution," *The Public Interest*, Spring 1970, pp. 69–85; R. U. Ayres and A. V. Kneese, "Production, Consumption and Externalities," *American Economic Review*, June 1969, pp. 282–97; and Hendrik S. Houthakker, "The Economy and the Environment" (remarks before the Cleveland Business Economists Club, April 19, 1971, available as a mimeographed release by the Council of Economic Advisers, Washington, D.C.).

interesting. Moreover, we have the wrong urban design for the purpose. As it happens, what we need for efficient heat and energy use is also optimal for transportation and communication. Whether we would tolerate the drastic changes in zoning ordinances and the degree of central planning that would be required to achieve the potential complementarities and economies is very doubtful. But we should not ignore the possibilities.[28]

It should also be recognized that anything short of a comprehensive system of materials-use fees will require taxes not just on discharges from productive processes but also on the purchases of products whose use inflicts injury on the environment. The case of herbicides and pesticides is most directly in point. Levying taxes on the sale of these products will bring their use more in line with total social costs. And it will produce revenue to help government cleanse the water of eutrophying residuals.

Removing Existing Governmental Subsidies to Pollution

Finally, as we work to terminate the subsidies that are implicit in our failure to charge for fouling the environment with liquid, solid, gaseous, and thermal wastes, we should also work to end the huge explicit subsidies in existing government programs that have the same effects, namely, to overstimulate high-pollution processes and technology, overproduce many products, and over-exploit natural resources. Agricultural subsidy programs that idle good land, with consequent chemical "overkill" to force more output from the remaining land, are one obvious example. Some aspects of transport regulation fall under a similar shadow.

But the most flagrant example is provided by our tax system. To continue stimulating the overexploitation of oil, coal, timber, and every mineral from iron to vermiculite and spodumene by big tax subsidies in the form of excessive depletion allowances, capital gains shelters, and special deductions becomes ever more anomalous. Here is another case where the believers in the market-pricing system ought to live by it. The public is subsidizing these industries at least twice—once by rich tax bounties and once by cost-free or below-cost discharge of waste and heat.

Far from stimulating conservation and rational use of fossil fuels, both the form and the price impact of the tax preferences work the wrong way. In the case of oil, neither the percentage depletion allowances nor the deductions for intangible drilling and development costs offer any incentive to more efficient and thorough exploitation of oil in the ground, no premium for fuller recovery of the potential oil in the well. And since much of the subsidy is reflected in higher prices of oil lands and lower prices of oil products, economic incentives for full use of the available technology to achieve higher recovery ratios are once

---

[28] My colleague, Ralph Hofmeister, provided the foregoing example.

again reduced. Adding to the diseconomies are refinery discharges of effluents into the air and water, tanker flushings and spillages, offshore oil well fires and spills, all of which inflict costs on the general public and do not now find their way into the costs of production. The net result is to underprice and overproduce petroleum products and the energy derived from them. (It should be noted that oil import quotas work, uneconomically, in the opposite direction, as do the tight oil allowables set by state regulatory commissions.)

Coal is another case in point. Its capital gains and percentage depletion preferences, while less flagrant than in the case of oil and gas, cut the price of mining coal below its social costs and hence speed up the rate of exploitation. The entire polluting sequence—from the strip mining that scores the land to the smoke and heat emissions involved in production—is magnified. With coal coming into generating plants at too low a cost, public utility commissions set the price of electricity below actual cost (private and social combined). Too much electricity is produced and sold. As a result, physical capital and other productive resources are pulled away from their optimal uses in other, less pollution-intensive industries. The net effect of tax subsidies interacting with failure to charge for the use of air and water is both a less efficient use of the nation's resources and greater pressure on the environment.[29]

In the environmental context, the temptation is to make the tax preferences conditional on proof of nondespoiling extraction and nonpolluting utilization of coal. But this would load onto the tax system and Internal Revenue Service agents a burden of policing environmental crimes that they should not have to bear. In this case, the simplest solution (conceptually, though not politically) is also the most effective: end the specific tax subsidies as well as the general spillover cost subsidies that mining and drilling now enjoy.

Distributional Effects

As we increasingly inject the costs of waste disposal into the prices of our products, GNP may not suffer greatly in quantity, but it will change in quality, containing more environmental safeguards and amenities and less material output. Given the high income-elasticity of demand for environmental services, the intuitive reaction of most readers of this paper will be inwardly to smile with satisfaction.

But how will the poor and the black ghetto dweller view the matter? What do environmental attractions, aesthetics, and amenities mean to them? Perhaps they mean somewhat cleaner air and water, but more pertinently they mean

---

[29] In the context of the earlier discussion of GNP impacts, one might note the resulting effect on the national accounts. Owing to resource transfers, the net effect on measured GNP has probably been limited. But NNP is overstated because the social costs of waste disposal and disamenities are not counted and subtracted, nor is the cost treated as a depreciation of our environmental capital.

higher prices of the goods that will now bear the costs of producing those three A's and little help with what Congressman Charles Rangel from Harlem says "ecology" means to his constituents: "Who's gonna collect the damned garbage!"

So before we at this forum take much solace in the improved mix of the national output as *we* see it, we had better be sure (1) that the ghetto dweller is cut in on the environmental dividends as *he* sees them, and (2) that as the prices of goods and services are raised because industry's free ride on public air and water and land is ended, the nation simultaneously compensates the poor through more effective measures to redistribute income and opportunity.

CONCLUSION

In the complex and often baffling field of environmental control, no one—surely not the economist—has all the answers. But good economics is the handmaiden, not the enemy, of the good environment. What the economist believes he can contribute is a better understanding of how economic growth, cost-benefit analysis, and the market-pricing system can be made to work for us rather than against us in the battle to protect our natural environment and improve the quality of existence.

Those who defend economic growth rest their case essentially on the following points:

1. For all the misallocations and mistakes, environmental and otherwise, that have been made in the process of growth, it is still demonstrably true that growth in per capita GNP has been associated with rising levels of human well-being.
2. Much if not most of the environmental damage associated with growth is a function of the *way* we grow—of the nature of our technology and the forms of production. By prohibiting ecologically deadly or dangerous activities and forcing producers to absorb the cost of using air, water, and land areas for waste disposal, growth, technology, and production can be redirected into environmentally more tolerable channels.
3. To provide social and financial lubrication for this painful process as well as to repair the ravages of past neglect of the environment requires the resources, revenues, and rising incomes that growth can put at our disposal.
4. Side by side with the problem of restoring our physical environment is the even greater problem of overcoming the ills of our human and social environment. Those ills seem to be cumulating even faster and to be even more stubbornly resistant to reversal than our environmental ills. How

we could hope to cope with them and avoid unbearable sociopolitical tensions within the context of a stationary state is not apparent.

Coupled with a conviction that economic growth can more than atone for its sins is a belief that its environmental vices can be diminished and its virtues magnified by greater use of the pricing system, by putting appropriate price tags on use of the public environment for private gain. The economist readily recognizes that environmental quality is a highly subjective good on which it will be difficult to put those price tags. He also readily acknowledges that where damage to health, life, or the biosphere—either now or in the future—are severe or even infinite, the pricing system has neither the speed nor the capacity to deal with the problem.

But even recognizing such limits, the economist rightly asserts that across a large part of the pollution spectrum the pricing system *is* applicable. By charging producers—and ultimately consumers—for the full cost of waste disposal, their self-interest will be put to work in slowing or even reversing the march toward a degraded or exhausted environment.

To make economic growth not only compatible with, but a servant of, a high-quality environment won't be easy. Even after ecologists identify the source of the trouble, engineers identify solutions and develop monitoring devices, and economists identify appropriate taxing and pricing schemes, there remain crucial tests of public will and political skill. To get producers and consumers to pay the full cost of using the environment for waste disposal and to get the public to accept the reordered priorities and pay the higher taxes that will be needed to redirect growth and clean up past environmental mistakes will require great acts of both will and skill.

The Environmental Cost of Economic Growth

BARRY COMMONER

This paper is an evaluation of the environmental costs of economic growth in the United States—a complex issue that has appeared rather suddenly on the horizon of public affairs and therefore suffers somewhat from a high ratio of concern to fact. In addition, the issue is one that happens not to coincide with the domain of any established academic discipline. For, until rather recently, environmental costs have been so far removed from the concerns of orthodox economics as to have been nearly banished from that realm under the term "externalities." And for its part, the discipline of ecology has also until very recently maintained a position of lofty disdain for such mundane matters as the price of ecological purity.

It is useful to begin with a brief summary of the ecological background of the issue.

1. The environment is defined as a system comprising the earth's living things and the thin global skin of air, water, and soil that is their habitat.

2. This system, the ecosphere, is the product of the joint, interdigitated evolution of living things and of the physical and chemical constituents of the

Barry Commoner is the Director of the Center for the Biology of Natural Systems at Washington University in St. Louis, where he has been a member of the university faculty since 1947. In 1946–47 he was Associate Editor of *Science Illustrated*. He is a member of the Board of Directors of the American Academy of Sciences and of the National Parks Association, and is Chairman of the Board of Scientists' Institute for Public Information. His service on advisory boards includes the Rachel Carson Trust for the Living Environment; the Law Center Commission, University of Oklahoma (1969–70); and the Special Study Group on the Sonic Boom, U.S. Department of the Interior (1967–68). Dr. Commoner was born in 1917 in New York City. He received his A.B. degree from Columbia College and his M.A. and Ph.D. from Harvard University.

earth's surface. On the time scale of human life, the evolutionary development of the ecosphere has been very slow and irreversible. Hence, the ecosphere is irreplaceable; if the system should be destroyed, it could never be reconstituted or replaced either by natural processes or by human effort.

3. The basic functional element of the ecosphere is the ecological cycle, in which each separate element influences the behavior of the rest of the cycle and is in turn influenced by it. For example, in surface waters fish excrete organic waste, which is converted by bacteria to inorganic products; in turn, the latter are nutrients for algal growth; the algae are eaten by the fish, and the cycle is complete. Such a cyclical process accomplishes the self-purification of the environmental system, in that wastes produced in one step in the cycle become the necessary raw materials for the next step. Such cycles are cybernetically self-governed, dynamically maintaining a steady state condition of indefinite duration. If sufficiently stressed, however, by an external agency, such a cycle may exceed the limits of its self-governing processes and eventually collapse. Thus, if the water cycle is overloaded with organic animal waste, the amount of oxygen needed to support waste decomposition by the bacteria of decay may be greater than the oxygen available in the water. The oxygen level is then reduced to zero; lacking the needed oxygen, the bacteria die, and this phase of the cycle stops, halting the cycle as a whole. It becomes evident, then, that there is an inherent limit to the turnover rate of local ecosystems and of the global ecosystem as a whole.

4. Human beings are dependent on the ecosphere, not only for their biological requirements (oxygen, water, food), but also for resources that are essential to all their productive activities. These resources, together with underground minerals, are the irreplaceable and essential foundation of all human activities.

5. If we regard economic processes as the means of governing the disposition and use of resources available to human society, then it is evident from the above that the stability of the ecosystem, which ensures the continued availability of resources that are derived from the ecosphere (i.e., nonmineral resources), is a prerequisite for the success of any economic system. More bluntly, any economic system that is to survive must be compatible with the continued operation of the ecosystem.

6. Because the turnover rate of an ecosystem is inherently limited, there is a corresponding limit to the rate of production of any of its constituents. Different segments of the global ecosystem (e.g., soil, fresh water, marine ecosystems) operate at different intrinsic turnover rates and therefore differ in the limits of their productivity. On purely theoretical grounds, it is self-evident that any economic system impelled by its own requirements for stability to grow by constantly increasing the rate at which it extracts wealth from the ecosystem must eventually drive the ecosystem to a state of collapse. Computation of the rate limits of the global ecosystem or of any major part of it are as yet in a

rather primitive state. Apart from the foregoing theoretical and as yet unspecified limit to economic growth, such a limit may arise much more rapidly if the growth of the economic system is dependent on productive activities that are especially destructive of the stability of the ecosystem.

7. Unlike all other forms of life, human beings are capable of exerting environmental effects that extend, both quantitatively and qualitatively, far beyond their influence as biological organisms. Human activities have also introduced into the environment not only intense stresses due to natural agents (such as bodily wastes) but also wholly new substances not encountered in natural environmental processes: artificial radioisotopes, detergents, pesticides, plastics, a variety of toxic metals and gases, and a host of other man-made substances. These human intrusions on the natural environment have thrown major segments of the ecosystem out of balance. Environmental pollution is the symptom of the resultant breakdown of the environmental cycles.

THE PROBLEM

In order to evaluate the cost of economic growth in terms of the resultant environmental deterioration, it is, of course, necessary to define both terms—if possible, in quantitative dimensions that might permit a description of their relationship. The common definition of economic growth would appear to be applicable here: the increase in the goods generated by economic activity. Environmental deterioration is a more elusive concept. On the basis of the foregoing discussion, it may be defined as degradative changes in the ecosystems that are the habitat of all life on the planet. The problem is, then, to describe such ecological changes in terms that can be related, quantitatively if possible, to the processes of economic growth—i.e., to increased production of economic goods.

To begin with, we can take note of the self-governing nature of the ecosystem. It is this property that ensures the stability and continued activity of the ecosystem. This basic property helps to define both the process of ecological degradation and the nature of the agencies that can induce it. We can define ecological or environmental degradation as a process that so stresses an ecosystem as to reduce its capability for self-adjustment and that, therefore, if continued, can impose an irreversible stress on the system and cause it to collapse.

An agency capable of exerting such an effect on an ecosystem must arise from *outside* that system. The cyclical nature of the ecosystem automatically brings about the system's readjustment to any *internal* change in the number or activity of any of its normal biological constituents, for a constituent of an ecological cycle both influences and is influenced by the remainder of the cycle. For example, organic waste produced by fish in a closed aquatic ecosystem, such as a balanced aquarium, cannot degrade the system, because the waste is con-

verted to algal nutrients and simply moves through the ecological cycle back to fish. In contrast, if organic waste intrudes upon this same ecosystem from without, it is certain to speed up the cycle's turnover rate and, if sufficiently intense, to consume all of the available oxygen and bring the cycle to a halt.

The internal changes in an ecosystem that occur in response to an external stress are complex nonlinear processes and are not readily reduced to simple quantitative indices. The aquatic ecosystem is one of the relatively few instances in which this goal can, to some degree, be approached—in that oxygen tension is a sensitive internal indicator of the system's approach to instability. In most cases, however, such internal measures of the state of an ecosystem have not yet been elucidated. Hence, as a practical but, it is to be hoped, temporary expedient, we need to fall back on a measure of the *impact* on the ecosystem of an external degradative agency as an index of environmental quality. This expedient has the virtue of enabling the quantitative comparison of the effects of ecological impacts of different origins, a matter of particular importance in connection with their relation to economic processes. Such data can later be translated to the resultant internal changes when the necessary ecological information becomes available. In what follows, then, the environmental cost of a given economic process will be represented by its *environmental impact*, a term that has the dimensions of the amount of any external agency that intrudes on the ecosystem and thereby tends to degrade the system's capacity for self-adjustment.

Turning now to the possible environmental impacts that may result from *human* activity, we find the situation somewhat complicated by the special role of human beings on the earth. In one sense, human beings are simply another animal in the earth's ecosystem, consuming oxygen and organic foodstuff and producing carbon dioxide, organic wastes, heat, and more people. In this role, the human being is a constituent part of an ecosystem and therefore in terms of the previous definition exerts no environmental impact on it. A human population, however, has a zero environmental impact only as long as it is in fact part of an ecosystem, which is the case, for example, if food is acquired from soil that receives the population's organic waste. If a population is separated from this cycle, for example, by settling in a city, its wastes are intruded, with or without treatment, into surface waters. Now the population is no longer a part of the soil ecosystem, and the wastes become *external* to the aquatic system on which they intrude. Here an environmental impact is generated, leading to water pollution.

On the basis of these considerations, then, people—viewed simply as biological organisms—generate an environmental impact only insofar as they become separated from the ecosystem to which, in nature, terrestrial animals belong. This is, of course, nearly universally true in the United States. The intensity of this environmental impact is generally proportional to the population size.

All other environmental impacts are generated not by human biological activities but by human *productive activities* and are therefore governed by economic processes. Such impacts may be generated in several different ways:

1. Certain economic gains can be derived from an ecosystem by exploiting its biological productivity. In these cases, a constituent of the ecosystem that has economic value—for example, an agricultural crop, timber, or fish—is withdrawn from the ecosystem. Insofar as the withdrawn substance or a suitable substitute fails to return as a nutrient to the ecosystem, it constitutes a drain that cannot continue indefinitely without causing the system to collapse. Destructive erosion of the soil following excessive exploitation or the incipient destruction of the whaling industry due to the extinction of whales are examples of such effects.

2. Environmental stress may also arise from an intrusion of opposite sign to that described above—that is, the amount of some component of the ecosystem is augmented from outside that system. This may be done either for the purpose of disposing of waste or in order to accelerate the system's rate of turnover and thus increase its yield. Examples of these effects are the intrusion of sewage into surface water and the intensive use of fertilizer nitrogen in agriculture. In the latter case, following a reduction in the nitrogen available from the soil's natural store of nutrient (its organic humus) due to a period of overexploitation through uncompensated crop withdrawal (i.e., a stress of the type described in point 1 above), the nitrate level is artificially raised by adding fertilizer to the soil's ecological cycle. Because of the low efficiency of nutrient uptake by the crop's roots (which is in turn a result of inadequate soil oxygen due to reduced porosity stemming from the decreased humus content), a considerable portion of the fertilizer leaches from the soil into surface waters. In these waters, the fertilizer becomes an external stress on the aquatic ecosystem, causing algal overgrowths and the resulting breakdown of the self-purifying aquatic cycle.

3. Apart from the above stresses—which represent the impact of externally altered concentrations of natural ecosystem constituents—environmental impact may be caused by the intrusion into an ecosystem of a substance wholly foreign to it. Thus, DDT has a powerful environmental impact, in part because it readily upsets the naturally balanced ecological relations among insect pests, the plants they attack, and the insects that, in turn, prey on the pests. DDT-induced outbreaks of insect pests often result. In general, there is a considerable risk of environmental pollution whenever productive activity introduces substances to the natural environment that are foreign to it.

We turn now to the practical problem of evaluating the environmental cost of economic growth. The most general theoretical aspect of this problem has already been alluded to. Given that the global ecosystem is closed and that its integrity is essential to the continued operation of any conceivable economic

system, it is evident that there must be an upper limit to the growth of productive activities on the earth.

Such a theoretical statement, however, is hardly an effective guide to follow. The chief reason is that the theory fails to specify the time scale in which the ecological limitation on economic growth is likely to take effect. For one can readily grant the truth of such an abstract theorem—for example, that economic growth will eventually be limited by the extinction of the sun—and disregard its practical consequences because of the rather long time scale involved, in this case some billions of years.

Accordingly, it would seem useful to make the problem more concrete by examining the relationship between growth and environmental impact in the real world. And since growth is, of course, a time-dependent process, this suggests the value of a historical approach.

THE ORIGINS OF ENVIRONMENTAL IMPACTS

In what follows, I wish to report the results of an initial effort to describe the origins of environmental impacts in the United States.[1] Most U.S. pollution problems are of recent origin. The postwar period, 1945-46, is a convenient benchmark because a number of pollutants—man-made radioisotopes, detergents, plastics, and synthetic pesticides and herbicides—are due to the emergence, after the war, of new productive technologies. The statistical data available for this period in the United States provide a useful opportunity to compare the changes in the levels of various pollutants with the concurrent activities of the U.S. productive system that might be related to the environmental effects of the pollutants.

Although, unfortunately, we lack sufficient comprehensive data on the actual environmental levels of most pollutants in the United States, some estimates of historical changes can be made from intermittent observations and from computed data on emissions of pollutants from their sources. Some of the available data are summarized in table 1, which indicates that since 1946 emissions of pollutants have increased by 200-2000 percent. In the case of phosphate, which is a pollutant of surface waters that enters mainly from municipal sewage, data on the long-term trends are available; these are shown in figure 1. In the thirty-year period between 1910 and 1940, phosphorus output from municipal sewage increased gradually from about 17 million pounds per year to about

---

[1] This study has been carried out as part of the program of the American Association for the Advancement of Science Committee on Environmental Alterations in collaboration with Michael Corr and Paul J. Stamler. For a preliminary report of this work, see Barry Commoner, Michael Corr, and Paul J. Stamler, "The Causes of Pollution," *Environment*, vol. 13, no. 3 (April 1971), p. 2.

Table 1. Postwar Increases in Pollutant Emissions

| Pollutant | Annual production | | | | Percentage increase over indicated period |
	Year	Amount	Year	Amount	
Inorganic fertilizer nitrogen	1949	0.91×10^6 tons	1968	6.8×10^6 tons	648
Synthetic organic pesticides	1950	286×10^6 lbs.	1967	$1,050 \times 10^6$ lbs.	267
Detergent phosphorus	1946	11×10^6 lbs.	1968	214×10^6 lbs.	1,845
Tetraethyl lead[a]	1946	0.048×10^6 tons	1967	0.25×10^6 tons	415
Nitrogen oxides[a]	1946	10.6^b	1947	77.5^b	630
Beer bottles	1950	6.5×10^6 gross	1967	45.5×10^6 gross	595

[a]Automotive emissions.

[b]Dimension = NO_x (ppm) $\times$ gasoline consumption (gal. $\times$ 10^{-6}); estimated from product of passenger vehicle gasoline consumption and ppm of NO_x emitted by engines of average compression ratio 5.9 (1946) and 9.5 (1967) under running conditions, at 15 in. manifold pressure. NO_x emitted: 500 ppm in 1946; 1,200 ppm in 1967.

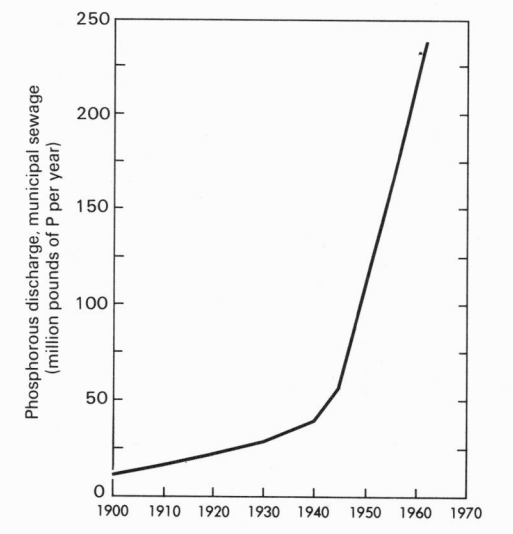

Figure 1. Phosphorus emitted by U.S. municipal sewage. *Source:* L. W. Weinberger and others in *The Adequacy of Technology for Pollution Abatement*, Hearings before the Subcommittee on Science, Research and Development of the House Committee on Science and Astronautics, vol. 2, 89 Cong. 2 sess. (1966), p. 756.

40 million pounds per year. Thereafter, the rate of output rose rapidly so that in the thirty-year period 1940-70 phosphorus output increased to about 300 million pounds per year.

It should be noted that these are data regarding the computed *emission* of pollutants, and they are not necessarily descriptive of the actual concentrations of pollutants in the environment or of the ultimate effects on the ecosystems or on human health. Numerous complex and interrelated processes intervene between the entry of a pollutant into the ecosystem and the expression of its biological effect. Moreover, two or more pollutants may interact synergistically to intensify the separate effects. Most of these processes are still too poorly understood to enable us to convert the amount of a pollutant entering an ecosystem to a quantitative estimate of its degradative effects. Nevertheless, it is self-evident that these effects (such as the incidence of respiratory disease due to air pollutants or of algal overgrowths due to phosphate and nitrate) have increased sharply since 1946, along with the rapid rise of pollutant levels. Since pollutant emission is a direct measure of the activity of the source, it is a useful way to estimate the contributions of different sources to the overall degradation of the environment.

If the amount of a given pollutant introduced annually into the environment is defined as the *environmental impact* (*I*), it then becomes possible to relate this value to the effects of three major factors that might influence the value of *I* by means of the following identity:

$$I = \text{Population} \cdot \frac{\text{Economic good}}{\text{Population}} \cdot \frac{\text{Pollutant}}{\text{Economic good}} \cdot$$

Here, "population" refers to the size of the U.S. population in a given year. "Economic good" refers to the amount of a designated good produced (or, where appropriate, consumed) during the given year. "Pollutant" refers to the amount of a specific pollutant (defined as above) released into the environment as a result of the production (or consumption) of the designated good during the given year. This relationship enables the estimation of the contribution of three factors to the total environmental impact: (1) the size of the population; (2) production (or consumption) per capita, i.e., "affluence"; (3) the environmental impact (i.e., amount of pollutant) generated per unit of production (or consumption) that reflects the nature of the productive technology.

Since we are concerned with identifying the sources of the sharp increases in the environmental impacts experienced in the United States from 1946 to the present, it becomes of interest to examine the concurrent changes in the nation's productive activities. The most general data relevant to these changes are presented in figure 2. In the period 1946-68, the U.S. gross national product (GNP), adjusted to 1958 dollars, increased exponentially by about 126 percent; GNP per capita also increased approximately exponentially by about 59 percent.

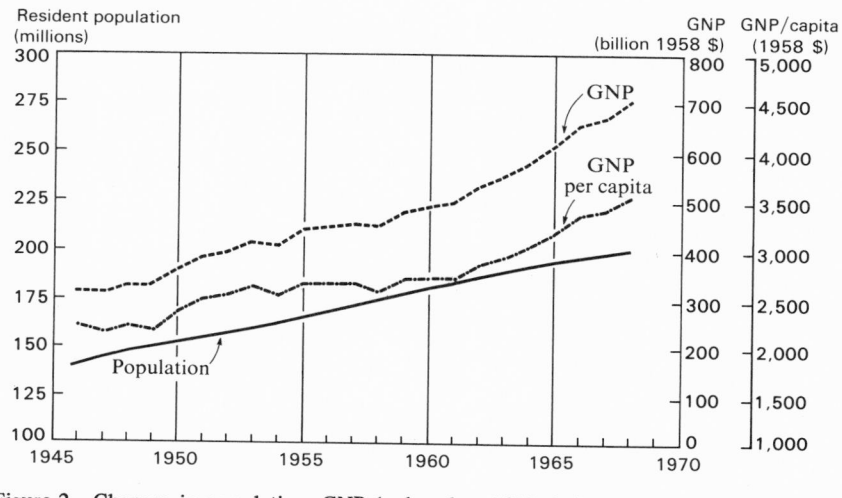

Figure 2. Changes in population, GNP (reduced to 1958 dollars), and GNP per capita for the United States since 1946. *Sources:* U.S. Department of Commerce, *Statistical Abstract of the United States* (1970), p. 5; and U.S. Department of Commerce, *The National Income and Product Accounts of the United States, 1929–1965* (1966), pp. 4–5.

It can be seen at once that, as a first approximation, the contribution of population growth to the overall values of the environmental impacts generated since 1946 is of the order of 40 percent. In most cases, this represents a relatively small contribution to the total environmental impact, since as indicated in table 1, the environmental impact indices increased by 200–2,000 percent in that period of time.

In order to evaluate the effects of the remaining factors, it is useful to examine the growth rates of different sectors of the productive economy. For this purpose a series of productive activities that are likely to contribute significantly to environmental impact and that are representative of the overall pattern of the economy have been selected. From the annual production (or, where appropriate, consumption) data for the United States as a whole the annual percentage rates of increase or decrease have been calculated by computer. The results of these computations are presented in figure 3, from which it is possible to derive certain useful generalizations about the pattern of economic growth that are relevant to environmental impacts in the United States.

1. Production and consumption of certain goods have increased at an annual rate about equal to the annual rate of increase of the population so that per capita production remains essentially unchanged. This group includes food; fabric and clothing; major household appliances; and certain basic metals and building materials, including steel and copper and brick. In effect, with respect

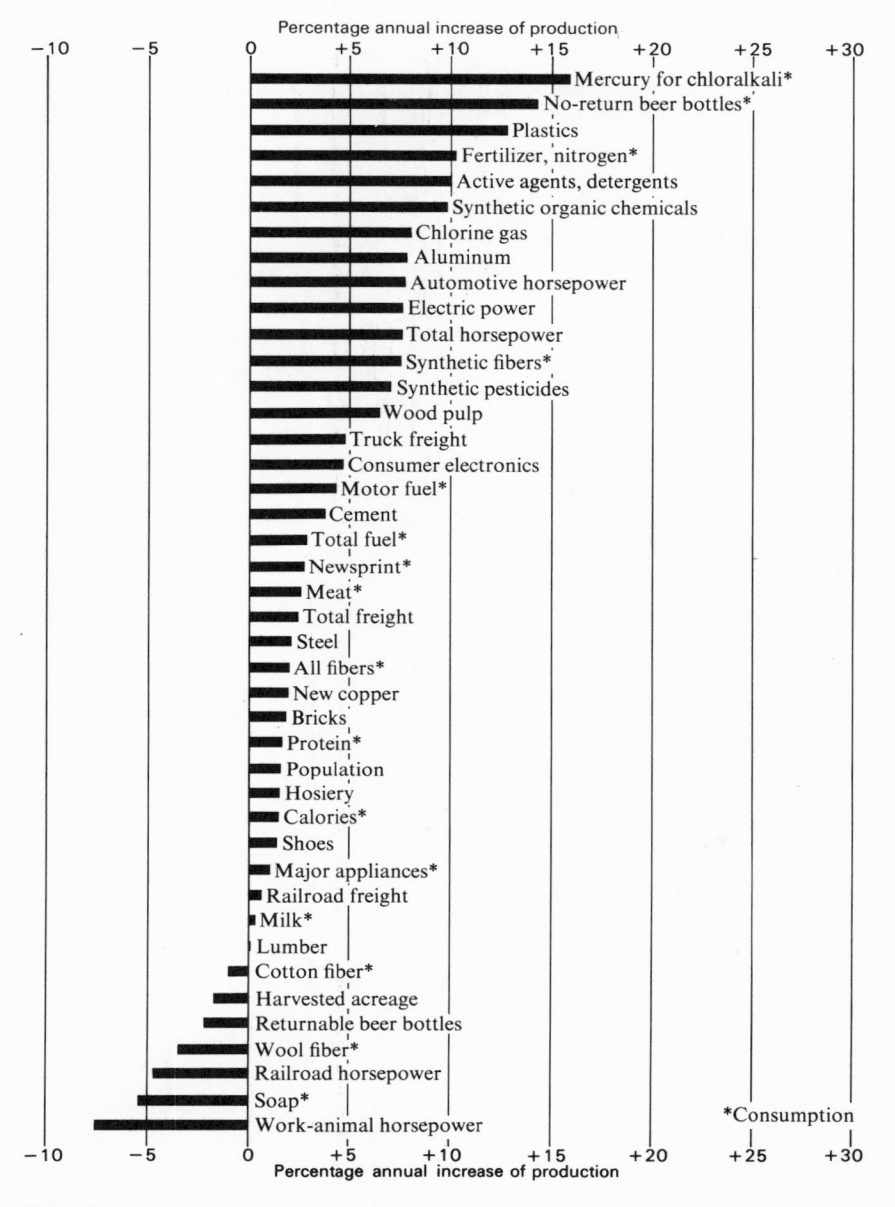

Figure 3. Annual growth rates of production (or consumption) in the United States, 1946–1968. *Source:* U.S. Department of Commerce, *Statistical Abstract of the United States,* for the years 1948–70. See text for method of computation.

to these basic items average "affluence," i.e., per capita production (or consumption) remained essentially unchanged in 1946–68.

2. The annual production of certain goods has decreased since 1946, or has increased at an annual rate below that of the population. Horsepower produced by work animals is the extreme case; it declined at an annual rate of about 10 percent. Other items in this category are saponifiable fat, cotton fiber, wool fiber, lumber, milk, railroad horsepower, and railroad freight. These are goods that have been significantly displaced in the pattern of production during the course of the overall growth of the economy. Cultivated farm acreage also declined in this period.

3. Among the productive activities that have increased at an annual rate in excess of that exhibited by the population, the following classes can be discerned:

(a) Certain of the rapidly increasing productive activities are substitutes for activities that have declined in rate, relative to population. These generally represent technological displacement of an older process by a newer one, with the sum of goods produced remaining essentially constant, per capita, or increasing somewhat. These processes include the displacement of natural fibers (cotton and wool) by synthetic fibers, lumber by plastics, soap by detergents, steel by aluminum and cement, railroad freight by truck freight, harvested acreage by fertilizer, and returnable by nonreturnable bottles.

(b) Certain of the rapidly growing productive activities evident in figure 3 are secondary consequences of displacement processes. Thus, the displacement of natural products by synthetic ones involves the use of greatly increased amounts of synthetic organic chemicals so that this category has increased sharply. Moreover, since many organic syntheses require chlorine as a reagent, the rate of chlorine production has also increased rapidly. Finally, because chlorine is efficiently produced in a mercury electrolytic cell, the use of mercury for this purpose has also increased at a very considerable rate. Similarly, the rapidly rising rate of power utilization is, in part, a secondary consequence of certain displacement processes, for a number of the new technologies are more power consumptive than the technologies they replace.

(c) Finally, among the rapidly growing productive activities evident in figure 3, there are some that represent neither displacements of older technologies nor sequelae to such displacements but true increments in per capita availability of goods. An example of this category is consumer electronics (radios, television sets, sound equipment). Such items represent true increases in "affluence."

In sum, the pattern of growth in the U.S. economy in 1946–68 may be generalized as follows: Annual production of basic life necessities, which represent perhaps one-third of the total GNP, grew at about the pace of population

growth so that no significant overall change in per capita production took place in that period. However, within these general categories of goods—food, fiber and clothing, freight haulage, household necessities—there was a pronounced displacement of natural products by synthetic ones, of power-conservative products by relatively power-consumptive ones, and of reusable containers by "disposable" ones.

THE ENVIRONMENTAL IMPACT OF ECONOMIC GROWTH

Given the foregoing conclusions, the original question can be rephrased as follows: What are the relative costs, in intensity of environmental impact, of the several distinctive features of the growth of the U.S. economy from 1946 to the present? Reasonably complete quantitative answers to this question are, unfortunately, well beyond the present state of knowledge. At the present time, it is possible in most cases to provide only an informal qualitative description of the changes in environmental impact that have been induced by the postwar transformation of the U.S. economy. In some cases it is also possible to produce a quantitative evaluation in the form of an environmental impact index, and in a few cases a partial environmental impact inventory can be constructed. As shown in the discussion below, such evidence leads to the general conclusion that in most of the technological displacements that have accompanied the growth of the U.S. economy since 1946 *the new technology has an appreciably greater environmental impact than the technology it displaced, and that the postwar technological transformation of productive activities is the chief reason for the present environmental crisis.*

Agricultural Production

As shown in figure 3, agricultural production in the United States, as measured by the U. S. Department of Agriculture (USDA) Crop Index, has increased at about the same rate as the population since 1946. The technological methods for achieving agricultural production, however, have changed significantly in that period. One important change is illustrated in figure 4, which shows that, although agricultural production per capita has increased only slightly, harvested acreage has decreased, and the use of inorganic nitrogen fertilizer has risen sharply. This displacement process—i.e., of fertilizer for land—leads to a considerably increased environmental impact.

Briefly stated, the relevant ecological situation is that nitrogen, an essential constituent of all living things, is available to plants in nature from organic nitrogen stored in the soil in the form of humus. Humus is broken down by bacteria to release inorganic forms of nitrogen, eventually as nitrate. The latter is taken up by the plant roots and reconverted to organic matter, such as the

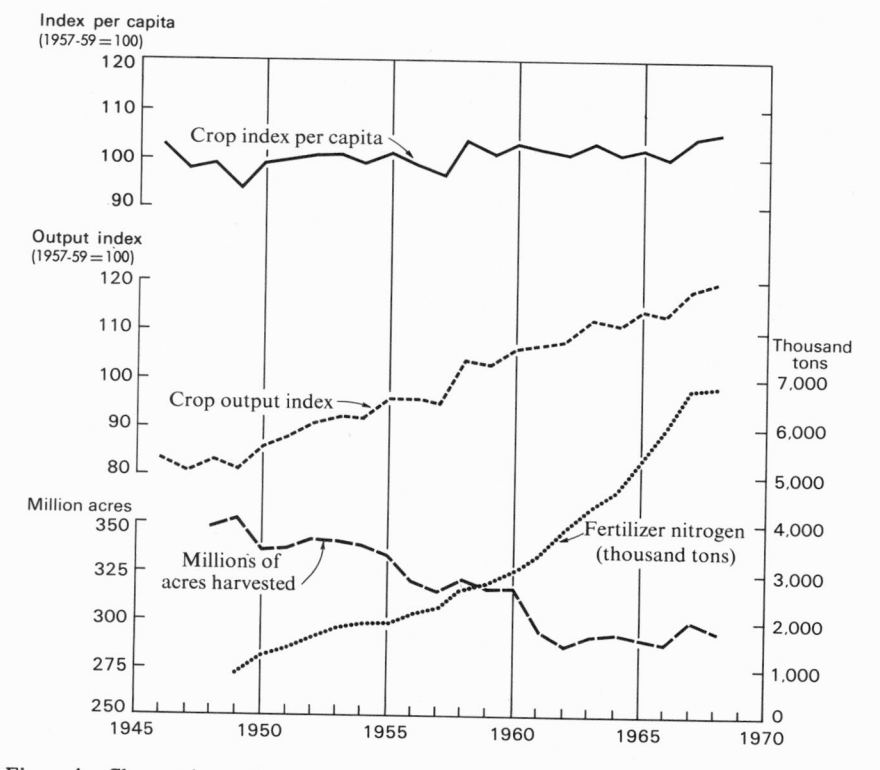

Figure 4. Changes in total crop output (as determined by the USDA Crop Index), in crop output per capita, in harvested acreage, and in annual use of inorganic nitrogen fertilizer in the United States since 1946. *Source:* USDA, *Agricultural Statistics* (1967), pp. 531, 544, 583; and (1970), pp. 444, 454, 481.

plant's protein. Finally the plant may be eaten by a grazing animal, which returns the nitrogen not retained in the growth of its own body to the soil as bodily wastes.[2]

Agriculture imposes a negative drain on this cycle. Nitrogen is removed from the system in the form of the plant crop or of the livestock produced from it. In ecologically sound husbandry all of the organic nitrogen produced by the soil system, other than the food itself—plant residues, manure, garbage—is returned to the soil where it is converted by complex microbial processes to humus and thus helps to restore the soil's organic nitrogen content. The deficit, if it is not

[2] See Barry Commoner, "Threats to the Integrity of the Nitrogen Cycle: Nitrogen Compounds in Soil, Water, Atmosphere, and Precipitation," in S. Fred Singer, ed., *Global Effects of Environmental Pollution* (Dordrecht, Netherlands: Reidel, 1970).

too large, can be made up by the process of nitrogen fixation, in which bacteria, usually in close association with the roots of certain plants, take up nitrogen gas from the air and convert it into organic form. If the nitrogen cycle is not in balance, agriculture "mines" the soil nitrogen, progressively depleting it. This process does more than reduce the store of organic nitrogen available to support plant growth, for humus is more than a nutrient store. Due to its polymeric structure, humus is also responsible for the porosity of the soil to air. And air is essential to the soil, not only as a source of nitrogen for fixation, but also because its oxygen is essential to the root's metabolic activity, which in turn is the driving force for the absorption of nutrients by the roots. In the United States, for example in corn belt soils, about half the original soil organic nitrogen has been lost since 1880. Naturally, other things being equal, such soil is relatively infertile and produces relatively poor crop yields. Beginning after World War II, however, a technological solution was intensively applied to this problem: sharply increasing amounts of inorganic nitrogen were applied to the soil in the form of fertilizer. Annual nitrogen fertilizer usage in the United States increased by an order of magnitude in 1946–68.

In effect, then, nitrogen fertilizer can be regarded as a substitute for land. With the intensive use of fertilizer, it becomes possible to accelerate the turnover rate of the soil ecosystem so that each acre of soil annually produces more food than before. The economic benefits of this new agricultural technology are appreciable and self-evident. But this economic advantage may be counterbalanced by the increased impact on the environment. This arises because, given the reduced humus content of the soil, the plant's roots do not efficiently absorb the added fertilizer. As a result, an appreciable part leaches from the soil as nitrate and enters surface waters where it becomes a serious pollutant. Nitrate may encourage algal overgrowths, which on their inevitable death and decay tend to break down the self-purifying aquatic cycle.

Excess nitrate from fertilizer drainage leads to another environmental impact that may affect human health. While nitrate in food and drinking water appears to be relatively innocuous, *nitrite* is not, for it combines with hemoglobin in the blood, converting it to methemoglobin—which cannot carry oxygen. Unfortunately, nitrate can be converted to nitrite by the action of bacteria in the intestinal tract, especially in infants, causing asphyxiation and even death. On these grounds, the U.S. Public Health Service has established 10 parts per million (ppm) of nitrate nitrogen as the acceptable limit of nitrate in drinking water. In a number of agricultural areas in the United States, nitrate levels in water supplies obtained from wells, and in some instances from surface waters, have exceeded this limit. Our own studies in the area of Decatur, Illinois, show quite directly that in the spring of 1970 when the city's water supply, which is derived from an impoundment of the Sangamon River, recorded 9 ppm of nitrate nitro-

gen, a minimum of 60 percent of the nitrate was derived from inorganic fertilizer applied to the surrounding farmland.[3]

The effect of this change in agricultural technology is evident in table 2, in which the influence of the several relevant factors on the total environmental impact due to fertilizer nitrogen is compared for 1949 and 1968. During that period the total annual use of fertilizer nitrogen, i.e., the total environmental impact, increased 648 percent. The influence of population size increased by 34 percent, the influence of crop production per capita ("affluence") increased by 11 percent, and the influence of the change in fertilizer technology increased by 405 percent. Clearly, the latter factor dominates the large increase in the total environmental impact of fertilizer nitrogen. Specifically, it should be noted that in 1949 about 11,000 tons of fertilizer nitrogen were used *per unit crop production*, while in 1968 about 57,000 tons of nitrogen were employed for the *same* crop yield. This means that the efficiency with which fertilizer nitrogen contributes to crop yield has *declined* fivefold. Obviously an appreciable part of the added nitrogen does not enter the crop and must appear elsewhere in the ecosystem.

Table 2. Fertilizer Nitrogen: Environmental Impact Index

	Index factors			Total impact index
	(a)	(b)	(c)	(a × b × c)
	Population (*1,000*)	$\dfrac{\text{Crop production}^a}{\text{Population}}$ (*prod. units/cap.*)	$\dfrac{\text{Fertilizer nitrogen}}{\text{Crop production}}$ (*tons/prod. unit*)	Fertilizer nitrogen (1,000 tons)
1949	149,304	5.43×10^{-7}	11,284	914
1968	199,846	6.00×10^{-7}	57,008	6,841
1968:1949	1.34	1.11	5.05	7.48
Percentage increase, 1949–1968	34	11	405	648

[a]The crop output index is an indicator of agricultural production; 1957-59 average = 100.

The biological basis for this effect is shown in figure 5, where the corn yield in Illinois is compared with the concurrent amounts of nitrogen fertilizer added to the soil.[4] This shows that as fertilizer levels increased, the yield per acre rose but eventually leveled off because of the natural limits of plant growth. Thus, between 1962 and 1968 fertilizer usage doubled, but crop yield rose only about 10-15 percent. Clearly, at the higher levels of fertilizer usage an increasingly

[3] D. H. Kohl, G. B. Shearer, and Barry Commoner, "Isotopic Analysis of the Movement of Fertilizer Nitrogen into Surface Water," *Science* (forthcoming).

[4] J. H. Dawes, T. E. Larson, and R. H. Harmeson, *Proceedings*, 24th Annual Meeting, Soil Conservation Society of America (Fort Collins, Colo.: SCSA, 1968).

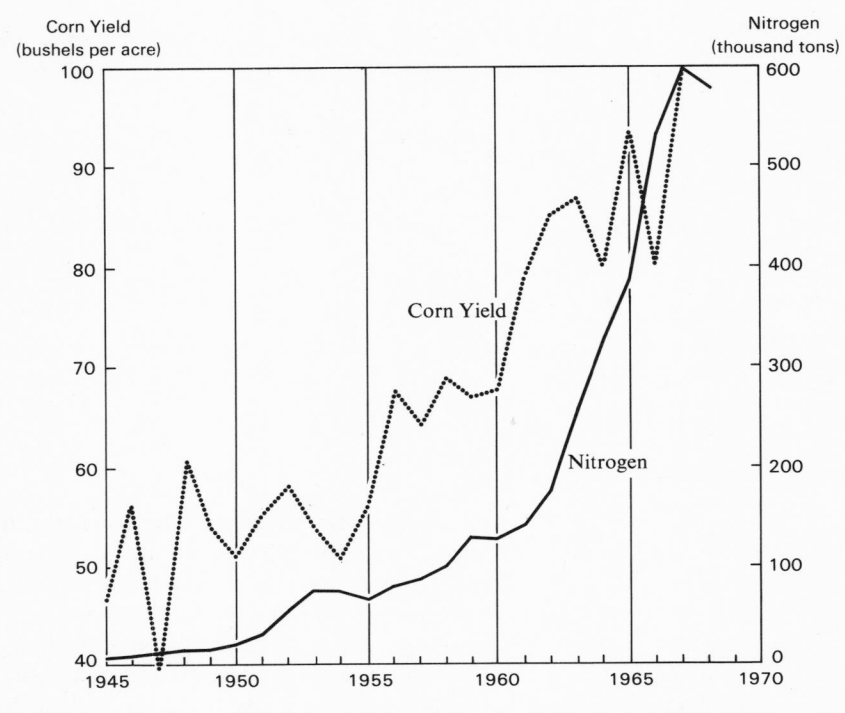

Figure 5. Corn yield and nitrogen usage for the state of Illinois. *Source*: J. H. Dawes, T. E. Larson, and R. H. Harmeson, *Proceedings*, 24th Annual Meeting, Soil Conservation Society of America (Fort Collins, Colo.: SCSA, 1968).

smaller proportion of the fertilizer contributes to the crop. As indicated earlier, the remainder leaches into surface waters where it causes serious pollution problems. Thus, this innovation in agricultural technology sharply increases the environmental stress due to agricultural production.

A similar situation exists in the case of pesticides. This is shown by the changes in the environmental impact index of pesticides between 1950 and 1967 (table 3). In that time there was an increase of 168 percent in the amount of pesticides used *per unit crop production*, as a national average. By killing off natural insect predators and parasites of the target pest—with the pest often becoming resistant to insecticides—the use of modern synthetic insecticides tends to exacerbate the pest problems that they were designed to control. As a result, *increasing* amounts of insecticides must be used to maintain agricultural productivity. Insecticide usage is, so to speak, self-accelerating—resulting in both a decreased efficiency and an increased environmental impact.

Another technological displacement in agriculture is the increased use of feedlots for the production of livestock in preference to range feeding. Range-

Table 3. Synthetic Organic Pesticides: Environmental Impact Index

	Index factors			Total impact index (a × b × c)
	(a)	(b)	(c)	
		Crop production[a] / Population	Pesticide consumption / Crop production	Synthetic organic pesticides
	Population (*1,000*)	(*crop production units/cap.*)	(*1,000 lb./prod. unit*)	(*million lb.*)
1950	151,868	5.66×10^{-7}	3,326	286
1967	197,859	5.96×10^{-7}	8,898	1,050
1967 : 1950	1.30	1.05	2.68	3.67
Percentage increase, 1950–1967	30	5	168	267

[a]The crop output index is an indicator of agricultural production; 1957–59 average = 100.

fed cattle are integrated into the soil ecosystem; they graze the soil's grass crop and restore nutrient to the soil as manure. When the cattle are maintained instead in huge pens, where they are fed on corn and deposit their wastes intensively in the feedlot itself, the wastes do not return to the soil. Instead the waste drains into surface waters where it adds to the stresses due to fertilizer nitrogen and detergent phosphate. The magnitude of the effect is considerable. At the present time the organic waste produced in feedlots is more than the organic waste produced by all the cities of the United States. Again, the newer technology has a serious environmental impact, and in this case has displaced a technology with an essentially zero environmental impact.

Textiles

In figure 6 changes in textile production since 1946 are shown. While total fiber production per capita has remained constant, natural fibers (cotton and wool) have been significantly displaced by synthetic ones. This technological change considerably increases the environmental impact due to fiber production and use.

One reason is that the energy required for the synthesis of the final product, a linear polymer (cellulose in the case of cotton, keratin in the case of wool, and polyamides in the case of nylon) is greater for the synthetic material. Although quantitative data are not yet available on this, it is evident in the comparison of two productive processes provided in table 4. Nylon production involves as many as ten steps of chemical synthesis, each requiring considerable energy in the form of heat and electric power to overcome the entropy associated with chemical mixtures and to operate the reaction apparatus. In contrast, energy required for the synthesis of cotton is derived free from a renewable source—

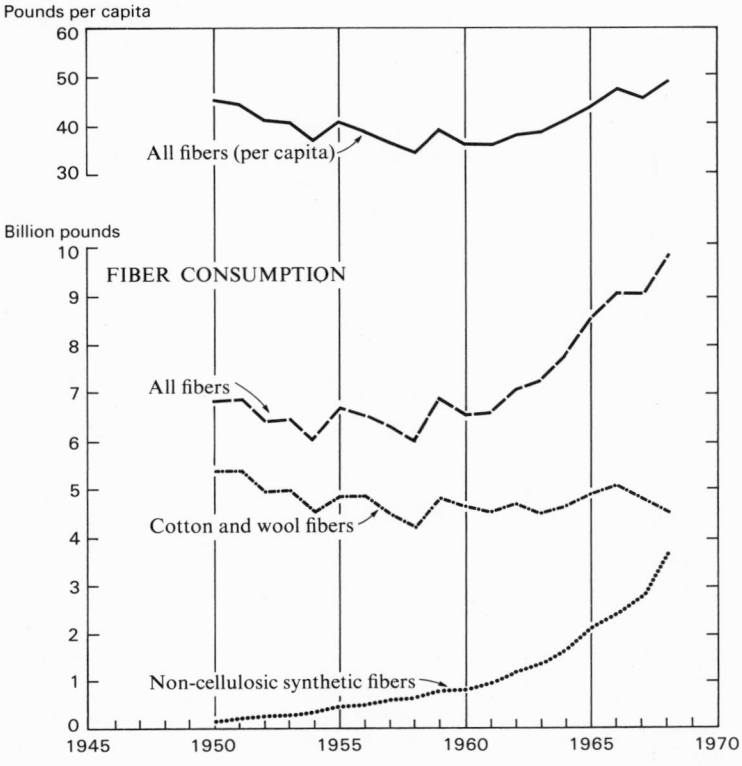

Figure 6. Natural and synthetic fiber production in the United States. *Source*: U.S. Department of Commerce, *Statistical Abstract of the United States* (1962), p. 198; (1966), p. 789; and (1970), p. 713.

sunlight—and is transferred without combustion and resultant air pollution. Moreover, the raw material for cellulose synthesis is carbon dioxide and water, both freely available renewable resources, while the raw material for nylon synthesis is petroleum or a similar hydrocarbon—nonrenewable resources. As a result it would appear that the environmental stress due to the *production* of such an artificial fiber is probably well in excess of that due to the production of an equal weight of cotton. This is only an approximation, for we need far more detailed quantitative estimates, in the form of the appropriate environmental impact indices, that would also take into account the fuel and other materials used in the production of cotton.

Because a synthetic fiber, such as nylon, is unnatural, it also has a greater impact on the environment as a waste material than have cotton or wool. The natural polymers in cotton and wool, cellulose and keratin, are important con-

Table 4. Cotton and Environmental Characteristics

	Cotton	Nylon	Comparative environmental impact
Raw materials	CO_2, H_2O	Petroleum	Cotton, renewable; nylon, nonrenewable
Process	CO_2 + H_2O + light	Petroleum (distilled)	Fuel combustion and resultant air pollution:
	→ Glucose → cellulose (ca. 70–90°F.)	→ Benzene (550°F.)	
	Cultivation, ginning, spinning, require power	→ Cyclohexane (300°F.)	probably nylon > cotton
		→ Cyclohexanol (200–400°F.)	
		→ Adipic acid (600–700°F.)	
		→ Adiponitrile (200–250°F.)	
		→ Hexamethylene diamine → Nylon 610	
		Distillation and other purification at most of above steps; power required to operate process	
Product	Cellulose	Polyamide	Cellulose wholly biodegradable; polyamide not degradable

stituents of the soil ecosystem. Through the action of molds and decay bacteria, they contribute to the formation of humus—a substance that is essential to the natural fertility of the soil. In this process, cellulose is readily broken down in the soil ecosystem. Thus, in nature, cellulose and keratin are simply *not* "wastes," because they provide essential nutrients for soil microorganisms. Hence they cannot accumulate. The crucial fact is that for every polymer that is produced in nature by living things, there exist in some living things enzymes that have the specific capability of degrading that polymer. In the absence of such an enzyme the natural polymers are quite resistant to degradation, as is evident from the durability of fabrics that are protected from biological attack.

The contrast with synthetic fibers is striking. The structure of nylon and similar synthetic polymers is a human invention and does not occur in natural living things. Hence, unlike natural polymers, synthetic ones find no counterpart in the armamentarium of degradative enzymes in nature. Ecologically, synthetic polymers are literally indestructible. Hence, every bit of synthetic fiber or polymer that has been produced on the earth is either destroyed by burning—

and thereby pollutes the air—or accumulates as rubbish. One result, according to a recent report, is that microscopic fragments of plastic fibers, often red, blue, or orange, have now become common in certain marine waters.[5] For technological displacement has been at work in this area too; in recent years natural fibers, such as hemp and jute, have been nearly totally replaced by synthetic fibers in fishing operations. A chief reason for this use of synthetic fibers is that they resist degradation by molds, which, as already indicated, readily attack cellulosic net materials, such as hemp or jute. Thus, the property that enhances the economic value of the synthetic fiber over the natural one—its resistance to biological degradation—is precisely the property that increases the environmental impact of the synthetic material.

Detergents

Figure 7 shows that synthetic detergents have largely replaced soap in the United States as domestic and industrial cleaners, with the total production of cleaners per capita remaining essentially unchanged. Soap is based on a natural organic substance, fat, which is reacted with alkali to produce the end product. Being a natural product, fat is extracted from an ecosystem (for example, that represented by a coconut palm plantation). When released into an aquatic ecosystem after use, soap is readily degraded by the bacteria of decay. Since most municipal wastes in the United States are subjected to treatment that degrades organic waste into inorganic products, in actual practice the fatty residue of soap wastes is degraded by bacterial action within the confines of a sewage treatment plant. What is then emitted to surface waters is only carbon dioxide and water. Hence, there is little or no impact on the aquatic ecosystem due to biological oxygen demand (which accompanies bacterial degradation of organic wastes) arising from soap wastes. Nor is the product of soap degradation, carbon dioxide, usually an important ecological intrusion, since it is in plentiful supply from other environmental sources; in any case, it is an essential nutrient for photosynthetic algae. Hence, compared with soap, the production of synthetic detergents is a more serious source of pollution.

Even the newer detergents that are regarded as degradable, because the paraffin chain of the molecule (which, unlike the earlier nondegradable detergents, is unbranched) is broken down by bacterial action, leave a residue of phenol that may not be degraded and may accumulate in surface waters. Phenol is a rather toxic substance, being foreign to the aquatic ecosystem.

Unlike soap, detergents are compounded with considerable amounts of phosphate in order to enhance their action as cleansers and as water softeners. Phosphate may readily induce water pollution by stimulating heavy overgrowths of algae, which release organic matter into the water when they die and thus

[5] See item in *Marine Pollution Bulletin 2*, February 1971, p. 23.

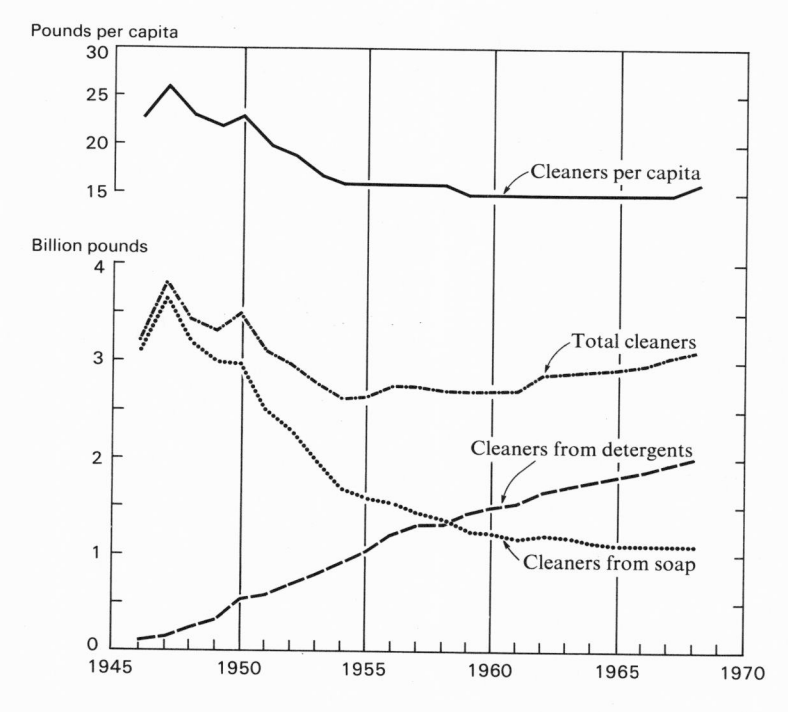

Figure 7. Total soap and detergent production and per capita consumption of total cleaners (soap plus detergent) in the United States, 1946–1968. Detergent data represent the actual content of the surface-active agent, which is estimated at about 37.5 percent of the total weight of the marketed detergent. *Source*: USDA, *Agricultural Statistics* (1970), p. 149.

overburden the aqueous ecosystem. Figure 8 shows that nearly all of the increase in sewage phosphorus in the United States can be accounted for by the phosphorus content of detergents. Since soap, which has been displaced by detergents, is quite free of phosphate, the environmental impact due to phosphate is clearly a consequence of the technological change in cleanser production.

The change in the environmental impact index of phosphate in cleaners between 1946 and 1968 is shown in table 5. In this period the overall environmental impact index increased 1,845 percent. The increase in the effect of population size was 42 percent; the effect of per capita use of cleaners does not change; the technological factor, i.e., that due to the displacement of phosphate-free soap by detergents containing an average of about 4 percent phosphorus, increased about 1,270 percent. The relative importance of this change in cleanser technology in intensifying environmental impact is quite evident.

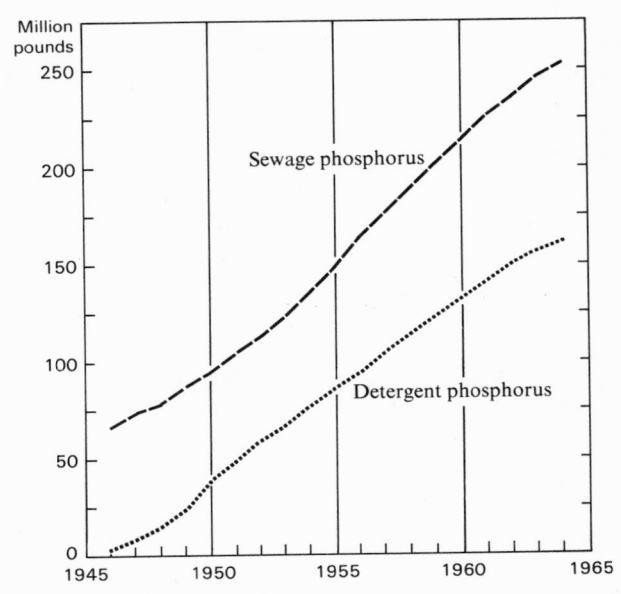

Figure 8. Concurrent values of the phosphorus output from municipal sewage in the United States and the phosphorus content of detergents produced. *Sources*: Values of the phosphorus output from U.S. municipal sewage are from L. W. Weinberger and others (see fig. 1). Detergent data are based on detergent production (see fig. 7), assuming an average of 4 percent P in marketed detergents.

Table 5. Detergent Phosphorus: Environmental Impact Index

	Index factors			Total impact index
	(a)	(b)	(c)	(a × b × c)
	Population	Cleaners[a] / Population	Phosphorus / Cleaners	Phosphorus from detergents[b]
	(1,000)	*(lb./cap.)*	*(lb./ton of cleaner)*	*(10⁶ lb.)*
1946	140,686	22.66	6.90	11
1968	194,846	15.99	137.34	214
1968 : 1946	1.42	0.69 (1.00)[c]	19.90 (13.70)[c]	19.45
Percentage increase, 1946–1968	42	(0)[c]	(1,270)[c]	1,845

[a]Assuming that 35 percent of detergent weight is active agent.
[b]Assuming average phosphorus content of detergents = 4 percent.
[c]Because of uncertainties regarding the content of active agent in detergents, especially soon after their introduction, the apparent reduction in per capita use of cleaners is not regarded as significant; the numbers contained in parentheses are based on the assumption that this value does not change significantly.

Secondary Environmental Effects of Technological Displacements

Increased production of synthetic organic chemicals leads to intensified environmental impacts in several different ways. This segment of industry has heavy power requirements; in contributing to increased power production, the industry adds as well to the rising levels of air pollutants that are emitted by power plants. In addition, organic synthesis releases into the environment a wide variety of reagents and intermediates that are foreign to natural ecosystems and often toxic, thus generating important and often poorly understood environmental impacts. A common example are massive fish kills and plant damage resulting from release of organic wastes, insecticides, and herbicides to surface waters or to the air.

Perhaps the most serious environmental impact attributable to the increased production of synthetic organic chemicals is due to the intrusion of mercury into surface waters. This effect is mediated by chlorine production. Chlorine is a vital reagent in many organic syntheses; about 80 percent of present chlorine production finds its end use in the synthetic organic chemical industry. Moreover, a considerable proportion of chlorine production is carried out in electrolytic mercury cells; until recent control measures were imposed on the industry, about 0.2–0.5 pounds of mercury were released to the environment per ton of chlorine manufactured in mercury electrolytic cells. This means, for example, that the substitution of nylon for cotton has generated an intensified environmental impact due to mercury, for nylon production (unlike cotton production) involves the use of chlorinated intermediates—therefore of chlorine—and hence the release of mercury into the environment. The rapid parallel rise in the production of synthetic organic chemicals, of chlorine production, and of the use of mercury in chlorine production is illustrated in figure 9.

Similarly, the displacement of steel and lumber by aluminum adds to the burden of air pollutants, for aluminum production is extremely power consumptive. Per pound of aluminum produced, about 29,860 British thermal units (Btu) of power are required to generate the necessary electricity, whereas about 4,615 Btu are used per pound of steel produced. Cement, which tends to displace steel in construction, is also extremely power consumptive in its production. The production of chemicals, aluminum, and cement account for about 28 percent of the total industrial use of electricity in the United States.

Packaging

The displacement of older forms of packaging by "disposable" containers, such as nonreturnable bottles, is another example of the intensification of environmental impact due to the postwar pattern of U.S. economic growth. This is illustrated in figure 10 and table 6. It is evident that there has been a very striking increase in environmental impact due to beer bottles, which are not

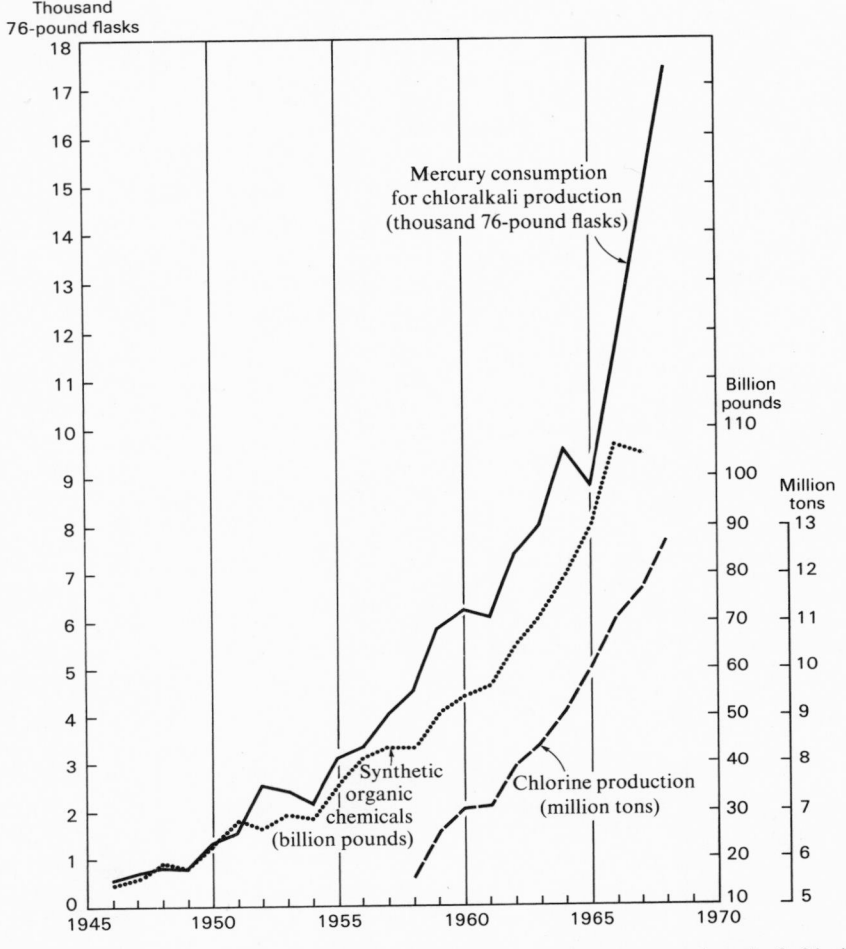

Figure 9. Changes in annual production of synthetic organic compounds and of chlorine gas, and consumption of mercury for chlorine gas production in the United States, 1946–1968. *Source*: U.S. Bureau of the Census, "Inorganic Chemicals and Gases," *Current Industrial Reports*, Series M28A; and U.S. Department of Commerce, *Statistical Abstract of the United States* (1962, 1968, and 1970).

assimilated by ecological systems and which, in their manufacture, are quite power consumptive. It is also evident that the major factor in this intensified environmental impact is the new technology—the use of nonreturnable bottles to contain beer—rather than increased population or "affluence" with respect to per capita consumption of beer. At the same time, a recent study showed that the total expenditure of energy (for bottle manufacture, processing, shipping)

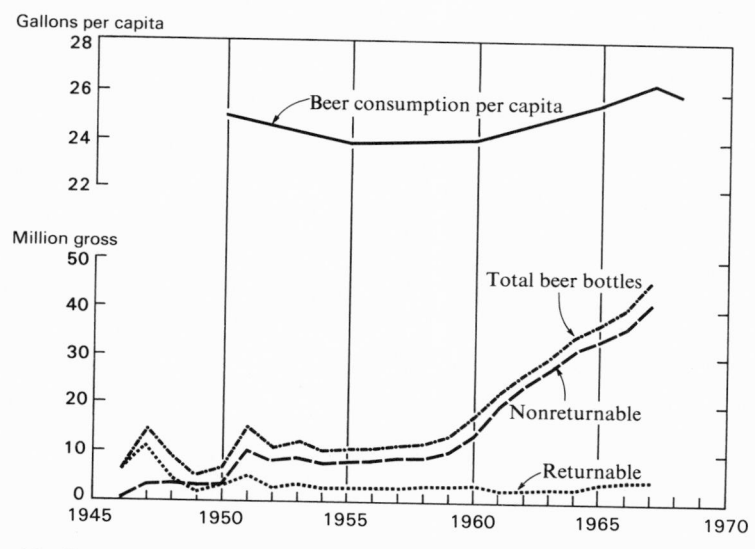

Figure 10. Per capita consumption of beer and production of beer bottles in the United States, 1946-1967. *Source*: U.S. Department of Commerce, *Statistical Abstract of the United States* (1951), p. 792; (1955), p. 833; and (1970), p. 12.

Table 6. Beer Bottles: Environmental Impact Index

	Index factors			Total impact index
	(a)	(b)	(c)	(a × b × c)
	Population	Beer consumption / Population	Beer bottles / Beer consumption	Beer bottles
	(*1,000*)	(*gallons/cap.*)	(*bottles/gallon*)	(*1,000 gross*)
1950	151,868	24.99	0.25	6,540
1967	197,859	26.27	1.26	45,476
1967 : 1950	1.30	1.05	5.08	6.95
Percentage increase, 1950–1967	30	5	408	595

required to deliver equal amounts of fluid in nonreturnable bottles is 4.7 times that for returnable ones.[6]

Automotive Vehicles

Finally, there is the problem of assessing the environmental impact of changes in patterns of passenger travel and freight traffic since 1946. Particularly important has been the increased use of automobiles, buses, and trucks.

[6] By personal communication with Bruce Hannon of the University of Illinois.

The environmental impact of the internal combustion engine is due to the emission of nitrogen oxides, carbon monoxide, waste fuel, and lead. The intensities of these impacts, as measured by the levels of these pollutants in the environment, is a function not only of the vehicle-miles traveled but also of the nature of the engine itself—i.e., technological factors are relevant as well.

The technological changes in automotive engines since World War II have worsened environmental impact. The results of these changes are illustrated in figure 11. Thus, for passenger automobiles, overall mileage per gallon of fuel declined from 14.97 in 1949 to 14.08 in 1967, largely because average horsepower increased from 100 to 240. Another important technological change was

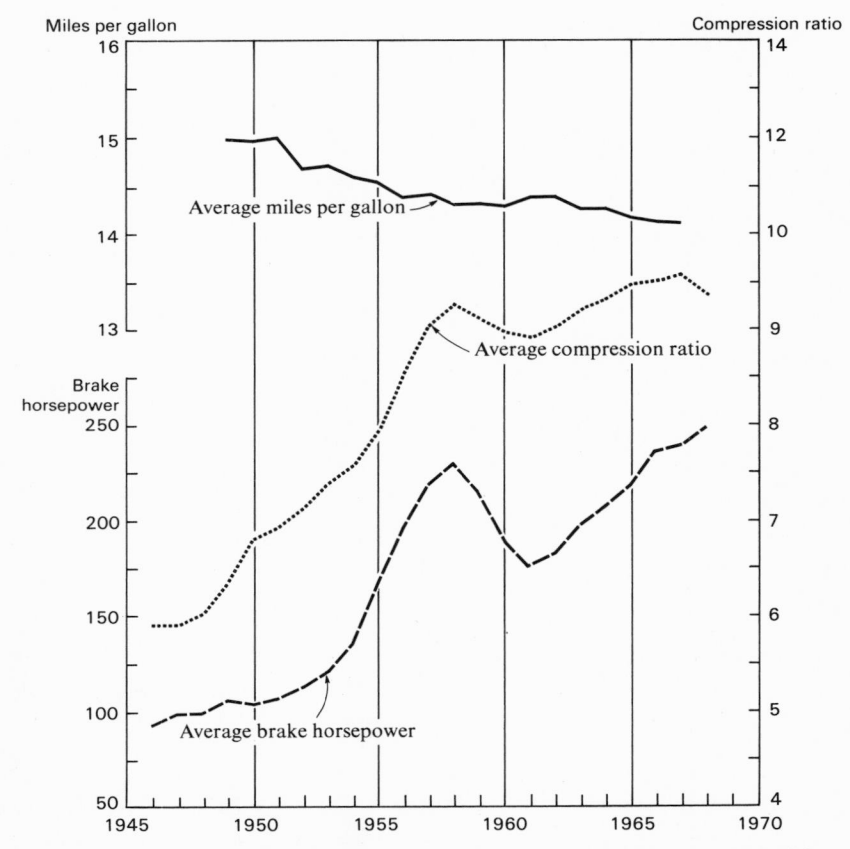

Figure 11. Average characteristics of passenger car engines produced in the United States, 1946–1968. *Sources*: Brake horsepower and compression ratio data are from the 1951 and 1970 volumes of *Brief Passenger Car Data*, Ethyl Corporation. Gasoline consumption data are from U.S. Department of Commerce, *Statistical Abstract of the United States*, for the years 1947–68.

in average compression ratio, which increased from about 5.9 to 9.5 in 1946-68. This engineering change has had two important effects on the environmental impact of the gasoline engine. First, increasing amounts of tetraethyl lead are needed as a gasoline additive in order to suppress the engine knock that occurs at high compression ratios. As shown in figure 12, annual use of tetraethyl lead increased significantly in 1946-68. Essentially all of this lead is emitted from the engine exhaust and is disseminated into the environment. Since lead is not a functional element in any biological organism and is in fact toxic, it represents an external intrusion on the ecosystem and generates an appreciable environmental effect.

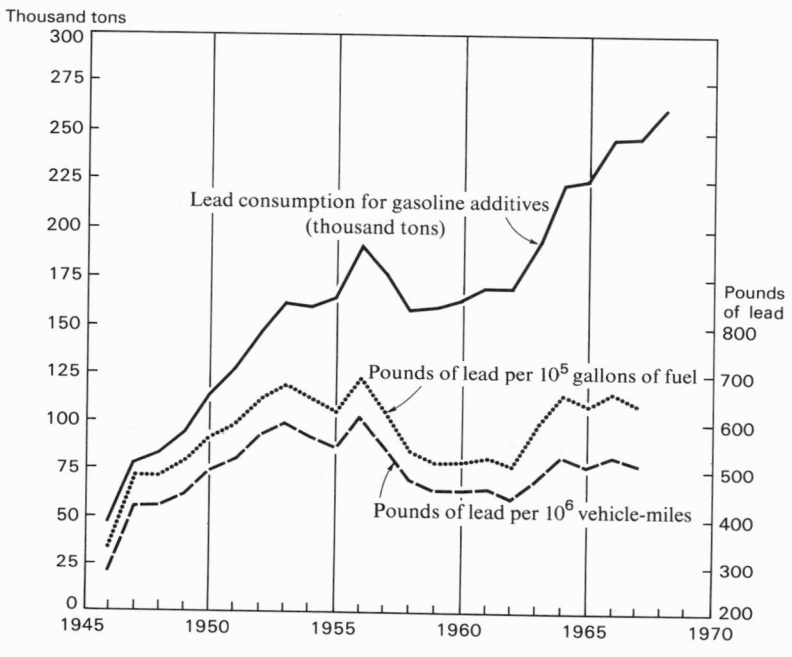

Figure 12. Lead emissions from tetraethyl lead in gasoline in the United States, 1946-1968. *Source*: U.S. Department of the Interior, Bureau of Mines, *Minerals Yearbook*, for the years 1947-68; and U.S. Department of Commerce, *Statistical Abstract of the United States* (1951, 1955, and 1970).

A second consequence of the increase in engine compression ratio has been a rise in the concentration of nitrogen oxides emitted in engine exhaust. This has occurred because the engine temperature increases with compression ratio. The combination of nitrogen and oxygen, present in the air taken into the engine cylinder, to form nitrogen oxides is enhanced at elevated temperatures. Nitrogen oxide is the key ingredient in the formation of photochemical smog. Through a

series of light-activated reactions involving waste fuel, nitrogen oxides induce the formation of peroxyacetyl nitrate, the noxious ingredient of photochemical smog. Smog of this type was first detected in Los Angeles in 1942–43; it was unknown in most other U.S. cities until the late 1950s and 1960s but is now a nearly universal urban pollutant. Peroxyacetyl nitrate is a toxic agent to man, agricultural crops, and trees. Introduction of this agent probably increased by about an order of magnitude in 1946–68.

The environmental impact indices for nitrogen oxides and lead are shown in tables 7 and 8. The total environmental impact for nitrogen oxides increased by about 630 percent between 1946 and 1967. The technological factor (the amount of nitrogen oxides emitted per vehicle-mile) increased by 158 percent, vehicle-miles traveled per capita increased by about 100 percent, and the population factor by about 41 percent. In the case of tetraethyl lead, the largest increase in impact was in vehicle-miles traveled per capita (100 percent), followed by the technological factor (83 percent) and the population factor (41 percent). It is evident that the major influences on automotive air pollution are increased per capita mileage (in part, because of changes in work-residence distribution due to the expansion of suburbs) and the increased environmental impact per mile traveled due to technological changes in the gasoline engine.

A similar situation obtains with respect to overland shipments of intercity freight. Truck freight has tended to displace railroad freight. And again the displacing technology has a more severe environmental impact than the displaced

Table 7. Nitrogen Oxides from Passenger Vehicles: Environmental Impact Index

	Index factors			Total impact index
	(a)	(b)	(c)	(a × b × c)
	Population (1,000)	Vehicle-miles Population	Nitrogen oxides[a] Vehicle-miles	Nitrogen oxides
1946	140,686	1,982	33.5	10.6
1967	197,849	3,962	86.4	77.5
1967:1946	1.41	2.00	2.58	7.3
Percentage increase, 1946–1967	41	100	158	630

[a]Dimension = NO_x (ppm) × gasoline consumption (gal. × 10^{-6}). Estimated from product of passenger-vehicle gasoline consumption and ppm of NO_x emitted by engines of average compression ratio 5.9 (1946) and 9.5 (1967) under running conditions, at 15 in. manifold pressure: 1946, 500 ppm NO_x; 1967, 1,200 ppm NO_x.

SOURCES: T. A. Huls and H. A. Nickol, "Engine Variables Influence Nitric Oxide Concentration in Exhaust Gas," SAE Journal, vol. 76, no. 8 (August 1968), pp. 40–45; and "The Effect of Engine Operating Variables on Oxides of Nitrogen: A Report to the Variables Panel of the Group on Composition of Exhaust Gases, CRC, from the General Motors Research Staff" (September 25, 1957, mimeo.).

Table 8. Tetraethyl Lead: Environmental Impact Index

	(a)	(b)	(c)	Total impact index
	Population	Vehicle-miles[a] / Population	Tetraethyl lead[b] / Vehicle-miles[a]	(a × b × c)
	(1,000)	*(veh. mi./cap.)*	*(lb./mill. veh. mi.)*	Tetraethyl lead[b] *(1,000 tons)*
1946	140,686	1,984[c]	300[c]	48[c]
1967	197,859	3,962	630	247
1967 : 1946	1.41	2.00	1.83	5.15
Percentage increase, 1946–1947	41	100	83	415

[a]Passenger vehicles only.

[b]Weight refers to lead content.

[c]Estimated, using 1949 breakdowns of vehicle miles and gasoline consumption into passenger and nonpassenger uses and extrapolating these percentages to 1946.

technology. This is evident from the energy required to transport freight by rail and truck: 624 Btu per ton-mile by rail and 3,462 Btu per ton-mile by truck. It should be noted as well that the steel and cement required to produce equal lengths of railroad and expressway (suitable for heavy truck traffic) differ in the amount of power required in the ratio of 1 to 3.6. This is due to the rather power-consumptive nature of cement production and to the fact that four highway lanes are required to accommodate heavy truck traffic. In addition, the divided roadway requires a 400 foot right-of-way, while a train roadbed needs only 100 feet. In all these ways the displacement of railroads by automotive vehicles, not only for freight but also for passenger travel, has intensified the resultant environmental impact.

THE ENVIRONMENTAL IMPACT INVENTORY

It will be recognized that the foregoing analysis represents only small fragments of a complex whole. What is required is a full inventory of the various environmental impact indices associated with the productive enterprise and the identification of the origins of these impacts within the production process and of the ecosystems on which they intrude. Such an assemblage of data, representing an environmental impact inventory, is derived as an exploratory exercise below, with reference to a productive item for which a certain amount of the needed data happens to be at hand—the production of chlorine and alkali by chlor-alkali plants employing mercury electrolytic cells.

The needed data include: (1) the environmental impact indices associated with the input goods, chiefly electric power, salt, and mercury; (2) the environmental impact indices representative of the wastes of the process and the prop-

erties of the ecological systems that are affected by them; and (3) the environmental impact indices representative of the ecologically significant wastes associated with the output goods (chlorine and alkali) of the process and the environmental fate of this material. Thus, the production of one megawatt of electricity by plants burning fossil fuels results in the release of 34.20 pounds of sulfur oxides to the atmosphere. Since 4,300 kilowatt-hours (kwh) are consumed by a mercury cell chlor-alkali plant per ton of chlorine produced, on the average, 147 pounds of sulfur oxides are released to the environment per ton of chlorine produced. In this way the corresponding values for other power plant pollutants (e.g., nitrogen oxides, dust) can be computed as well.

The major ecologically significant waste from chlor-alkali production is mercury metal. Two studies provide data on the amounts of mercury released to the air or to surface waters or buried in landfill per ton of chlorine produced. For example, per ton of chlorine produced, about 17–35 grams of mercury vapor are emitted to the air as waste. Chemical engineering data indicate a total "mercury loss" of 0.2–0.5 pounds per ton of chlorine for the process. This agrees rather well with the total losses to the environment estimated directly in the studies, 0.13–0.57 pounds of mercury per ton of chlorine.

The present data indicate that as much as 20 grams of mercury may become incorporated in the alkali produced in the course of producing a ton of chlorine; this alkali is used in some forty-two separate products. From an input-output analysis of the chlor-alkali industry, one could construct a comprehensive matrix for the movement of mercury contained in alkali through various manufacturing processes into the environment. Recently, economic input-output methods (Leontief and Isard) have been adapted to include environmental externalities.[7] For present purposes, I will restrict the analysis to a group of products—wood pulp and paper, soap, lye, and cleansers—that use about 26 percent of the alkali output. Hence, it may be estimated that of every 20 grams of mercury that go into alkali, 26 percent, or 5 grams, appears in the products listed above. The environmental fates of these products are known. Waste water containing cleansers goes into waterways, as do the fluid wastes from pulp and paper production. Paper is eventually burned, releasing its mercury to the air as vapor.

The ecological data relevant to an environmental impact inventory for chlor-alkali production are just beginning to be investigated. When metallic mercury is dumped into surface waters, it sinks into the bottom mud as droplets. There it may be acted on by certain species of bacteria that convert the mercury to an organic form, methyl mercury. While metallic mercury does not dissolve in water, methyl mercury does. Hence, in this form the mercury is readily taken up by living organisms in the water, ultimately contaminating fish that may be

---

[7] See, for example, Walter Isard and others, "On the Linkage of Socio-Economic and Ecologic Systems," *The Regional Science Association Papers*, vol. 21 (1968), p. 79.

eaten by people. In recent months, it has been found that mercury wastes from a number of chlor-alkali plants have caused mercury levels in fish in adjacent surface water to exceed acceptable public health limits. Emitted into the air, mercury may be taken up directly by human beings through absorption in the lungs or may be washed down into soil and water by precipitation—and thus enter into these ecosystems. Very little is known as yet about the ecological transfer of mercury in the soil. Finally, since mercury is very volatile, when heated (as in an incinerator), it is vaporized and emitted into the air. A recent study showed that domestic incinerators in St. Louis emit about 2,000-3,000 pounds of mercury into the air annually. Much of this originates in the incineration of paper and wood pulp products.

On the basis of such data, one can now produce (here in a quite incomplete and tentative form) an environmental impact inventory for chlor-alkali production. This is presented in table 9.

SOME CONCLUSIONS

The data presented above reveal a functional connection between economic growth—at least in the United States since 1946—and environmental impact. It is significant that the range of increase in the computed environmental impacts agrees fairly well with the independent measure of the actual levels of pollutants occurring in the environment. Thus, the increase in the environmental impact index for tetraethyl lead computed from gasoline consumption data for 1946-67 is about 400 percent. A similar increase in environmental lead levels has been recorded from analyses of layered ice in glaciers.[8] Similarly, the 648 percent increase in the nineteen-year period 1949-68 in the environmental impact index computed for nitrogen fertilizer is in keeping with the few available large-scale field measurements. Thus, field data show that nitrate entering the Missouri River as it traversed Nebraska in the six-year period 1956-62 increased a little over 200 percent.[9] The environmental impact indices computed for several aspects of automotive vehicle use are also in keeping with general field observations. It is widely recognized that the most striking increase in the several aspects of environmental deterioration due to automotive vehicles has occurred with respect to photochemical smog. This pollutant was detected for the first time in Los Angeles in 1942-43. Since then it has increased, nationally, by probably an order of magnitude, appearing in nearly every major city and even in smaller ones in the last five years. However, in the period 1946-68 total use of automotive vehicles, as measured by gasoline consumption, increased by only

[8]Clair C. Patterson and Joseph D. Alvia, "Lead in the Modern Environment: How Much Is Natural?" *Scientist and Citizen*, vol. 10, no. 3 (April 1968), p. 66.
[9]Commoner, "Threats to the Integrity of the Nitrogen Cycle."

Table 9. Environmental Impact Inventory: Chloralkali Production by Means of
          Mercury Electrolytic Cells

	Production process	Relevant ecological systems[a]	Environmental impact (per ton of chlorine produced)
Input goods[b]	Electric power (4,300 kwh/ton Cl)	Air	SO_x: 147.1 lb. NO_x: 29.4 lb. Particulates: 5.9 lb. Mercury: 0.004 gm. Heat: 5.51×10^6 Btu
		Surface waters	Heat: 16.56×10^6 Btu
Production process step[b]	H_2 gas ventilation	Air	Mercury: 17–35 gm.
	H_2 condensate, wash water	Surface waters via settling pond or drainage system	Mercury: 35–121 gm.
	Brine sludge removal	Surface waters	
	Anode, sweepings removal	Soil via landfill	Mercury: 6–97 gm.
Output goods[b]	Selected alkali-using goods (soap, lye, cleansers, pulp and paper)	Air, surface waters	Mercury: 1–5 gm.
			Total Mercury: 59–258 gm./ton Cl (0.10–0.57 lbs/ton Cl

[a]In an actual index, reference would be made to a standardized description of each of the indicated relevant ecological systems.

[b]Only a few of the actual items are shown, for purposes of illustration.

about 200 percent—an increment too small to account for the concurrent rise in the incidence of photochemical smog. It is significant, then, that this disparity between the observed increase in smog levels and the increase in vehicle use is accounted for by the environmental impact index computed for nitrogen oxides, the agent that initiates the smog reaction, for that index increased by 630 percent in 1946–67.

These agreements with actual field data support the conclusion that the computations represented by the environmental impact index provide a useful approximation of the changes in environmental impact associated with the relevant features of the growth of the United States economy since 1946. In particular, we can therefore place some reliance on the subdivision of the total impact index into the several factors: population size, per capita production or consumption, and the technology of production and use.

It is of interest to directly compare the relative contributions of increases in population size, in "affluence," and in changes in the technology of production with the increases in total environmental impact that have occurred since 1946.

The ratio of the most recent total index value to the value of the 1946 index (or to the value for the earliest year for which the necessary data are available) is indicative of the change in the total impact over this period of time. The relative contributions of the several factors to these total changes is then given by the ratios of their respective partial indices. Figure 13 shows such comparisons for the six productive activities evaluated. The population factor contributes only between 12 and 20 percent of the total changes in the impact index. For all but the automotive pollutants, the affluence factor makes a rather small contribution—no more than 5 percent—to the total changes in the impact index. For nitrogen oxides and tetraethyl lead (from automotive sources), this factor accounts for about 40 percent of the total effect, reflecting a considerable increase in the number of vehicle-miles traveled per capita since 1946. The technological changes in the processes that generate the various economic goods, contribute from 40–90 percent of the total increases in impact.

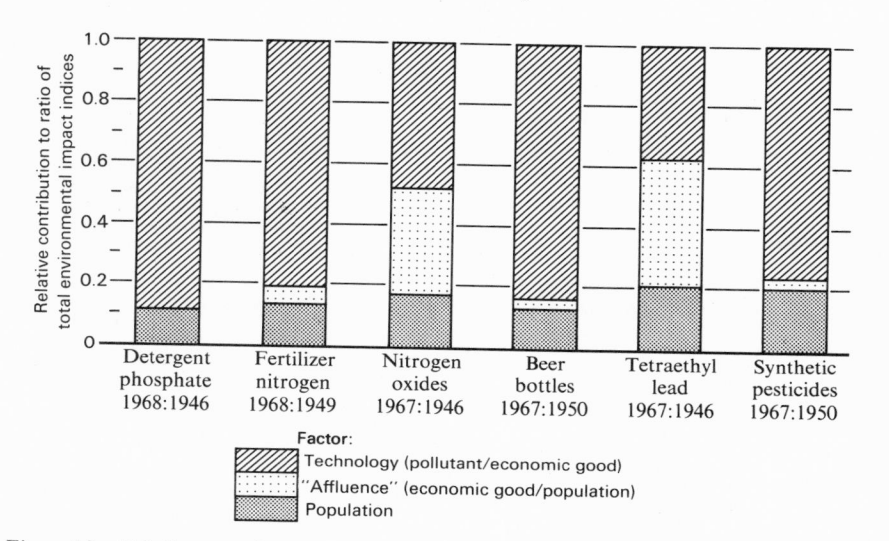

Figure 13. Relative contributions of several factors to changes in the environmental impact indices. The contributions of population size, "affluence" (production per capita), and technological characteristics (amount of pollutant released per unit production) to the total environmental impact indices were computed as shown in the text. Each bar is subdivided to show the *relative* contributions, on a scale of 1.0, of the several factors to the ratio of the total impact index value for the later year to the value for the earlier year.

In evaluating these results, it should be noted that automotive travel is itself strongly affected by a kind of technological transformation: the rapid increase of suburban residences in the United States and the concomitant failure to provide adequate railroad and other mass transportation to accommodate to this change. That the overall increase in vehicle-miles traveled per capita since 1946 (about 100 percent) is related to increased residence-work travel incident upon

this change is suggested by the results of a 1963 survey. It was found that 90 percent of all automobile trips, representing 30 percent of total mileage traveled, are 10 miles or less in length. The mean residence-work travel distance was about 5.5 miles. Thus, it is probably appropriate to regard the increase in per capita vehicle-miles traveled by automobile as a response to new work-residence relationships that require more transportation, rather than to attribute it to increased affluence.

During the period from 1946 to the present, pollution levels in the United States have increased sharply—generally by an order of magnitude or so. It seems evident from the data presented above that most of this increase is due to one of the three factors that influence environmental impact—the technology of production—and that both population growth and increasing affluence exert a much smaller influence. Thus, the chief reason for the sharp increase in environmental stress in the United States is the sweeping transformation in production technology in the postwar period. *Productive activities with intense environmental impacts have displaced activities with less serious environmental impacts; the growth pattern has been counter-ecological.* This conclusion is easily misconstrued to mean that technology is therefore, per se, ecologically harmful. That this interpretation is unwarranted can be seen from the following examples.

Consider the simple transformation of the present ecologically faulty relationship among soil, agricultural crops, the human population, and sewage. Suppose that the sewage, instead of being introduced into surface waters as it is now, whether directly or following treatment, is instead transported from urban collection systems by pipeline to agricultural areas, where—after appropriate sterilization procedures—it is incorporated into the soil. Such a pipeline would literally reincorporate the urban population into the soil's ecological cycle. It would restore the integrity of that cycle and incidentally remove the need for inorganic nitrogen fertilizer—which also stresses the aquatic cycle. Hence, the urban population would no longer be external to the soil cycle and therefore would be incapable either of generating a negative biological stress on it or of exerting a positive ecological stress on the aquatic ecosystem. But note that this state of zero environmental impact is not achieved by a return to "primitive" conditions; it is achieved by an actual technological advance, the construction of a sewage pipeline system.

Or consider the example provided by the technological treatment of gold and other precious metals. Gold is, after all, subject to numerous technological manipulations that generate a series of considerable economic values. Yet we manage to accomplish all of this without intruding more than a small fraction of all the gold ever acquired by human beings into the ecosphere. Because we value it so highly, very little gold is "lost" to the environment. In contrast, most of the mercury that has entered commerce in the last generation has been disseminated into the environment with very unfortunate effects. Clearly, given adequate technology—and motivation—we could be as thrifty in our handling of mercury

as we are of gold, thereby preventing the entry of this toxic material into the environment. Again, what is required is not necessarily the abandonment of mercury-based technology, but rather the improvement of that technology to the point of satisfactory compatibility with the ecosystem.

Generally speaking, it would appear possible to reduce the environmental impact of human activities by developing alternatives to ecologically faulty activities. This can be accomplished, not by abandoning technology and the economic goods it can yield, but by developing *new* technologies that incorporate the knowledge of the physical sciences (as most do moderately well; the new machines do, after all, usually produce their intended goods) and ecological wisdom as well.

These considerations show that the deterioration of the environment, whatever its cost in money, social distress, and personal suffering, is chiefly the result of the ecologically faulty technology that has been employed to remake productive enterprises. The resulting environmental impacts stress the basic ecosystems that support the life of human beings, destroy the "biological capital" that is essential to the operation of industry and agriculture, and may, if unchecked, lead to the catastrophic collapse of these systems. The environmental impacts already generated are sufficient to threaten the continued development of the economic system. Witness the current difficulties in the United States in siting new power plants at a time of severe power shortage and the recent curtailment of industrial innovation in the fields of detergents, chemical manufacturing, insecticides, herbicides, chlorine production, oil drilling, oil transport, supersonic aviation, nuclear power generation, and industrial use of nuclear explosives—all resulting from public rejection of the concomitant environmental deterioration.

The actual cost of the degradation that has been the response of the environmental system to the intensified impacts upon it is, of course, a very difficult matter. As indicated earlier, the theory linking environmental impact to ecological effect is poorly developed for the most part. At the same time, there are formidable difficulties confronting the economist who attempts to return the "externalities" represented by ecological damage to the realm of economic evaluation. These efforts, which appear to be developing increasingly useful information, need not be reviewed here. For there is, I believe, a simpler and more direct way to express the cost to the economic system represented by environmental deterioration. It seems to me that a meaningful way to evaluate this cost is somewhat along the following lines:

1. Given that the deterioration of the environment, whatever its cost in money, social distress, and personal suffering, is chiefly the result of the ecologically faulty technology employed to remake productive enterprises in the United States since 1946; and

2. Given that the resulting environmental impacts stress the basic ecosystems that support the life of human beings, destroy the "biological capital"

that is essential to the operation of industry and agriculture, and may in a period of a few decades lead to the catastrophic collapse of these systems; and

3. Given further that the environmental impacts already generated are sufficient to threaten the continued development of the economic system—witness the difficulties in siting new power plants at a time of severe power shortage and the recent curtailment of industrial innovation in many fields because of public rejection of the concomitant environmental deterioration;

4. Then, it seems probable that, if we are to survive economically as well as biologically, much of the technological transformation of the U.S. economy since 1946 will need to be, so to speak, redone in order to bring the nation's productive technology much more closely into harmony with the inescapable demands of the ecosystem. This will require the development of massive new technologies for systems to return sewage and garbage directly to the soil; for the replacement of synthetic materials by natural ones; for supporting the reversal of the present trend to retire soil from agriculture and to elevate the yield per acre; for the development of land transport that operates with maximal fuel efficiency at low combustion temperatures; and for the sharp curtailment of the use of biologically active synthetic organic agents. In effect, what is required is a new period of technological transformation of the economy that will reverse the counter-ecological trends developed since 1946. The cost of the new transformation might be estimated from the cost of the former one, which must represent a capital investment in the range of hundreds of billions of dollars. To this must be added, of course, the cost of repairing the ecological damage that has already been incurred, such as the eutrophication of Lake Erie—again, a bill to be reckoned in the hundreds of billions of dollars.

The enormous size of these costs raises a final question: Is there some functional connection in the economy between the tendency of a given productive activity to inflict an intense impact on the environment (and the size of the resultant costs) and the role of this activity in economic growth? For it is evident from even a cursory comparison of the productive activities that have rapidly expanded in the U.S. economy since 1946 with the activities they displaced that the displacing activities are also considerably more profitable than those displaced. The correlation between profitability and rapid growth is one that is presumably accountable by economics. Is the additional linkage to intense environmental impact also functional, or only accidental?

It has been pointed out often enough that environmental pollution represents a long-unpaid debt to nature. Is it possible that the U.S. economy has grown since 1946 by deriving much of its new wealth through the enlargement of that debt? If this should turn out to be the case, what strains will develop in the economy if, for the sake of the survival of our society, that debt should now be called? How will these strains affect our ability to pay the debt—to survive?

II.
ON ENERGY GROWTH AND THE ENVIRONMENT

Possible Impacts of Environmental Standards on Electric Power Availability and Costs

PHILIP SPORN

In my opinion, the projections of U.S. energy consumption for the end of this century cited by Joel Darmstadter[1] overstate the likely rate of growth. The projections indicate 190,014 trillion British thermal units (Btu) of total energy input for the year 2000, net electric energy generation of 10,802 billion kilowatt-hours (kwh), and installed generating capacity of 2,228,400 megawatts (mw). I believe the requirements are likely to be 20–25 percent less—152,000 trillion Btu of total energy input, 8,640 billion kwh of electric generation, and 1,780,000 mw of electrical generating capacity. Even so, these are formidable estimates in view of the figures for 1970 of 68,000 trillion Btu of total energy input, 1,529 billion kwh generated, and 340,000 mw of installed generating capacity.

Some factors, it seems to me, have not been taken into account in the projections of total gross energy input given in table 12 in the appendix—the likely acceptance of the minicar, the net effect on energy input of even a moderate development of the electric car, and the probable moderating influence on the U.S. gross national product (GNP) of increased social expenditures whose associated energy requirements presumably will be lower than those

Philip Sporn is a consultant. A former President of the American Electric Power Company, which he joined in 1921, he has also served the company as Chairman of the System Development Committee (1961–67), Executive Vice President (1945–47), Chief Engineer (1932–45), and Chief Electrical Engineer (1927–32). He has been a consultant to the Atomic Energy Commission and the Joint Committee on Atomic Energy and has taught at the Massachusetts Institute of Technology as a visiting professor. Mr. Sporn was born in Austria in 1896. He received his E.E. degree from Columbia University.

[1] See appendix.

embodied in the traditional relationship between GNP and energy use. Also, in the next three decades we most certainly will have our share of recessions, inflationary binges, and major manufacturing and construction industry strikes—none of which provide a climate particularly favorable to industrial expansion.

As for the electric energy figures for the year 2000 shown in table 14 in the appendix, assuming that 96,000 mw of the 114,000 mw of conventional steam capacity in service in 1960 will have been retired forty years later, then an average annual addition of 64,900 mw will be made to generating capacity between 1971 and 2000; an average of only 15,600 mw were added annually in the last ten years and 13,200 mw in the last eighteen years. On the basis of the increases in the past, I do not believe the United States can or will add the projected large blocks of generating capacity annually between now and the end of the century. Even though some deceleration toward the end of the century is assumed in the projections of electricity growth given by Darmstadter, this assumed slowdown, in my opinion, is not sufficiently great.

My lower projections will not satisfy those who believe with David Inglis that

> if, through wise regulations limiting advertising and certain types of consumption, and by readjusting power rates, we should keep the increase in the next decade down to 60 per cent instead of the expected 100 per cent, we could dispense with nuclear power completely and still have no greater demands on fossil-fuel production of electricity. We should be able to limit the demand more than that and still have a healthily, though less rapidly, expanding economy.[2]

I doubt that it is in the best interests of the American people to adopt Professor Inglis's program for limiting energy growth. Since every projection of population, GNP, and industrial production indicates major increases in total energy use, electric energy use, and per capita use, I shall discuss the impacts of environmental costs on the program of expansion and growth as I visualize that growth.

Will the required energy be available? Can the present rate of energy exploitation be continued without risking catastrophe in the form of melting ice caps, higher ocean levels, and the flooding out of the coastal cities of the world? Many evaluations of this threat have been made. Alvin M. Weinberg and R. Philip Hammond have carefully analyzed the problem, and they have demonstrated that the expressed fears are completely without foundation. In a paper in which he discussed this point, Dr. Weinberg said:

> If the entire world became developed, and each person used energy at an annual rate of 20 kilowatts of heat, then a world of 20,000,000,000 people

---

[2] "Nuclear Energy and the Malthusian Dilemma," *Science and Public Affairs*, vol. 27, no. 2 (February 1971), p. 18.

would dissipate 400,000,000,000 kilowatts of heat. This is 100 times the present energy budget of man; it is 1/300th of the sun's energy budget actually absorbed (and in equilibrium, re-emitted) by the earth. If one assumed that this additional energy would not change, say, the cloud cover on the earth so that the earth's reflectivity will remain as it is today, this increment of man-made energy would, on the average, increase the temperature of the earth by only ¼°C. Of course local heating effects would be serious; but if power plants were located on the oceanside or even offshore, the heat could be dissipated to the ocean with what are probably small ecological effects. However, the precise ecological implications of each installation would have to be carefully examined.[3]

The dismissal of this basic fear is important, because it is this fear that presents the greatest obstacle to building the facilities and providing the means to meet the five-and-a-half-fold growth in electric energy requirements that I have conservatively projected for the year 2000.

No limit will be imposed on growth by the unavailability of primary energy sources. Please note, however, that this does not mean that it will be possible to utilize these resources in compliance with regulations and restrictions that may be invoked in connection with their use.

And there will be no restrictions on growth due to a lack of manufacturing facilities to provide the additional equipment—boilers, reactors, generators, and transmission and distribution facilities—required for this increased capacity. Nor will the need to spend roughly $500 billion (in today's prices) to pay for this capacity present any obstacles. Rather the question is how the rapidly multiplying codes and regulations designed to protect the environment will limit growth.

The desire to protect our environment without further delay—to bring about compatibility between our technological society, which increasingly exploits resources and energy, and our environment—is legitimate enough. But surely we cannot beat a technological retreat. If U.S. population growth makes the Census Bureau's highest projection a reality and we become a nation of 320 million people by the year 2000, we will have a great deal of work ahead of us. If we are to keep this 320 million fed, clothed, housed, educated, employed, and living at increasing levels of welfare, we must expand our economy and increase our productivity. This means more tools and more energy. The increased production and productivity simply cannot come about in any other way.

We cannot go back. To quote Loren Eiseley, "Increasingly there is but one way into the future: the technological way."[4] Nor can we afford to act under the pressure of the panic that has developed across the nation. To find out what

[3] "Prudence and Technology: A Technologist's Response to Predictions of Catastrophe" (paper presented at the Institute of Electrical and Electronics Engineers Nuclear Science Symposium, New York City, November 4, 1970, mimeo.).

[4] *The Unexpected Universe* (Harcourt, Brace & World, 1969), pp. 38-39.

was going on in environmental activities, I recently sent a letter to the top people in ten leading electric utilities extending from coast to coast and covering companies serving large metropolitan areas, large integrated systems serving an extensive geographic area, and systems limited to a single major city—in other words, representative systems of the U.S. electric utility industry, both public and private. I asked them several questions, including:

1. Which of the following factors do you believe will significantly influence the planning, building, or operation of your power facilities over the next ten to twenty years?

    Air pollution
    Water pollution
    Visual pollution, or esthetics
    Noise pollution
    Use of herbicides and pesticides
    Conservation
    Recreation

2. Which of the above factors or problems have become major state or community issues in your territory to date?

3. What programs or policies have the concerned communities adopted, or are they discussing programs to minimize the effects of the pollution factors listed in 1 above?

There was almost unanimous agreement that the three most pressing questions were air, water, and visual pollution. All three have become major local and state issues. A number of the respondents pointed out that some of these issues have been important concerns in their areas for more than fifteen years. In the less-urbanized areas, these matters are becoming a subject of active interest but have not reached the point of bitter controversy and conflict reached elsewhere. None of the utilities executives seemed surprised or indicated a resentful attitude toward these developments. Most of those surveyed clearly recognized that the reaction of their communities is not a temporary thing and that the programs being developed for meeting these concerns will have to be geared to a long-time schedule of action.

On question 3, regarding programs or policies that the concerned communities have adopted, the replies were revealing and a little frightening. An executive of one company pointed out that in the major city served by his company the approach has been largely one of progressively more restrictive environmental regulations, to the extent that there is concern that no new power plant construction will be permitted and that operation of existing plants may become almost impossible. A respondent with another company that serves one very large city and large suburban and rural areas as well said that, with minor exceptions, the communities served by the company have adopted programs or policies that can be summed up in three words: "Put it elsewhere."

We are, of course, all familiar with the $1°F$. limitation on condenser effluent proposed for Lake Michigan by the Department of the Interior in May 1970. While this fortunately has been withdrawn, the thermal pollution situation on Lake Michigan and the potential problems that may be created there from the standpoint of power generation certainly have not been cleared up. In many parts of the country, city and county governments are striving to outdo each other in adopting more stringent requirements than those proposed by their states, and this is particularly true of air pollution, land use, and esthetics.

In one of the major U.S. industrial cities, current regulations with regard to sulfur content in fuel call for a limit of 1 percent sulfur in oil, which will be reduced to 0.5 percent in 1972 and 0.3 percent in 1973. In coal, this limitation is now 2 percent and is scheduled for reduction to 1 percent in 1971 and 0.3 percent in 1972. It is significant that sulfur in fuel, which hurts no one until it is converted to sulfur dioxide, is sharply limited, whereas in the state in which this industrial city is located, there is no regulation on sulfur dioxide emission. In other areas a 1 percent sulfur limitation on fuel is either in effect or will go into effect well before 1971 comes to an end.

In many cases, the setting of standards has become a technique of local governing bodies to force the reduction of the level of undesirable combustion by-products without regard to the necessity for such low standards, their effect on costs, or the ability to get fuels to meet the standards. Preventing the pollution of our seashores, our estuaries, our lakes, and our rivers is an objective to which no socially minded person can fail to lend his fullest support. As for the air we breathe that sustains us, surely we want to protect it from pollution and corruption. And the streets, avenues, and squares of our cities and other centers of habitation—the landscape, the highways, and the byways of the country in general—need to be guarded against the invasion of the ugliness that does such violence to our esthetic sensibilities. All this, however, needs to be carried out and implemented in the context of a rational, unbiased scientific evaluation of existing conditions and of the means proposed to ameliorate them, including the effects on the economic life of the country.

But what is one to say about regulations that outlaw the use of many of our national fuel resources, not on the basis of contributions of harmful concentrations of effluent end-products at any level, but rather on the extent of the existence of a foreign body, or impurity if you will, in the fuel in its mineral state? What can one say except that it is unnecessarily destructive? This kind of regulation leads to economic lunacy, such as the hauling of low-sulfur coal from Wyoming and Montana to Chicago—1,200 miles away—with a freight cost of $10 per ton.[5] Since coal is one of the great resources of Illinois, it is hard to refrain

[5] Based on information communicated to the Joint Committee on Atomic Energy in February 1971.

from saying, "What a corkscrewy way for a people to grow strong and evolve into a great society!"

Americans today are impatient with conditions in their society that are the result of accepting the validity of a great many fallacies, social as well as technological. Since these fallacies have already influenced legislation, rules and regulations, research and development, and projected or contemplated action in the general areas of energy and the environment, I shall critically examine them in the hope that this will not only lead to better answers to the questions posed by the title of this paper but may even contribute to more rational conduct in programming our technological and administrative actions and procedures.

Here are the major fallacies:

1. *We are experiencing a trend of rapid energy growth and even more rapid electric energy growth that has been doubling every ten years, will double in the next ten years, redouble in the following ten, then redouble, and so on, for as long as one cares to project.*

The members of one utility organization could foresee no limitation to the continued growth of electrical energy at the rate of a doubling every six years. If this continued for forty-eight more years, the use of energy by the utility's customers would have grown 250-fold.

Recently Weinberg and Hammond published a perceptive paper on limits to the use of energy, in which they showed that the present annual U.S. energy budget is 10 kw thermal (kw^t) per person.[6] On the assumption that energy is convertible into the basic necessities for man's future, they drew up an energy budget for a society using energy as its basic raw material. After a series of calculations, and without specifying when such a state could or would be reached in the United States, they concluded that this budget figure would be roughly 600 million Btu per capita per year, or 20 kw^t per capita.

To check my conclusions about the fallacy of an essentially unrestricted exponential growth of energy and electricity use, I decided to assume that the United States would become a society using energy as its basic raw material by 2000. Thus, I arrived at the following energy and electric energy figures for that year, using the perhaps high population estimate of 320 million and an efficiency of conversion into electric energy of 40 percent (a 20 percent improvement over 1969):

$$\text{total energy} = 600 \times 10^6 \times 320 \times 10^6 = 192{,}000 \text{ trillion Btu;}$$

$$\text{total electric energy} = \frac{0.50 \times 192{,}000 \times 0.40 \times 10^{12}}{3{,}412} = 11{,}250 \text{ trillion kwh.}$$

[6] Alvin M. Weinberg and R. Philip Hammond, "Limits to the Use of Energy," *American Scientist*, vol. 58, no. 4 (July–August 1970), pp. 412–18.

It will be noted that the figures for total energy use and for electrical energy generation are substantially the same as those reported by Darmstadter for the year 2000. But since it is utterly inconceivable that the United States can be completely converted to the use of energy as its basic raw material in the short span of thirty years, the figures suggesting unlimited energy growth must be too high. At the same time, the calculation provides backing for what I consider to be my more conservative projections.

2. *Sulfur dioxide is the great atmospheric pollutant, and therefore sulfur must be eliminated from any fossil fuel burned.*

Sulfur dioxide is a most amazing example of how a component of fossil fuels can be indicted, tried, and condemned without anyone stopping long enough to ask: "How do we know?" or "What is the evidence?" The mere mention of sulfur results in a throwback to the medieval witch and witchcraft and "guilty as charged."

I recognized sulfur dioxide as a potential pollutant in power plant operation some nineteen years ago. A solution was worked out whereby the sulfur dioxide was dispersed to harmless levels through the use of a record-breaking high stack of 682 feet. A full account of the successful performance of the stack was given in 1966.[7] Recently, an excellent paper on the performance of the tall stack in Great Britain was presented in Washington, D.C., by three members of the Central Electricity Generating Board, F. F. Ross, A. J. Clarke, and D. H. Lucas.[8] I shall refer to their paper throughout my discussion of the second fallacy, for it includes an excellent account of the British adoption of the tall stack for control of sulfur dioxide pollution, and it is worthy of study by every responsible American scientist, technologist, and public administrator. I particularly feel this because so responsible and able a scientist as Alvin Weinberg declared recently: "Well, tall stacks are OK and go a certain distance, but when you have 500 million kilowatts or even 1,000 million kilowatts of electricity being generated, you finally realize that tall stacks are not the complete answer to the whole question."[9]

[7] Philip Sporn and T. T. Frankenberg, "Pioneering Experience with High Stacks on the OVEC and American Electric Power Systems," *Proceedings: Part 1*, International Clean Air Congress, London, October 4–6, 1966 (London: National Society for Clean Air, 1966), pp. 102–5.

[8] "Tall Stacks—How Effective Are They?" (paper prepared for the Second International Clean Air Congress, Washington, D.C., December 6–11, 1970, mimeo.). F. F. Ross is technical secretary of the Station Environment Steering Committee of the Central Electricity Generating Board and a recognized authority on pollution. A. J. Clarke heads a group of specialists in air and water pollution and other environmental factors of power station planning and operation. D. H. Lucas is head of the Physics Division, Central Electricity Research Laboratories. He has played a leading part in making air pollution a scientific subject.

[9] From the transcript of a taped discussion before the Institute of Electrical and Electronics Engineers Power Engineering Society, New York City, February 2, 1971.

My points of difference with Weinberg are:

(a) When will the American power industry have 1,000 million kw of fossil fuel capacity on the line? On the basis of my modification of Darmstadter's figures, the coal- and oil-burning generating capacity in effective service in the year 2000 will be only 448 million kw.

(b) Although tall stacks perhaps are not the final answer, why are they not a good answer for the next thirty years, considering the opinion of Ross, Clarke, and Lucas that "it would be a tragedy for the cause of clean air if the campaign for low-sulphur fuels and for sulphur removal led to underestimation of the potentiality of chimneys."

According to Ross and his associates, evidence of the ill effects of sulfur dioxide has been extraordinarily difficult to come by. The Hazelton Laboratories have kept monkeys in atmospheres containing 2,800 pgm^{-3} (1 part per million) for several months with no adverse effects.

The reduction of sulfur dioxide emissions either by some removal process or by using low-sulfur fuel will not, in general, reduce emissions to zero but will merely lessen the concentrations in the atmosphere. Ross and his associates point out that tall stacks are sometimes criticized because they "only spread the pollution further afield." But if the pollution is a gas that is not absorbed by the ground, the implication is false. Furthermore, there is no evidence that if a chimney is sufficiently tall to give satisfactory ground-level concentrations of sulfur dioxide there is any other gaseous pollutant in normal furnace flue gas that is not also diluted satisfactorily. Once again, for large plants in general, use of low-sulfur fuels is unnecessary and undesirable.

Ross, Clarke, and Lucas have stated that sulfur dioxide extraction processes are not promising. Processes that simultaneously cool the gases tend to defeat their own object because of the loss of thermal buoyancy.

In the light of all the above, is it possible that we are overreacting in the ways in which we are combatting the sulfur dioxide problem? I cannot do any better than to quote Ross and his associates again: "A high chimney is a cheap, reliable, and indeed indispensable means of reducing pollution by gases. The criticism of chimneys is largely misguided."

3. *Heat is a major pollutant of our water bodies.*

Unused heat from the bottom end of a thermodynamic power cycle has to be discharged into a heat sink. Almost universally, waterways have served as sinks for steam plants. To date, these waterways have not been damaged to any significant degree by such discharges. Yet mainly as a result of publicity about the increased heat burden that nuclear plants are bound to place on the waterway systems, there has been an enormous amount of public apprehension about the threatened life and character of communal waterways.

"What happened to Lake Erie will not, we are determined, happen to Lake Michigan," was, I am certain, the principal motivating idea behind the recent ill-conceived determination to impose a 1°F. limit on rises of temperature of the

effluents discharged into Lake Michigan. The fact that Lake Erie is a victim of discharges of sewage and some of the worst industrial wastes over many decades was apparently lost sight of in tagging as culprit the cooling water of steam electric condensers. And the fact that if the proposed limit of 1°F. had been sealed into a regulation it would have resulted in shutting down millions of kilowatts of electric generating capacity already in operation—needed to supply scores of communities in Wisconsin, Illinois, Indiana, and Michigan—would have meant little to the zealous defenders of the antipollution measures suggested for Lake Michigan.

There is still another point. Whether the effects of waste heat on water bodies are deleterious is highly controversial. The severity of the effects depends on the area in which the waste heat is discharged and the kinds of water life involved; these effects can range from a more productive yield of marine life to killing large numbers of fish. Although we know this and can forecast and plot patterns of heat dissipation, our ability to forecast the ecological results of heating water are not as well advanced. Hence, it is more important than ever to simplify this problem by taking rigorous steps against the known enemies of the ecology, while at the same time sharpening our technological knowledge and our evaluations of the factors having more complex effects on living matter.

The utilities of the country could play a more effective part in helping to demolish fallacy and in successfully establishing a more accurate relationship between cause and effect.

4. *Water is an indispensable heat sink for an efficient power cycle.*

Of course, this is not so, although water is a very convenient heat sink, and it is almost always a highly economical one. But as shown in the discussion of fallacy 3, it is becoming very difficult to use water as a heat sink—difficult for fossil fuel cycles and even more so for nuclear fuel cycles. Perhaps this can be straightened out. But if not?

It may be that the best answer to the heat sink problem is the dry cooling tower. But this solution, even disregarding its apparently greater economic price, may add esthetic problems on account of size and bulkiness. The dry cooling tower is not a new idea. It was brought into the realm of the practicable only recently, however, by the Heller cycle. In this cycle, the condensing medium is cooled in the same way as is the jacket water in the standard water-cooled car engine, except that a great deal more cooling surface is required. Thus, for example, a 1,000 mw unit requires about 1.75 million square feet of tubing, covered with approximately 40 million square feet of fins. The electric utility industry—its engineers, architect engineers, and associated manufacturers—is well aware of the concept of the dry cooling tower. But development of the tower is being neglected.

In 1970 at a symposium on thermal considerations in the production of electric power that brought together eighteen experts from the industry, the dry cooling tower was mentioned—as one would expect—by several of the partici-

pants, but without any sense of urgency. In the one paper devoted entirely to cooling towers, this discouraging judgment on the dry cooling tower was made:

Although apparently feasible, dry type cooling towers are not economically competitive due to high investment costs and lower steam cycle efficiency due to high condenser pressures. Some may be installed under special circumstances. Experience in operation is not available at this time and potential problems may be difficult to solve.[10]

I venture the judgment that just as nuclear power has given the world a fuel that has a universal ease of transportability so may the dry cooling tower free the steam electric plants of the future from the confinement of contiguity to large bodies of water. With this liberation, the rejected heat will be put directly into the atmosphere, interconnecting transmission lengths will be reduced, and all the terrors of thermal pollution of cherished water bodies will be eliminated. And this may be possible at no significant net increase in cost. The dry cooling tower is exciting enough to warrant an extensive development program at several levels.[11]

But if we are going to have a dry cooling tower, why not simplify some of the problems of the cooling cycle—possible freeze-up in winter, for example—by introducing a binary cycle using a freon condenser boiler to condense the steam and in the process to generate freon vapor? This can then be used to drive a freon turbine, and the freon exhaust will be condensed in the dry condenser. This offers possibilities of savings on the dry condenser, in the elimination of the steam condensers, and in the number and size of turbines. The binary cycle was first discussed in a paper presented in 1961 by Aronson,[12] and as far as I know has never been developed further.

5. *For the future, atomic power is the obvious clean, essentially nonpolluting, and practically inexhaustible power source.*

This judgment, shared by many, has a great deal of qualified truth in it. But from the standpoint of a categorical program for action in the present and the immediate future, it is a fallacy, nevertheless. How this fallacy originated is interesting. Its acceptance undoubtedly was enormously stimulated by the apparently favorable economies initially contained in the Oyster Creek (New Jersey) and Browns Ferry TVA plant promotions. In 1971 the fallacy was reinforced by the action of "the most turbulent of America's basic industries"—

---

[10] Riley D. Woodson, "Cooling Towers for Large Steam-Electric Generating Stations," in Merrill Eisenbud and George Gleason, eds., *Electric Power and Thermal Discharges* (New York: Gordon and Breach, 1969), p. 370.

[11] A sense of this excitement was conveyed by Charles T. Chave, an engineer with imagination, in "Applicability of Air Cooling to Siting Problems in the Pacific Coast Area" (paper presented at the Engineering and Operating Conference of the Pacific Coast Electrical Association, San Francisco, March 27, 1970, mimeo.).

[12] David Aronson, "Binary Cycle for Power Generation," *Proceedings of the American Power Conference, 1961*, vol. 23 (Illinois Institute of Technology, 1961), pp. 261–71.

coal—and the reaction of those in the utilities who were "disgusted by recent sharp increases in coal prices and by chaotic delivery schedules."[13] And surely the recent instability in oil prices in the international markets—with the Organization of Petroleum Exporting Countries demanding increases that would have raised the posted cost of oil to almost $2.60 a barrel, or nearly twice what the cost had been six months before[14]—contributed significantly.

Weinberg, relying on King Hubbert, has adopted the judgment that the long-term survival of man depends on an inexhaustible energy source that "almost surely will have to be nuclear," and has stated that "we shall therefore have to learn to live with the peaceful atom."[15] I share that judgment. The question is whether the public is ready to accept this view. Men have a fear, not merely cerebral but deeply visceral, of a nuclear accident that could cause destruction of life and property on a large scale. The technologists who have designed into their reactor systems what they believe to be an almost infallible defense against serious release of radioactivity cannot as yet point to an instance when the defense system was called upon to function and demonstrated its complete ability to prevent harm to the public. I do not believe that we can completely allay this fear until the demonstration has taken place.

This raises serious questions about the soundness of our current program of phasing nuclear energy into our rapidly growing overall energy requirements. When this question is examined critically, I am sure it will be found that a carefully balanced program of phasing-in harmonizes with the desirable provision of maximum diversity and flexibility in utilizing all our primary energy sources so as to be in the best shape to face up to coal, oil, and gas shortages and to a serious nuclear accident.

6. *We have reached a plateau on our almost century-old downward trend of costs and, beclouded by inflation, lower productivity, and environmental requirements, can only look forward to major increases in energy costs.*

This is a particularly dangerous fallacy. With the kind of growth in electric energy requirements that is being projected, an increase in energy costs of 1 mill per kwh means an annual increase in the nation's energy costs of $8.6 billion by the year 2000. This is an economic item of sufficient significance to be seriously concerned about and to try to do something about, particularly since, as I shall show later, the cost of meeting compatible environmental standards is going to be quite high.

There is so much that can be done. In generation alone, at least half a dozen basic ideas cry for exploration and development—topping gas turbine cycles, bottoming binary cycles, fluidized bed combustion, the atomic breeder, mag-

---

[13] Editorial, *New York Times*, March 8, 1971.

[14] Petroleum Press Service, February 1971.

[15] Alvin M. Weinberg, *New York Times Book Review*, March 8, 1971.

netohydrodynamics (MHD), and thermionic generation in a topping cycle with fossil or nuclear fuel. All these are well known to our utility organizations, but except for MHD practically nothing of consequence is being done to develop them.

In other areas, too, a great many challenging ideas await exploration and development. With the cost of construction labor climbing faster than any other item in our economy, the potentials for cutting construction costs by sharply increasing the percentage of shop-assembled large equipment items in generation, transmission, and distribution are being left unexplored.

Costs can be lowered. They never will be, however, if we do not adopt the idea that they can be and then proceed to make that idea good.

I have explored these six fallacies concerning energy because I believe no well-founded answer could be given to the main questions raised in this paper without digging down to foundations and determining the solidity of present trends both in electric energy availability and in costs. Against this background, I would now like to comment in more detail on the availability and cost of energy.

Earlier, I indicated that there would be no restraints on availability except possibly those stemming from environmental codes and regulations. We are perhaps at a peak of our social impatience with the environmental situation in the United States. The fallacies we are laboring under will gradually be displaced by better understanding.

I am optimistically hopeful that the current fears of overexploitation of inanimate energy will subside in the face of better understanding of the limits to potential dangers and with better handling of expanded use. Recognition of the basic importance of additional energy supplies to the further growth and improvement of our societies—to the development of a better life—will gradually spread.

I believe that by and large the regulations affecting the use and combustion of fossil fuels; the location and operation of nuclear plants; the use of our estuaries, rivers, lakes, oceans, and the atmosphere itself as heat sinks will gradually settle down to reasonable bases, if the utilities constructively oppose the irrational. I am encouraged by the example other great industrial countries (England, for one), whose reactions to the problems of the environment are less emotional than ours, have set before us.

Achieving reasonable antipollution regulations will require a great deal of work and large expenditures on the part of the utilities of the United States. But on the whole, the U.S. power supply is in good hands, certainly as good as in any other part of the world.[16] The utilities' response to the environmental develop-

---

[16] Elsewhere, I have given a detailed critical analysis of this situation. See Philip Sporn, *The Social Organization of Electric Power Supply in Modern Societies* (Massachusetts Institute of Technology Press, 1971).

ments in their communities is a healthy one, generally free of resentment and buoyed by a determination to solve the problems of compatibility between adequate supply and environmental requirements. And I am genuinely hopeful that they will resourcefully employ technology to help in that solution.

Thus, in spite of some troublesome local situations, which have been exacerbated by bad system planning for several decades, there will be no general problem of meeting electric demands even at the optimistic levels I have projected for the balance of this century.

Another question I asked my friends in the utilities was: What additional costs do you visualize will be necessary to take care of environmental protection in (1) generation, (2) transmission, (3) distribution, and (4) overall?

My correspondents made a valiant effort to help me with this difficult question, and in several cases they expended a large amount of time on it. But the range of costs developed was an astonishing one. For generation, for example, the range of increased costs was from 5 percent to 80 percent; for transmission, from 10 percent to 2,400 percent; for distribution, from zero to 700 percent. The overall costs were from 1 to 20 mills per kwh.

By extrapolating past and current experience into the future, one company estimated the increased costs[17] as follows:

	1970	1980	1990
Generation (*percent*)	10–15	25	40
Transmission (*percent*)	20	35	50
Distribution (*percent*)	35	45	60
Total (*mills/kwh*)	2	3	4

Not knowing the basis for these figures, I attempted to break down all potential increases into fourteen environmental components and estimated in table 1 the cost of each component carried to completion in the power system, both for a fossil fuel energy source and for a nuclear fuel source. Then, to find the effect on power production costs of expenditures for these components, the thirty-year period 1971–2000 was divided into three ten-year intervals. In each of these periods, a rational division between nuclear and fossil fuel was assumed on the basis of complete flexibility and optimum economic results. A gradual improvement was visualized in system performance thermodynamically and in

[17] Environmental components of costs given for generation, transmission, and distribution represent capital cost for new construction. The total covers overall annual costs, including capital, fuel, operating, and maintenance costs.

Table 1. Increased Generating Costs Due to Environmental Control Expenditures

	Cost per kw	
Steam electric generation	Fossil[a]	Nuclear[b]
	(- - - - - - - *dollars* - - - - - -)	
1. Tall stack	4.00	2.00
2. SO$_2$ removal, minus credit	8.00	–
3. Advanced electrostatic precipitator	2.00	–
4. Wet cooling tower, induced draft	4.00	6.00
5. Wet cooling tower, natural draft	5.50	8.25
6. Dry cooling tower, minus credit	18.00	27.00
7. Noise suppression	0.50	–
8. Monitoring devices	0.50	0.50
9. Improved architectural design and landscaping	3.00	4.00
10. Intake and discharge structures, improved design	3.00	4.00
11. General improved design standards	2.00	8.00
	(- - - - - - *mills/kwh* - - - - - -)	
12. Higher-cost fuel[c]	⌈ 0.510	
	⟨ 0.864	–
	⌊ 1.125	
13. Operating cost of monitoring devices	0.012	0.020
14. Increased research	0.050	0.050

NOTE: These costs apply to both new and old plants.

[a] 1,300 mw unit size.
[b] 1,100 mw unit size.
[c]

Calculation of Higher-Cost Fuel

	Total increase in fuel costs (¢/mil. Btu)	Heat rate (Btu/kwh)	Total fuel cost increase ascribed to environment (percent)	Increased fuel cost due to environment (mills/kwh)
1st interval (1971–80)	10	8,500	60	0.510
2nd interval (1981–90)	18	8,000	60	0.864
3rd interval (1991–2000)	25	7,500	60	1.125

The remaining 40 percent fuel cost rise can be attributed to inflation, the increased social cost of mining, the higher cost of mining or drilling for oil or gas due to less favorable natural conditions, and the higher cost of imported fuels.

other areas where environmental protection was the objective sought. This work yielded tables 2 and 3. Obviously, for the generation component, the total increase in energy costs due to increases in environmental expenditures is the sum of the values developed in tables 2 and 3; thus for the three intervals ending with 1980, 1990, and 2000, the increase is 1.016 mills per kwh, 1.668 mills per kwh, and 2.008 mills per kwh, respectively.

To complete the cost picture, I made a study of increased costs in transmission, distribution, rights of way, and public information. These costs are reduced to an increase in cost per kwh in tables 4a–4d. It will be noted in these tables

Table 2. Increased Generating Costs Due to Environmental Control Expenditures, Fossil Fuel

Item[a]	At end of 1970–80			At end of 1980–90			At end of 1990–2000		
	Application factor	Dollars/ kw	Mills/ kwh[b]	Application factor	Dollars/ kw	Mills/ kwh[b]	Application factor	Dollars/ kw	Mills/ kwh[b]
1	0.60	2.40	0.067	0.43	1.72	0.048	0.35	1.40	0.039
2	0.05	0.40	0.01	0.30	2.40	0.067	0.40	3.20	0.090
3	0.60	1.20	0.033	0.43	0.86	0.024	0.40	0.80	0.022
4,5	0.40	1.90	0.053	0.33	1.58	0.044	0.33	1.58	0.044
6	—	—	—	0.10	1.80	0.051	0.15	2.70	0.076
7,8	0.33	0.33	0.009	0.35	0.35	0.010	0.35	0.35	0.010
9,10	0.25	1.50	0.042	0.35	2.10	0.059	0.35	2.10	0.059
11	0.25	0.50	0.014	0.35	0.70	0.020	0.35	0.70	0.020
12	—	—	0.510	—	—	0.864	—	—	1.125
13	—	—	0.012	—	—	0.012	—	—	0.012
14	—	—	0.050	—	—	0.050	—	—	0.050
Total			0.791			1.249			1.547

NOTES: Dashes indicate "not applicable." Application factor is a weight describing the percentage of the total plant to which this expenditure will apply in a particular interval; it implicitly takes into consideration assumed environmental improvement factors in average plant design and operation over the period in question.

[a] See table 1.
[b] Based on 15 percent annual capital cost and 5,350 hours' use (61 percent load factor).

Table 3. Increased Generating Costs Due to Environmental Control Expenditures, Nuclear Fuel

Item[a]	At end of 1970–80			At end of 1980–90			At end of 1990–2000		
	Application factor	Dollars/ kw	Mills/ kwh[b]	Application factor	Dollars/ kw	Mills/ kwh[b]	Application factor	Dollars/ kw	Mills/ kwh[b]
1	0.22	0.44	0.012	0.40	0.80	0.022	0.45	0.90	0.025
2	—	—	—	—	—	—	—	—	—
3	—	—	—	—	—	—	—	—	—
4, 5	0.20	1.43	0.040	0.30	2.14	0.060	0.30	2.41	0.060
6	—	—	—	0.10	2.70	0.076	0.15	4.05	0.113
7, 8	0.20	0.20	0.006	0.40	0.40	0.011	0.45	0.45	0.113
9, 10	0.20	1.60	0.045	0.40	3.20	0.090	0.40	3.20	0.090
11	0.20	1.60	0.045	0.40	3.20	0.090	0.40	3.20	0.090
12	—	—	—	—	—	—	—	—	—
13	—	—	0.020	—	—	0.020	—	—	0.020
14	—	—	0.050	—	—	0.050	—	—	0.050
Total			0.218			0.419			0.461

NOTES: Dashes indicate "not applicable." Application factor is a weight describing the percentage of the total plant to which this expenditure will apply in a particular interval; it implicitly takes into consideration assumed environmental improvement factors in average plant design and operation over the period in question.

[a] See table 1.
[b] Based on 15 percent annual capital cost and 5,350 hours' use (61 percent load factor).

Table 4a. Summary of Increased Electric Power Transmission Costs, Reflecting
Environmental Control Expenditures

	End of decade		
	1970–1980	1980–1990	1990–2000
1. Investment cost, new, no allowance for environmental costs ($/kw)	68.00	53.30	45.50
2. Investment cost, weighted new and old, no allowance for environmental costs ($/kw)	74.00	65.20	57.80
3. Environmental cost to modify old equipment ($/kw)	10.00	10.00	10.00
4. Environmental cost component of new equipment ($/kw)	7.80	8.00	8.53
5. Sum of lines 2, 3, and 4	91.80	83.20	76.33
6. Incremental cost (line 5 minus $80) ($/kw)	11.80	3.20	−3.67
7. Annual incremental capital charge (line 6 at 15%) ($/kw)	1.77	0.48	−0.55
8. Total incremental cost (mills/kwh)	0.331	0.090	−0.103

NOTES: These calculations apply to a system having a 1970 peak of 10,000 mw and a net utility plant (original cost minus depreciation reserve) of $325/kw of maximum demand, and consisting of the following costs: generation, $140; transmission, $80; distribution, $85; miscellaneous, $20.

These judgments and calculations of the author are based in part on the following assumptions and considerations, each of which relates to the corresponding line in the table.

(1) New investment cost shown in line 1 declines by approximately 33 percent every 20 years due to technological improvement (including higher voltages).

(2) Demand doubles in the first decade, increases 75 percent in the second decade, and increases 60 percent in the third decade.

(3) Modification of old plant, shown in line 3, is based on the following estimated costs:
$1.33/kw/year in first decade
$0.55/kw/year in second decade
$0.46/kw/year in third decade

(4) Environmental cost of new equipment, shown in line 4, assumes the following increments to new equipment costs:
20 percent in first decade
35 percent in second decade
50 percent in third decade

(6) Calculated as the difference from new investment cost in 1970.

(8) Based on 5,350 hours per year. Note that the figures in this line reflect the combined effect of changes in power costs arising from environmental factors, on the one hand, offset to a limited extent by assumed technological improvements—hence reduced real costs—in transmission, on the other.

that for the three successive ten-year intervals, I adopted increased costs in environmental components of transmission equal to 20 percent, 35 percent, and 50 percent, respectively, of new investment in transmission, exclusive of environmental costs. For distribution, the corresponding figures are 35 percent, 45 percent, and 55 percent. The other increased costs are clear from inspection of

Table 4b. Summary of Increased Electric Power Distribution Costs, Reflecting Environmental Control Expenditures

	End of decade		
	1970–1980	1980–1990	1990–2000
1. Investment cost, new, no allowance for environmental costs ($/kw)	79.05	73.52	68.37
2. Investment cost, weighted new and old, no allowance for environmental costs ($/kw)	82.03	78.50	74.50
3. Environmental cost to modify old equipment ($/kw)	10.00	10.00	10.00
4. Environmental cost component of new equipment ($/kw)	13.84	14.20	14.10
5. Sum of lines 2, 3, and 4	105.87	102.70	98.60
6. Incremental cost (line 5 minus $85) ($/kw)	20.87	17.70	13.60
7. Annual incremental capital charge (line 6 at 15%) ($/kw)	3.13	2.65	2.04
8. Total incremental cost (mills/kwh)	0.585	0.495	0.381

NOTES: System characteristics are described in note to table 4a.

These judgments and calculations of the author are based in part on the following assumptions and considerations, each of which relates to the corresponding line in the table.

(1) New investment cost shown in line 1 declines by 7 percent every 10 years due to technological improvements (including higher distribution voltages).

(2) Demand doubles in the first decade, increases 75 percent in the second decade, and increases 60 percent in the third decade.

(3) Modification of old plant, shown in line 3, is based on the following estimated costs:

$1.33/kw/year in first decade
$0.55/kw/year in second decade
$0.46/kw/year in third decade

(4) Environmental cost of new equipment, shown in line 4, assumes following increments to new equipment costs:

35 percent in first decade
45 percent in second decade
55 percent in third decade

(6) Calculated as the difference from new investment cost in 1970.

(8) Based on 5,350 hours per year. Note that the figures in this line reflect the combined effect of changes in power costs arising from environmental factors, on the one hand, offset to a limited extent by assumed technological improvements—hence reduced real costs—in distribution, on the other.

the tables. The total estimated increase in environmental costs or expenditures, including those associated with generation noted above, are given as:

2.50 mills per kwh at the end of 1980
2.90 mills per kwh at the end of 1990
3.00 mills per kwh at the end of 2000

These figures are reasonably close to those of one of my correspondents whose general approach I followed, but for the year 1980 I arrived at a cost that

Table 4c. Summary of Increased Costs of Rights-of-Way and Public Information
due to Environmental Control Expenditures

	End of decade		
	1970–1980	1980–1990	1990–2000
Incremental costs (*mills/kwh*) for:			
1. Rights-of-way	0.017	0.017	0.017
2. Public information	0.020	0.020	0.020
Total	0.037	0.037	0.037

NOTES: The distinguishing characteristics of rights-of-way and public information components of electricity costs should be noted: a rights-of-way cost can be amortized over a period of years, while a public information charge cannot be amortized and has to be charged off in the year it is made.

Data on system characteristics, capital charge, and load factor appear in Table 4a.

These judgments and calculations of the author are based in part on the following assumptions and considerations, each of which relates to the corresponding line in the table.

(1) The calculation for the first decadal interval is based on a total system rights-of-way cost of $9 million per year, which reduces to an average of $0.60/kw/year or 0.017 mills/kwh. The estimates for the succeeding two decades were computed so as to equalize costs with the first decade.

(2) Based on a system public information cost during the first decade of $1.5 million per year, which reduces to $0.10/kw/year or 0.020 mills/kwh. Succeeding decades estimated as in line 1.

Table 4d. Summary of Total Increases in the Cost of Electric Power, Reflecting
Environmental Control Expenditures

			(*mills/kwh*)
	End of decade		
	1970–1980	1980–1990	1990–2000
1. Generation:			
Fossil fueled	0.791	1.249	1.547
Nuclear fueled	0.218	0.419	0.461
2. Transmission	0.331	0.090	−0.103
3. Distribution	0.585	0.495	0.381
4. Miscellaneous (rights-of-way and public information)	0.037	0.037	0.037
Subtotal	1.962	2.290	2.323
5. Factor of ignorance (25 percent)	0.491	0.573	0.581
Total of above	2.453	2.863	2.904
Total (rounded)	2.50	2.90	3.00

NOTES: See notes for tables 2, 3, 4a, 4b, and 4c.

is a full half-mill per kwh higher and for the year 2000 a full mill lower.[18] One cannot help offering such a set of figures with diffidence, but I would hope that in time they will be found to have been accurate within plus or minus 25 percent—barring any major inflationary effects. The figure for the year 2000 is, incidentally, a sobering one. If we assume that it proves to be at the low end of the range of 25 percent, then the annual increase in the nation's electric energy bill in the year 2000 due to environmental expenditures will be over 32 billion. This is almost one and two-thirds times the total national electric energy bill of slightly over $20 billion paid by nearly 70.5 million customers in 1969.

When in 1776 Tom Paine said: " 'Tis dearness only, that gives everything its value," he was speaking of freedom. But could he also have been prophetically alluding to the activities of his countrymen two centuries later in environmental control?

[18] The figures shown above indicate the combined effect of changes in power costs arising from environmental factors, on the one hand, offset to a limited extent by assumed technological improvements—hence reduced real costs—in transmission and distribution, on the other.

The Possible Impact of Environmental Standards on the Availability and Cost of Petroleum

RICHARD J. GONZALEZ

Much needs to be done to provide cleaner air and water as more waste products are created by an expanding population, as consumption rises per capita, and as people concentrate increasingly in metropolitan areas. In the United States the major national commitment to improve the quality of air and water during this decade can be compared with the goal of the 1960s to land a man on the moon. The cases are similar in that we start not knowing how the task is to be done, how much it will cost, nor how the costs will affect us. In order to avoid later disenchantment with environmental programs, strenuous efforts must be made to focus attention on the full cost of each action so that choices may be made, not on the basis of emotion, but on evaluation of the relationship between costs and benefits.

It has been suggested that a better environment can be achieved only by reducing population growth or by prohibiting the use of internal combustion engines. When aspirations to reduce poverty in the United States are analyzed, it becomes clear that we cannot and need not reduce consumption and return to the horse and buggy era. The nineteenth century formula of "forty acres and a mule" long ago ceased to be an acceptable basis on which to provide for a large population. We need not give up the benefits of industrialization, cities, and

Richard J. Gonzalez, an authority on petroleum economics and on the mineral industries, is an economic consultant. Formerly, he was Director of the Humble Oil and Refining Company (1951–65), and Economic Advisor to the company (1937–51). He also has served as Chairman of the Economics Advisory Committee, Interstate Oil Compact Commission (1946–49); and as Director of the National Industrial Conference Board (1956–65). Dr. Gonzalez was born in San Antonio, Texas, in 1912. He received his A.B., M.A., and Ph.D. degrees from the University of Texas.

suburban living to enjoy a healthy environment. A high-energy society improves productivity so much that it can afford to spend part of the additional output to improve the environment to enjoyable standards, provided that costs are kept in relation to the results achieved.

PETROLEUM AND THE ENVIRONMENT

The petroleum industry and the automobile are under great attack as major sources of pollution. The picture needs to be balanced by consideration of the contributions of inanimate energy and convenient transportation to economic growth, of the reduction in air pollution that has been and is being achieved, of the true relation of oil spills to the total volumes handled, and of the consequences for the public and the nation of standards that may reduce the availability and increase the costs of oil and gas produced in the United States.

Crude oil and natural gas, the joint products of the petroleum industry, are better fuels than coal from the standpoint of environment and convenience of use. Marked improvement in air quality has been attained in London, Pittsburgh, and many other cities by shifting from coal to the use of oil and gas. Gas is an ideal fuel for improving air quality because of the low level of undesirable emissions from combustion, and low-sulfur fuel oil is much better than coal. U.S. wells now produce more energy in the form of gas than oil, a major contribution to a better environment.

Advantages in use plus increasing availability at attractive prices have made oil and gas the principal fuels of the world. Oil products have transformed transportation and brought us to the space age. Mechanization in agriculture and industry has been the basis of higher productivity and rising real income per capita. For homes, oil and gas provide central heat and part of the power for electricity to run air-conditioning units, lights, and appliances.

Of total energy consumption in the United States in 1970 of nearly 69 quadrillion British thermal units (Btu), oil supplied 43 percent and gas 33 percent. The amounts used were 5.4 billion barrels of petroleum liquids (about 800 million tons, or nearly 4 tons per capita) and almost 22 trillion cubic feet of gas. Imports provided about 23 percent of the liquids and less than 5 percent of the gas.

In 1970 about 640,000 oil and gas wells in the United States produced 3.5 billion barrels of crude oil and more than 21 trillion cubic feet of wet natural gas from which 0.6 billion barrels of gas liquids were extracted for use. (Based on an average energy content of 5.8 million Btu per barrel of crude oil and 1,075 Btu per cubic feet of wet gas, 5.4 million cubic feet of wet gas contain as much energy as a barrel of crude oil.) Oil and gas are moved over long distances. The liquids must be handled several times in moving them from wells to processing plants, thence to terminals, and finally to points of distribution and consump-

tion. In the process some spills occur. For pipelines, it has been estimated that spills account for only six-thousandths of 1 percent of the total volume handled.[1] For all operations, it is reported that in 1969 there were 1,007 oil spills of over 100 barrels each in U.S. waters, and 532 of these spills were from vessels.[2] As few of these spills were large, it appears that combined losses from all petroleum operations are only a small fraction of 1 percent of 5.4 billion barrels.

PETROLEUM AND ECONOMIC PROGRESS

The use of energy to operate machines, which increase productivity, and to provide transportation and other comforts means that our economic progress depends on energy, particularly on oil and gas. With less than 6 percent of the world's population, the United States consumes about one-third of world energy. Our energy use per capita is about seven times that of the rest of the world, reflecting the difference in average living standards.

Greater efficiency in the use of energy over a period of time may reduce the amount of energy needed per dollar of real income measured in stable prices, as was the case in the United States until about 1960. During the past decade, however, energy use increased as rapidly as real income, at about 4 percent a year, as it became harder to improve efficiency and as air conditioning increased the role of electricity. For the long run, higher costs for energy might induce consumers to use smaller and lighter cars, to insulate buildings completely, and to make other economies.

THE U.S. PETROLEUM POSITION

Since 1956 the number of exploratory and development wells drilled for oil and gas in the United States has decreased nearly 50 percent to the lowest levels of the postwar period. Meanwhile, production increased about one-third for crude oil and doubled for natural gas. Known recoverable reserves available through existing facilities, excluding those of the North Slope of Alaska—which will require transportation facilities still to be approved and built—declined for crude oil and remained relatively stable for natural gas in the 1960s. Withdrawal rates from these reserves in 1970 were more than 10 percent on petroleum liquids and 8 percent on natural gas, at or close to the limits of efficient productive capacity.

[1] National Petroleum Council, *Environmental Conservation*, vol. 1, pt. 1 (Washington, D.C.: NPC, June 1971), p. 71.
[2] Council on Environmental Quality, *Environmental Quality,* First Annual Report (August 1970), p. 38.

The spare productive capacity that proved so useful in many emergencies has been exhausted. Even with production at capacity, domestic supplies are falling further behind demands. The deficits are being covered by imports. Unless production rises steadily, dependence on imports will increase sharply.

Energy requirements for the next twenty years have already been determined in large measure by decisions on where Americans live, work, and shop; by the fuels used in plants that will be in operation for many years; and by the long time-lag in bringing about a major change in energy use. If sufficient petroleum supplies can be made available at prices that remain attractive relative to rising real incomes, consumers will probably double their use of oil and gas within twenty years. In that case, potential use for 1971–90 would be 165 billion barrels of oil and 660 trillion cubic feet of gas, or several times the known U.S. reserves, even including those of the North Slope.

The magnitude of future petroleum requirements poses problems of shortages similar to those that have aroused public concern in the past. Widespread fears of shortages in the 1920s disappeared when better exploration methods, especially through geophysics, led to many new discoveries and a temporary surplus. Lower costs, conservation, and better engineering resulted in very attractive prices.

The tight supply situation after World War II was corrected by a marked recovery in real oil and gas prices from the low levels of 1930–46, despite a general belief that the nation had reached its peak ability to produce oil by 1946. Better real prices stimulated a sharp rise in exploration and drilling that soon resulted in a higher rate of discovery and development and in expanded capacity to produce oil and gas. After 1957, declining real prices for petroleum and other factors brought about the decrease in activity that has led to the imbalance between the rate of development of new reserves and capacity and growth in demand. The stage is now set for another repetition of the cycle characteristic of resource operations in which prices move as needed to restore long-run balance.

In order for petroleum supplies to keep pace with prospective demands, the rate of development of U.S. resources needs to be stepped up sharply, unless the nation is to become much more dependent on imports, particularly on the East Coast where imports now provide nearly 50 percent of the total use of liquid fuels. Those who think that foreign oil and gas will always be available without interruption or who have greater concern about the risks of environmental problems from petroleum production here than abroad will prefer to see the United States rely on imports. From an environmental viewpoint, however, we must ask whether a rich nation should act in a manner that shifts risks of pollution to poorer areas. In terms of economic costs we must (1) consider oil and gas together, because the domestic development of these resources is inseparably interrelated; (2) analyze the outlook for long-run prices, including taxes, of foreign supplies; and (3) weigh the prospects of the total costs of foreign fuels

(in the forms consumers prefer) approaching or exceeding the competitive equilibrium level set by domestic fuels. Even now, imports of liquefied natural gas are much more expensive than gas from domestic wells. Finally, from the standpoint of consumers and the nation, we must evaluate the risks of lengthy disruptions of imports, the cost of which would quickly run into billions of dollars, and the consequences for our position in world affairs. As Secretary of the Interior Rogers Morton stated at a meeting of the National Petroleum Council in Washington, D.C., on March 4, 1971: "The nation's entire capacity to act in a crisis may become restricted by its dependence on energy sources over which it has no control." The embargo by several countries on exports to the United States in 1967 illustrates this point.

I believe that the present petroleum outlook means that the United States will find it desirable to increase reserves and the production of oil and gas well above current levels. This conclusion leads to the questions of whether potential resources exist for expansion at costs below those of other domestic alternates, such as conversion of coal into oil and gas or extraction of oil from shales, and whether expansion can be made in a manner compatible with a good environment.

THE POTENTIAL FOR EXPANSION OF U.S. PETROLEUM PRODUCTION

The major potential for large new discoveries of oil and gas at reasonable cost appears to be in two vast provinces in the early stages of exploration and development, namely, the continental margin (the shelf and slope) and Alaska.

Formations favorable for petroleum deposits on the continental margin are nearly 55 percent as large in area as on land and 90 percent as large in terms of the volume of sediments.[3] The director of the U.S. Geological Survey has estimated the petroleum potential of this area at 100 billion to 200 billion barrels of oil and 300 trillion to 1,000 trillion cubic feet of natural gas, including the offshore-Alaska portion.[4] The resources of this area aroused great interest when it became harder and more expensive to find onshore resources. Well-known exploration techniques can be used effectively in this virgin area to locate structures with conditions favorable for accumulation of commercial deposits of oil and gas, in some cases adjacent to onshore fields and productive trends.

Alaska is a large area with a high potential both onshore and offshore. Oil seepages along the Arctic Coast (presumably with little impact on the environment) have been known to exist since early in this century. In 1923 President

[3] U.S. Department of the Interior, *Petroleum and Sulphur on the United States Continental Shelf* (December 1969), p. 47.

[4] William Pecora, "Mineral Resource Potential of Continental Margin of United States" (speech delivered to the American Association of Petroleum Geologists, Dallas, Texas, April 14, 1969, mimeo.).

Harding set aside 37,000 square miles of the North Slope as Naval Petroleum Reserve Number 4. The Navy explored this reserve by drilling fifty-seven test wells from 1944 to 1953 and found a number of oil and gas fields.[5]

Subsequently, oil companies spent many millions of dollars on the North Slope, including the costs of exploration and some ten dry holes. In 1968 the large Prudhoe Bay field was found on the North Slope. While the magnitude of the reserves of this field remains to be determined by experience with its behavior under actual production, the field is generally rated as the largest discovery in North America, exceeding by a substantial margin the next largest field found in East Texas in 1930. In 1969 a number of oil companies paid the State of Alaska $900 million for the right to explore for and to produce oil and gas on 451,000 acres on the North Slope. These bids indicate confidence that large additional reserves remain to be found in this area. Estimates of recoverable oil range from 5 billion to 50 billion barrels.[6]

The continental margin and Alaska offer the best hope for large new fields and highly productive wells in the United States. If these hopes are realized, unit costs for expanded output may be kept at reasonable levels despite the difficult conditions that cause wells to be more expensive than in well-explored land areas.

U.S. land areas outside of Alaska have been explored intensively for many years. Consequently, new discoveries are generally smaller and deeper and result in higher unit costs. The National Petroleum Council noted that a high percentage of the new petroleum foreseen on land is expected to be in stratigraphic traps (which cannot yet be found by geophysics), in combination stratigraphic-structural traps, and in complex structural traps.[7] These conditions result in very high exploration and dry-hole costs and stimulate interest in newer provinces.

A substantial potential for additional recovery of oil from known fields exists if cost conditions and the long-term outlook for prices warrant the required outlays. Of some 400 billion barrels of oil in place found in the United States (excluding the North Slope), it is estimated that 36 percent will be recoverable under existing conditions. The recovery factor is limited by reservoir conditions, by the poor production practices in many old fields before conservation became effective, and by the cost of the facilities and processes for increasing recovery. It has been estimated that the recovery factor increased from 26 percent in 1945 to about 36 percent in 1965.[8] If costs for new oil were to increase and real prices were to develop an upward trend, the recovery factor

[5] National Petroleum Council, *Future Petroleum Provinces of the United States* (Washington, D.C.: NPC, 1970), p. 19.

[6] Ibid., p. 19.

[7] Ibid., p. 1.

[8] National Petroleum Council, *Impact of New Technology on the U.S. Petroleum Industry, 1946–1965* (Washington, D.C.: NPC, 1967), p. 3.

might be improved further to a maximum range of 50-60 percent, thereby adding some 56 billion to 96 billion barrels to recoverable reserves from known fields.

The preceding analysis leads me to conclude that the U.S. oil supply may be able to keep pace with demand for the next 15-20 years (contrary to the indications in many forecasts that the nation cannot escape greater dependence on foreign supplies), provided that governmental policies encourage rather than discourage exploration and development of new resources. Policies in recent years (controls on the price of natural gas, steady liberalization of imports in a manner creating doubt about the future, a cut in depletion rates for oil and gas taxation, and efforts to keep the price of oil from reflecting higher costs) have drastically discouraged new investment in exploration and drilling, which is evident from the decline in the number of smaller operators who have played an important part in past discoveries. Quite a change will be required to restore the confidence of the oil companies in the fact that expansion of investments in exploration and drilling makes good economic sense compared with less risky investments in other businesses.

A major new factor that may limit the development of additional domestic oil and gas for economic progress—environmental regulation under the National Environmental Policy Act of 1969, signed by the president on January 1, 1970—deserves careful consideration.

ENVIRONMENTAL REGULATIONS AFFECTING PETROLEUM PRODUCTION

Until recent years the principal environmental regulations affecting petroleum production were those of the producing states. Most of these states have a long record of controls designed to prevent waste, to promote conservation of resources, and to protect the rights of competing producers in the interest of equity and efficient operation of reservoirs. These measures have protected the environment by preventing wasteful practices, such as bringing wells in as gushers, storing oil in earthen pits, flaring casinghead gas produced with crude oil, and contaminating streams with salt water and wastes. In addition, state controls have reduced the number of wells drilled, even though allocation of production favoring small tracts and small operators still caused the drilling of unnecessary wells and greatly increased the recovery of oil. Market demand proration assured small operators of a share of the market, thereby attracting more operators and increasing the number of discoveries and the competitive pressures between gas and oil companies and between states.

State regulations have not only contributed to a much better environment in producing areas but also have benefited all consumers of energy by increasing the availability of oil and gas and by encouraging the efforts of industry to

control costs at levels that result in very attractive prices for petroleum products and natural gas. Costs and prices might have been even lower under unit operation of all fields, but in that case the opportunity for small operators would have been greatly reduced, and the number of discoveries would have been reduced.

Although the full effect of federal environmental regulations on the production of oil and gas remains to be determined, developments to date indicate that the impact on availability and costs may be quite serious. Thus far, actions taken under the Environmental Policy Act have (1) delayed by several years the availability of large new supplies from the North Slope, (2) slowed down development on the continental shelf and increased the cost of such development, (3) created uncertainty about the large sums risked in acquiring federal and state leases before the act was passed, and (4) raised doubts about whether industry will be allowed—or will find it economically attractive in the face of extraordinary obstacles—to continue with petroleum developments offshore and in Alaska.

In the arctic region, permafrost, tundra, and difficult terrain subject to earthquakes present problems that threaten to raise the cost of handling North Slope oil and gas. After evaluating the risks and the costs of various alternate means of transportation, the companies involved propose to spend several billion dollars on moving the oil to the West Coast by pipeline and tankers. They have a vital interest in seeing that these facilities will operate successfully with a minimum of down time and extra cost due to spills and have submitted designs for elevated lines where required because of permafrost conditions. The question now arises whether environmental standards will be applied on a reasonable basis or used instead to block development in an effort to maintain all of arctic Alaska as a frozen wilderness. Proposals that these potential resources be kept as a reserve for future emergencies ignore the great cost to taxpayers of such action and also the fact that only fully developed supplies deliverable when and where needed will be useful in an emergency. Naval Petroleum Reserve Number 4, for example, has been of no help in emergencies.

In California, the federal government sold seventy-two leases in the Santa Barbara channel for more than $600 million in February 1968, and the companies have spent large additional sums on exploration and drilling. The Administration is working on proposals that about half of these leases be reclaimed and placed in a national energy reserve, with leaseholders being compensated from the sale of production from the Elk Hills Naval Reserve. Quite apart from the serious problems of determining the value of these leases, such action would curtail availability from a major potential province and create doubts about what may happen on any other offshore leases on which a company may be successful in finding oil and gas. Environmental review of permits to drill exploratory wells and construct drilling platforms will mean more delay and higher costs.

In the Gulf of Mexico, sales of leases have been delayed, and new regulations have been imposed that increase costs. These actions may be entirely reasonable

in terms of reducing the risk of water pollution, but they have already delayed operations in areas where it is hoped that gas supplies will be developed to meet the urgent needs of customers endeavoring to reduce air pollution.

Of more than 14,000 wells drilled offshore, only 25 have gotten out of control and caused spills. Under the conditions that must be coped with, including hurricanes, the question to be answered is whether failure in two cases out of a thousand constitutes an acceptable performance when environmental protection is considered. If the answer is negative, then we may have to forget the large potential oil and gas resources of the offshore area, because it is unreasonable to expect complete freedom from accidents in any operation of this scale and complexity.

The question of unlimited liability for oil spills, even if all regulations have been complied with and there has been no negligence on the part of the operator, must also be mentioned. Any natural catastrophe can mean high unexpected costs for operators, some of which may be covered by insurance, but exposure to unlimited liability for spills incident to such disasters would add expensive insult to injury.

To forgo or curtail drastically the development of the potential resources of the continental margin and of arctic areas would have a major effect on the availability and the cost of oil and gas. In my judgment, such action would require extraordinary efforts to develop alternate domestic supplies of oil and gas from tar sands, coal, and shale at much higher costs by means of operations also involving environmental problems. Dependence on imported energy is not a satisfactory answer from a global viewpoint, because it merely shifts the location of the small amount of pollution that is associated with production and that cannot be avoided at reasonable cost.

OTHER EFFECTS OF ENVIRONMENTAL STANDARDS ON THE USE AND COST OF PETROLEUM

Environmental standards will affect energy consumers, not only in regard to the availability and cost of crude oil and natural gas, but also because of regulations designed to improve the quality of the air. In the United States an average of about 5 million tons of fuels are burned daily, or about 50 pounds per person. Emissions from this combustion include particulates, such as soot, and gases of various kinds. Particulates can be eliminated by burning gas or can be controlled by precipitators. Great strides have been made in reducing these undesirable emissions. Now the focus of attention has shifted to the reduction of sulfur compounds, lead, carbon monoxide, hydrocarbons, and nitrogen oxides.

Fuels vary widely in sulfur content, with the most serious problems arising in the use of coal. Some low-sulfur fuel oil is available from crude oils with a low-sulfur content, and sulfur can also be extracted from fuels before combus-

tion. Tax-reference prices recently set by Venezuela at $2.41 for fuel oil with 2 percent sulfur or more, $3.23 for 1 percent sulfur, and $3.52 for 0.3 percent sulfur indicate the substantial cost involved in reducing sulfur emissions.[9] For coal, the best hope appears to be recovery of the sulfur from exhaust fumes after combustion, and the cost remains to be determined by equipment now being tested at some plants.

Air pollution regulations have already had a substantial effect on the use and cost of fuels. In 1969 and 1970 there was a sharp rise in the use of gas and fuel oil by utilities. The Federal Power Commission reported that utility use of fuels in 1970 increased 32.3 percent for fuel oil, 11.7 percent for gas, and 3.8 percent for coal, while the gain for all fuels was 11.2 percent. The commission reported that utility fuel expenses increased 24.3 percent.[10]

The proposed tax on the sulfur content of fuels would also alter relative costs to the disadvantage of coal. On coal with 3 percent sulfur, for example, a tax of 1 cent a pound would amount to 60 cents a ton, equivalent to an increase of about 10 percent for utilities. For fuel oil with 3 percent sulfur the tax on the same energy input in a ton of coal would be much less because of the greater energy content per pound of fuel oil. (Bituminous coal has about 13,000 Btu per pound and fuel oil about 50 percent more.) The higher cost of coal and fuel oil due to a tax on sulfur would increase demands for natural gas, which is already in short supply.

Fuels constitute a substantial part of the cost of generating electric power, and the added costs incident to cleaner air will be reflected in utility bills. For other industrial users, the importance of fuel costs varies widely, but it must be expected that the additional expense for clean air will increase the cost and prices of commodities, both wholesale and retail.

Consumers may find that the greatest effect of regulations designed to improve air quality will be on the operation of automobiles. A law passed in 1970 stipulates that by 1975 emissions of carbon monoxide and hydrocarbons must be reduced 90 percent below the 1970 standards. The more detailed and specific standards for 1975 proposed by the Environmental Protection Administration (which asked for comments on the standards within sixty days) would cut automotive emissions 97 percent below pre-1968 levels before controls were imposed. The feasibility and cost of these standards remain to be determined.

Reducing automotive air pollution will affect the cost of vehicles and of the fuels they use. The cost of achieving specific goals will depend on what happens to the interrelated factors of car weight, compression ratios of engines, the composition of gasoline, and the period of time over which the transition is

[9] "Libya Easing Tough Oil-Price Stance?" *Oil and Gas Journal*, March 15, 1971, p. 34.

[10] "Utilities Gobbled Startling 32.3% More Oil in 1970," *Oil and Gas Journal*, March 15, 1971, p. 43.

made. Intelligent choices by regulators and the public require well-informed judgments about the relation of the costs and benefits of various alternates.

The average life of automobiles is about ten years. People with lower incomes tend to use the older cars and to prefer the cheapest gasoline because they have less money for all purposes, including transportation. By 1975 there will still be many pre-1968 cars in operation, and the cost of gasoline will be an important matter to their owners. Decisions on the components of the gasoline, particularly lead, may affect costs by several cents a gallon.

If leaded gasoline were banned by 1975, for example, many cars would still need high-octane gasoline, which would cost more if lead could not be used for octane improvement. It would be easier and less expensive for us to move steadily toward lighter cars with low-compression engines; thus, a decade hence the car population could realize as many miles per gallon, or more, with the average unleaded gasoline now being made at refineries as our heavy cars now realize with the use of leaded gasoline. In this case, no expensive changes in refining processes would be required. On the other hand, if average octane requirements remain at the current level, the more intensive processing needed to achieve the same octane without lead will inevitably result in larger investments and higher costs. In that case, gasoline itself might cost several cents more per gallon, and more crude oil and gasoline could be required per mile, aggravating problems of securing enough supplies at reasonable cost.

Environmental standards will increase costs and reduce the availability of oil and gas, but the degree of change will be determined by the nature of the choices made in the process of defining and administering the standards. To date, there seems to have been inadequate consideration of the full long-run costs. If the public is to be served well, more attention must be paid to the total long-run results of each decision on the availability and the cost of all forms of energy for the next twenty years.

Energy and the Environment

GORDON J. MacDONALD

The development of an energy policy is a key element in maintaining and improving the environment, because the use of energy affects the environment in an almost infinite number of ways. The conversion of fossil fuels to electricity produces thermal and chemical pollutants. The location of power plants raises the most complex of land use issues, and the production of raw fuels emphasizes similar questions of the use of land and natural resources. Beyond these serious but obvious questions lie the tremendously complex sociological and economic problems associated with the ever-increasing energy demands of our society. Only in the past few years has the question of "saturation" arisen. Can there be changes in human values leading to a gradual reduction in the rate of increase in the demand for energy, particularly electrical energy?

Rather than attempt a detailed evaluation of the myriad environmental impacts of energy use, I will concentrate on some of the thermal consequences. The emission of such pollutants as sulfur dioxide, carbon monoxide, nitrogen oxides, radioactivity, and particulate matter can, in principle, be controlled. Indeed, great progress has been made in the past few years toward achieving such

Gordon J. MacDonald is a member of the Council on Environmental Quality and a consultant to the National Aeronautics and Space Administration. Previously, he served as Chairman of the Department of Planetary and Space Science of the University of California at Los Angeles, and as Vice Chancellor for Research and Graduate Affairs of the University of California at Santa Barbara. He has also been a member of the President's Science Advisory Committee (1965–69); the Committee on Atmospheric Sciences, National Academy of Sciences (1961–70); the Space Science Board (1962–70), and the Environmental Studies Board (1968–70). Born in 1929 in Mexico City, Dr. MacDonald received his A.B., A.M., and Ph.D. degrees from Harvard University.

control over both stationary and moving sources. Thermal pollution is a different matter. The energy used to produce the material benefits we have become accustomed to will eventually return as heat. Because of the low efficiency of most processes that utilize raw fuel to produce useful energy, the waste heat put into the environment is a substantial fraction of the energy used. A consideration of the thermal balance provides, if nothing more, a gross measure of the environmental impact of energy use.

Joel Darmstadter's discussion[1] provides detailed documentation of the exponential growth in the generation and use of energy, particularly electrical energy, at a rate much faster than population growth. Almost all this energy reaches the lower atmosphere, either directly through combustion or dissipation processes or indirectly in the form of waste heat injected into water and then into the atmosphere by means of radiation, conduction, or evaporation. This excess heat eventually must be radiated into outer space. The earth, in order to rid itself of this excess thermal load, must increase in average temperature. Changes in average temperature will be accompanied by a vast variety of changes in weather and climate.

In order to assess the potential impact on the earth's thermal balance, I will first review briefly the natural flow of thermal power within the atmosphere. Next I will examine current trends of energy use and then consider the potential effects. The conclusion of this discussion is simple. We need to develop a rational energy policy. Uncontrolled growth in energy use not only decimates natural resources but also presents severe and, because of thermodynamics, unavoidable problems with very serious consequences.

NATURAL THERMAL POWER FLOWS

The energy resources of the world that are suitable for power production are of two kinds. First, there is the continuous flow of energy from the sun and other extraterrestrial sources, and there is the energy produced within the earth and flowing outward. A second source is the chemical and nuclear energy available to us in the outer parts of the earth's crust. The chemical energy has been stored over the geological times and is now being released at an increasing rate.

The energy flux into the earth's atmosphere is shown in table 1. The unit of flux is kilowatts per hectare.[2] The intensity of the solar radiation at the outer limit of the earth's atmosphere is known as the solar constant, which has a mean value of about 14,000 kilowatts per hectare. The amount of solar radiation reaching a unit area of any part of the surface in one day depends not only on the solar constant but also on the transparency of the atmosphere, the latitude,

---

[1] See appendix.
[2] One hectare equals 10,000 square meters, or 2.471 acres.

Table 1. Thermal Power Budget

(kilowatts per hectare)

Input	Output
Solar radiation = 3,500	Direct reflection to space = 1,225
	Direct conversion to heat and radiation at long wavelength to space = 1,505
	Evaporation, precipitation, storage, and eventual radiation to space = 770
	Winds, currents convection = 7.3
	Photosynthesis = 0.8
Terrestrial energy = 0.606	
Heat conduction = 0.6	
Heat convection (volcanoes, hot springs) = 0.006	
Tidal energy = 0.05	

and the time of year. For example, for a perfectly transparent atmosphere, a unit area at the equator at the equinox with the sun at the mean distance receives 0.32 times the energy it would receive if it were exposed to full solar radiation for twenty-four hours.

For the purposes of this discussion, an average value of one-fourth the solar constant is used in table 1. The impact of radiation from the sun on the atmosphere is thus 3,500 kilowatts per hectare. Of this energy, about 35 percent is reflected directly into outer space. Another 43 percent is directly converted into heat and radiated outward at long wavelengths. The remaining solar energy is absorbed either through evaporation or photosynthesis or is transformed directly into the mechanical motion of the atmospheres or oceans. It is roughly estimated that 770 kilowatts per hectare, or about 20 percent of the total input, are stored—in a sense—within the hydrosphere; about 1 percent of the 770 kilowatts goes into winds, waves, and convections and 1 percent is captured by plant leaves and stored chemically by the process of photosynthesis (whereby such inorganic materials as water and carbon dioxide are synthesized into complex compounds).

In addition to the direct energy of the sun, there are small contributions of energy from tides raised in both the oceans and the solid earth that are converted in part into heat by frictional processes. Heat flowing from the earth's interior by conduction and heat carried by volcanic activity contribute another small amount of energy to the atmosphere.

In examining the impact of man's activities on the thermal budget, we need to compare man's thermal load with the various natural inputs into the atmosphere. The relevant natural average flux is that which is stored within the atmos-

phere-ocean system and not lost to space on a very short time scale. According to table 1, 770 kilowatts per hectare are thus stored. On this basis, we can expect man's activities to have a minor effect on the thermal balance if the total thermal power load is small compared with about 1,000 kilowatts per hectare and, conversely, major effects can be expected when this number is large compared with 1,000 kilowatts per hectare.

MAN'S THERMAL POWER OUTPUT

The growth in total energy flux for the world as a whole from 1925 to 1968 is shown in table 2. Today, on the average, the thermal power output per capita is 1.8 kilowatts. With the present world population of about 3.5 billion, this average thermal power output is equivalent to 0.12 kilowatts per hectare, only a tiny fraction of the thermal input from the sun and only one-fifth of the heat flowing from the earth's interior. On the average, then, man's contribution to the thermal power budget of the atmosphere is insignificant. (In a completely primitive society, food consumed by the individual generates about one-tenth of a kilowatt.)

Table 2. World Power Output

Year	Population (*million*)	Thermal output (*kw/capita*)
1925	1,890	0.78
1950	2,504	1.03
1955	2,726	1.22
1960	2,990	1.39
1965	3,281	1.64
1968	3,484	1.82

The thermal output of various nations differs greatly, and within the nations there are significant variations. Using Darmstadter's values for years prior to 1970 and estimates for 1970, the historical variation of total thermal output per capita in the United States has been calculated in table 3.

Several features of the historical data are worth noting. Since well before 1900 the U.S. thermal power input into the atmosphere has been substantially greater than the *present* world average. Today the U.S. per capita input is six times the current world average. In 1925 this ratio was almost eight so that while the U.S. output has continued to grow, the world output has increased at a greater level. In terms of gross effects, even if the world power output were at U.S. levels, the total man-made contribution would still be small compared with that of natural processes.

A further point of environmental importance is illustrated in table 3. The amount of thermal output per dollar of gross national product (GNP) decreased

Table 3. Power Output in the United States

Year	Power output per capita (kilowatts)	Power output per dollar GNP[a] (watts)
1905	4.53	3.80
1910	5.36	4.12
1915	5.35	4.32
1920	6.21	4.72
1925	6.03	3.89
1930	6.06	4.07
1935	5.02	3.77
1940	6.03	3.51
1945	7.51	2.96
1950	7.50	3.20
1955	8.05	3.04
1960	8.29	3.07
1963	8.76	3.01
1965	9.25	2.91
1966	9.67	2.89
1967	9.89	2.92
1968	10.38	2.95
1969	10.80	3.02
1970	11.37	3.19

[a]1958 dollars.

during the early part of the century but has begun to increase in recent years. This is probably due in part to the leveling off of gains in efficiency of fossil-fueled power plants and also to increased uses of electricity, for example, air conditioning.

While the overall U.S. thermal power inputs into the atmosphere are small even at the nation's level of industrialization, in some localities they can become very significant. Using the average per capita value of 11.37 kilowatts, the average thermal flux in a few densely populated areas is large when compared with natural values. Table 4 illustrates this point for several cities. Although average values are used, the figures are in close accord with more detailed studies. For example, Bornstein reported results for Manhattan.[3] During the winter, heat produced from combustion alone was two and a half times greater than that of the solar energy reaching the ground; during summer this factor dropped to one-sixth. Thus, in densely populated areas, the thermal contribution of man's activities can be very substantial.

DIRECT WEATHER EFFECTS OF THERMAL OUTPUT

Observations decisively show that the climate of built-up urban areas differs from the surrounding rural regions. The average temperature in large cities is 1 to

[3]R. D. Bornstein, "Observation of the Urban Heat Island Effect in New York City," *Journal of Applied Meteorology*, vol. 2 (1968), p. 574.

Table 4. Thermal Flux in Densely Populated Cities

City	Population density (no./hectare)	Average thermal flux (kw/hectare)
New York	101	1,148
Manhattan	256	2,911
Chicago	58	659
Los Angeles	24	273
Philadelphia	58	659
Detroit	42	477
Baltimore	45	512

2°F. higher than in the surrounding countryside, while the minimum winter temperatures can be as much as 2 to 3°F. higher. Precipitation in cities is greater than in the nearby countryside, and the frequency of clouded skies and of fog is much greater.

These differences are partly due to the direct thermal input from man's activities and partly to the different thermal characteristics of the city. When we change a rural area to an urban one, we convert an essentially spongy surface of low-heat conductivity into an impermeable layer with a high capacity for absorbing heat that is re-radiated at night, increasing the local temperature.

The effects of the warmer, more cloudy environment in the cities on the inhabitants have not been studied. In the long term, however, serious problems are sure to arise. In today's urban centers, the area subjected to man's influence is fairly restricted, and changing weather patterns partly relieve the man-made alterations. As megalopolis grows, man's effect will become more regional in character. The total thermal influence will be correspondingly greater, and the climatic changes could indeed present serious problems.

EMISSIONS IN THE USE OF ENERGY

The conversion of energy also changes the chemical characteristics of the atmosphere. Some of these changes are global in nature, for example, increased carbon dioxide content; others are more nearly regional or local, for example, sulfur dioxide content.

The burning of fossil fuels now releases about 1.5×10^{16} grams of carbon dioxide per year. This figure should be compared with the amount consumed annually in photosynthesis of about 1.1×10^{17} grams. Not only is the artificially introduced amount large compared with natural processes, but it is 10,000 times greater than the return of carbon to the fossil reservoir.

Observations of man-made carbon dioxide show that about one-third of it remains in the atmosphere and that two-thirds is dissolved in the oceans. At the current rate of disposition in the atmosphere, the amount of man-made carbon dioxide doubles every twenty-three years, and the total amount of carbon dioxide in the atmosphere has increased by about 8 percent since 1900.

Other additions to the atmosphere are indicated in table 5, with the per capita values calculated from the 1968 inventory of emissions. The oxides of sulfur are derived largely from fossil fuel, while the other components result largely but not entirely from the burning of fuels for transportation.

Table 5. Nationwide Emissions of Pollutants per Capita, 1968

Pollutant	Tons/year
Carbon monoxide	0.50
Sulfur oxides	0.17
Hydrocarbons	0.16
Nitrogen oxides	0.10
Particulates	0.14

The flux of emissions in any given situation will depend on the density of industry and the location of highways as well as on the density of dwelling units. On the basis of the values given in table 5, the average flux of each constituent as a function of population density is indicated in table 6. Thus, in densely populated areas, on the average, some three-tenths of a gram of carbon monoxide are produced each second on a hectare of urban land. This rate becomes significant in terms of health effects when compared with maximum allowable concentrations.

Table 6. Average Flux of Pollutant Emissions as a Function of Population Density

(grams/hectare/second)

Pollutant	Density		
	10/hectare	50/hectare	100/hectare
Carbon monoxide	0.034	0.17	0.34
Sulfur oxides	0.01	0.05	0.10
Hydrocarbons	0.01	0.05	0.10
Nitrogen oxides	0.007	0.035	0.07
Particulates	0.009	0.045	0.09

Little is known of the fate of these pollutants in the atmosphere. The average background concentration of carbon monoxide has not been increasing, but where the carbon monoxide goes is uncertain. The same can be said of the oxides of nitrogen. Sulfur dioxide is soluble in water and for the most part rains out.

As I indicated earlier, these emissions can be controlled, with the exception of carbon dioxide. Already the effects of auto emissions and industrial control technology are being shown. Thus, in the United States, 1966 was probably the year with the highest levels of carbon monoxide, and the amounts emitted since

then have decreased by a few percent over what would have been expected in the absence of control.

EFFECTS OF EMISSIONS

Carbon dioxide can directly affect the climate of the earth by changing the radiation balance of the atmosphere. Indeed, carbon dioxide is one of the three important radiation-absorbing constituents of the atmosphere. The other two are water vapor and ozone. While man-made activities may have affected the latter two constituents, the changes in concentration are much smaller than the change in carbon dioxide.

The total amount of carbon dioxide added to the atmosphere by man's activities is about 1.7×10^{17} grams. Of this amount, a majority has been injected in the past two decades. Since about half the coal produced has been burned in the past thirty-one years and half the petroleum consumed has been burned in the past thirteen years, 9×10^{16} grams of carbon dioxide have been introduced since 1950 and 1.3×10^{17} grams since the mid-thirties.

An estimate of the maximum amount of carbon dioxide that man might introduce into the atmosphere can be made from estimates of the total fossil fuel available. Assuming 8×10^{12} metric tons of coal are available—about twice the coal resources mapped geologically—and assuming 2×10^{12} barrels of oil, burning these fuels would add 3.3×10^{18} grams of carbon dioxide. This is about one and a half times the 2.2×10^{18} grams of carbon dioxide in the atmosphere now.

Any attempt at long-term forecasting must be viewed with some caution. The oceans, for example, contain sixty times more carbon dioxide than the atmosphere. If the average temperature of the earth increases, either as a result of increasing carbon dioxide content or by some other means, the heating would tend to drive some of the carbon dioxide now dissolved in the oceans back into the atmosphere. It cannot be said with any precision what the carbon dioxide content of the atmosphere actually will be. What can be said is that man has changed the total amount of carbon dioxide by several percent; further, he is capable of doubling the carbon dioxide content over the next 100 years.

The effects of carbon dioxide on climate are also uncertain. Various calculations suggest that an increase of 10 percent in the carbon dioxide content would raise the average temperature the world over by 0.3 to $0.4°F$. Yet during the period of maximum input of carbon dioxide into the atmosphere—the past three decades—the average temperature has decreased by about the amount it was expected to rise. This implies that other natural processes are at work, which in the absence of the additional carbon dioxide would have led to a greater decrease in temperature, or that the calculations are deficient in some unknown respect. Similar calculations indicate that a doubling of carbon dioxide would

raise the temperature by about 3 to 4°F. Although this temperature fluctuation may seem small, it can have substantial effects, particularly on marginal economies. The small observed decrease in world temperature has been accompanied by increased ice coverage in the North Atlantic, which has had a major effect on Icelandic fisheries, and the economy of Iceland has been further adversely affected by the shorter growing season.

Various attempts have been made to estimate the economic cost associated with air emissions related directly to energy use.[4] Table 7 summarizes these estimates. A number of basic assumptions lie behind these figures:

1. Technology is assumed to be frozen at the 1968 levels, and no new controls are instituted.
2. Health costs include the present value of future earnings forgone because of reduced longevity, as well as the costs of medical treatment and absenteeism.
3. Energy use is proportional to growth in GNP, and GNP grows at an average rate of 4 percent.

Although the estimates in table 5–7 are certainly very rough, they do indicate the order of magnitude of the social cost of energy use. In 1968 the economic cost of air contaminants amounted to about $20 billion. To this figure must be added the cost in lowered water quality, the cost in terms of acres of strip-mined land, the cost of land no longer usable because of tailings, the cost of oil spills, and so on. The list is virtually endless. Without additional controls and the application of new technology, the estimated cost due to air pollution would double by 1985.

Table 7. Economic Effects of Energy-Related Air Emissions, 1968 and Projected for 1985

| | Health | | Property, materials, vegetation | |
	Stationary sources	Transportation	Stationary sources	Transportation
Year				($ billion)
1968	8.2	2.8	8.4	0.5
1985	16.7	3.9	19.0	1.2

CONCLUSIONS

The high cost that can be attributed to emissions resulting from energy conversion makes the development of the relevant technology important. In

[4] See Lester B. Lave and E. P. Seskin, "Air Pollution and Human Health," *Science*, vol. 169 (August 21, 1970), p. 723; and Ronald Ridker, *Economic Cost of Air Pollution* (Praeger, 1967).

part, the answer to emission problems lies in the further development of nuclear energy. Such development would have to be accompanied by environmentally safe means of disposing of high-level waste at costs that are not prohibitive. Another disadvantage of current reactor technology is its relatively low thermal efficiency compared with that of fossil fuel plants. Again, increased efficiency is not an insurmountable technical problem.

In addition to emission control technology, advances in the removal of potential pollutants prior to combustion afford a hopeful alternative. In particular, coal gasification represents a way of tapping the very large coal reserves and producing a relatively clean fuel.

The thermal load on the atmosphere as a result of energy use is not a problem of global concern today, nor is it expected to be in the future. On the other hand, densely populated regions that are highly industrialized could face undesirable alterations in weather and climate if alternatives for the disposal of thermal waste heat over larger areas are not developed.

In the longer term, the issue of continually increasing energy per capita and per dollar of GNP must be faced. The development of a recycling industry will help, of course. Developments in mass transit offer major opportunities. But any one of these developments by themselves will not be sufficient. What is required is a national energy policy that spells out in detail the needs and the means to achieve an efficient and environmentally sound use of energy.

III.
ON PROBLEMS OF
PUBLIC POLICY

Reconciling Energy Policy Goals

EDWARD S. MASON

My particular interest is in the reconciliation of the goals of economic efficiency and environmental quality. I shall discuss this problem at some length, commenting briefly as well on the goals of resource adequacy and national security.

The adequacy of a group of resources, such as energy resources, to meet requirements will obviously be influenced by the possibility of substituting one energy source for another in particular uses, by relative prices and prospective changes in these prices, and by the state of technology. At present prices, supplies of natural gas will not long be adequate to meet demands in current uses. But a price increase can generate new supplies and possibly lead to a substitution of other fuels in certain uses. For some time, U.S. oil production has been inadequate to supply American consumption, but oil imports have substituted for domestic sources. As the price of imported oil increases, and it certainly will, production of oil from shale and coal become possibilities, and the greater the technological advance, the more competitive these sources will become. Existing supplies of uranium that are easily available to the United States will not long support nuclear power generation using existing techniques, but effective

Edward S. Mason is University Professor Emeritus of Harvard University and a consultant to the World Bank. A member of the Harvard faculty since 1923, he served as Dean of the Graduate School of Public Administration, 1947–58. In 1951–52, he was a member of the President's Materials Policy Commission and has served as Chairman of the Advisory Committee on Economic Development, the Agency for International Development, and the Research Advisory Board of the Committee for Economic Development. From 1964 to 1970, he was a member of the Board of Directors of Resources for the Future and is now an honorary member. Dr. Mason was born in 1899 in Clinton, Iowa. He received his A.B. degree from the University of Kansas and, as a Rhodes Scholar, earned the B. Litt. degree at Oxford University. He holds A.M. and Ph.D. degrees from Harvard University.

breeder reactors are not far over the technological horizon, and this development should dispose of the potential scarcity of uranium. When one takes these and other possibilities into account, it is difficult to envisage any overall inadequacy of energy supplies for the United States over the next few decades. There may well be shortages of particular energy resources for particular uses and temporary failures of supply, such as those we have seen recently in electricity availability along the Eastern Seaboard, but no overall energy shortages. What we do probably confront is a shift toward higher-cost inputs. The days of low-cost energy inputs for the United States seem to be over.

Let me now comment briefly on the relation of energy supplies to security goals. Here, apart from the possibility of nuclear engagement, we are concerned almost exclusively with oil; oil to power land vehicles, ships at sea, and military aircraft. I take it for granted that assured access to Western Hemisphere sources of oil in sufficient volume to meet our own military requirements is essential. But again, I see no particular failure in resource adequacy, at least not over the next few decades,[1] nor is there any significant conflict between this and other national goals over and above the inevitable conflict between the use of all resources for military as against civilian uses. Oil is simply one of many resource inputs that, if not earmarked for security goals, would be available for other purposes. To consider in detail the energy requirements for all the possible security contingencies that could be imagined, including the requirements of any number of possible combinations of allies arrayed against any number of possible combinations of opponents, would take me far away from the subject I want to discuss. Let me then limit myself to a few observations that to me seem relevant to the security problem.

If we find ourselves engaged in nuclear combat with the Soviet Union, there is reason to believe that requirements for oil will diminish at least as rapidly as supplies. Destruction of populations, cities, and industrial establishments could be expected to occur mainly in oil-using, rather than oil-producing, areas. A close calculation of the security aspects of petroleum availability and requirements is simply irrelevant to nuclear warfare.

Second, if we accept the advice of the joint chiefs of staff and consider that the United States should be prepared to employ conventional weapons in two full-scale wars, one in Western Europe and one in the Far East, in addition to a small-scale war in Latin America, the oil requirements for ourselves and our allies simply could not be met without unimpaired access to Middle Eastern oil.[2] It

---

[1] This is not to deny that there may well be a security argument for impounding more already discovered North American oil, while relying for a period on larger imports.

[2] According to Charles L. Schultze, *Setting National Priorities: The 1971 Budget* (Brookings Institution, 1970), p. 24:

> With these limitations in mind, it was determined in the 1960's that, taking into account allied forces, U.S. planning should provide the active and high priority reserve forces needed to wage the initial stages of major and simultaneous conflicts in Europe and Asia

would be quite impossible to meet military and essential civilian requirements in Western Europe and Japan by shipments from the Western Hemisphere, no matter how closely we tightened our belts. Considering our potential antagonists in such wars, this might tell us something about possible theaters of action.

Third, considering how extremely vulnerable Western Europe and Japan are to interruption of Middle Eastern oil supplies, it would seem highly desirable from their point of view as well as ours to lessen this vulnerability by stockpiling oil and developing additional sources outside the Middle East. It appears unlikely, however, that Western Europe and Japan will take the necessary steps unless they become convinced that the Western Hemisphere in general and the United States in particular cannot and will not carry this load. It is high time they came to this realization.

This is all I want to say under the head of security. I am conscious that I have started any number of hares, but I am not going to stay around to see them run down, since, to mix my metaphors, I have other fish to fry.

Let me turn now to the question of reconciling economic efficiency and environmental quality. Stated in this form there is really no problem. Efficiency is a favorable or optimum relation of inputs to outputs, and everything depends on what is included in the inputs and the outputs. A productive process that takes full account of social costs, including damage to the environment, and social benefits, including improvement of the environment, can be as efficient as a process that minimizes costs per unit of output, calculating inputs and outputs at market prices. The real questions are these: If full account were taken of environmental costs and benefits, how would the combination of goods and services produced differ from the combination that in fact gets produced? Is there any reason to believe that the first combination would be better in some sense than the second? If so, how do we move from the second combination toward the first? It is this set of questions that I want to talk around, and I emphasize "talk around," since I am certainly not going to be able to present any definitive conclusions.[3]

(as in the Second World War), and a sufficient capability to deal with a much smaller conflict involving U.S. forces in the Western Hemisphere at the same time.

The limitations have to do with the undesirability of locking "capabilities irreversibly into some fixed geographic location" and with the recognition that reserve forces would be sufficient only to cope with initial enemy action while other forces were being mobilized.

[3] These questions involve the thorny problem of assessing the extent to which an increase in GNP, as presently measured, reflects an increase in that part of economic welfare that is connected with the output of goods and services. The view taken in this paper is that:

(a) Adequate care for the environment will indeed involve a substantial change in the combination of goods and services produced.

(b) The diversion of resources required to protect the environment will not necessarily adversely affect the rate of growth of GNP as it is conventionally measured. The cost of attachments required to control automotive exhausts, for example, and increased expenditures on sewage disposal facilities will enter into GNP calculations, even though the effect is merely to undo damage already done.

The crux of the difficulty in market economies is the result of decentralized decision making in which air and water are considered to be free goods, and noise, odors, and other affronts to the senses are considered to be irrelevant. It might be thought that the centralized planning of a socialist society would avoid this miscalculation, but the Soviet Union seems to be at least as enamored of a growth rate that takes no account of these considerations as any capitalist society.

How serious a matter is it that environmental costs and benefits are not taken into account in the production calculus? If one takes at face value the words of the 1971 report of the President's Council of Economic Advisers, the answer would appear to be "not much." While recognizing that the gross national product (GNP) "is not a perfect measure of all the activities comprehended in the idea of economic output," the council found that, on the whole, a high rate of growth of GNP is what the people want: ". . . whatever may be true about the relative values of the product included in the GNP and the product excluded from it—the automobile on the one hand and the clean air on the other—there is little evidence that we are witnessing a decline in the value assigned to economic output as a whole." Concern for the environment is firmly put in its place in a sentence: "For anyone to whom clean water is the only valuable product there has been no economic growth since the time of Hiawatha."[4]

But the problem is not as simple as this. In a free market economy, a consumer will purchase an automobile no matter how foul the atmosphere and no matter how many others are adversely affected by his addition to the number of cars on the road. And why should he not have an automobile? According to his calculus, his addition to the foulness of the atmosphere is minimal, and his desire for the automobile is great. This is true of all the products whose increased output inevitably increases air, water, noise, and other types of pollution. The free market measures the value of the output to an individual consumer, but it takes no account of the damage done to all other inhabitants of the area. So, government is inevitably drawn into the picture. Even the Council of Economic Advisers recognizes this necessity, and, if the decision-making process is democratic, the council appears to have considerable hope that the economic calculus can be righted.

However, in a society whose legal and economic institutions and ways of thought were developed in an era when environmental considerations were much

---

(c) The diversion of resources from current output will, in some respects, make GNP a better measure of welfare than it otherwise would be, even though it necessitates a decrease in the output of goods and services that would otherwise be produced.

(d) Whether the costs of increased inputs is covered by increased prices or taxes, the burden imposed on current consumption is apt to be seriously regressive.

[4]*Economic Report of the President, January 1971*, pp. 88, 86.

less important, drawing government into the process is easier said than done. In the case of automobile exhaust, it required near-catastrophe in metropolitan areas to bring about government participation in decisions regarding this problem—over the protests of the automobile industry and the objections of a considerable portion of the citizenry who do not want to pay $100 to $200 for effective control of exhaust emissions. Parenthetically, this added cost that will appear in the price of the car will thus take its place in GNP, even though the addition merely represents an attempt to get us back to where we once were in terms of quality.[5] But short of impending catastrophe, it is difficult indeed to stimulate action necessary to the preservation of the environment.

Of course, external economies and diseconomies—or spillover effects—have long been recognized by economists and others, and it has been noted that, if these effects are substantial, customary uses of GNP do not fully measure output. But, in general, they have not been considered substantial and have, in fact, been treated as one of those examples of "market failure" that should be mentioned in any respectable textbook before more important matters are touched upon. In particular, it has not been recognized until recently that environmental pollution, as an external diseconomy, tends to grow rapidly in importance with increases in population density and in per capita GNP. It is to the credit of Resources for the Future that it has been among the leaders in pressing for such a recognition.[6] External diseconomies become increasingly important primarily because water, air, and space continue to be drawn on by private producers without incurring costs, or at least without incurring costs that fully measure social disadvantages, and are used for the disposal or dilution of wastes, again, without incurring costs.

According to Kneese and d'Arge:

There are three classes of physical exchange for which current private property arrangements provide no basis of counterpart economic transactions; these are—

(1) Private use for production inputs of "common property" resources, notably air, streams, lakes, and the ocean (e.g., water from streams in industrial production; oxygen from the air in combustion, etc.);

---

[5] Increasingly, our GNP statistics not only fail to measure important dimensions of welfare but are becoming ambiguous measures of output itself. In contrast to an earlier period when discharges to the environment did not enter into national accounts, in the future we can expect to devote a growing share of measured output to cleaning up the consequences of our activities. Even so, we are likely to suffer a loss of amenity not presently recorded in national accounts or to see it preserved at a cost that inflates the figures but not our welfare.

[6] For example, see Allen V. Kneese and Ralph C. d'Arge, "Pervasive External Costs and the Response of Society," *The Analysis and Evaluation of Public Expenditures: The PPB System*, A compendium of papers submitted to the Subcommittee on Economy in Government of the Joint Economic Committee, 91 Cong. 1 sess. (1969), pp. 87–115 (Resources for the Future Reprint 80).

(2) Private use of the assimilative capacity of the environment to "dispose of" or dilute wastes and residuals; and

(3) Inadvertent or unwanted material inputs to productive processes—diluents and pollutants.

The authors go on to say, "All these services or disservices are physically transferred at zero price, because there exist no social institutions which would permit the resources in question to be 'owned,' and exchanged in the market."[7]

By how much would the combination of goods and services now produced be affected if resources devoted to increasing output were diverted to protection of the environment? A lot depends, of course, on whether we are content with present air and water quality standards, noise pollution levels, and urban congestion or whether we insist on improvement. But there can be little doubt that merely to preserve the standards we now have, under the influence of another 100 million of population, will require a very serious diversion of resources. Whether or not we can achieve such preservation of standards is another matter. We do not necessarily have to agree with Mishan that "the continued pursuit of economic growth by western societies is more likely on balance to reduce rather than to increase welfare," or that "the invention of the private automobile was one of the great disasters to have befallen the human race,"[8] to be convinced that putting a stop to the degradation of the environment will appreciably change the types and quantities of goods now produced. There is a very real conflict between the goals of economic growth and environmental preservation; although technological changes can mitigate this conflict, it is difficult to see how it can be avoided.

The production and use of energy resources lie at the center of the sources of pollution, and it is difficult to enumerate all their crimes.[9] In the case of oil production, refining, and use, there are leakages from underwater production, as in Santa Barbara; oil discharges from ships at sea or in other waters, either by accident or design; the destruction of terrain by pipelines, as in the proposed Alaska pipeline; sulfur and other chemical discharges in oil refining and oil use; and worst of all, exhausts from the combustion engine. Coal has to its discredit the leakage of mine acids into streams, the devastation of strip mining, the immediate human damage through black lung and other diseases, and, of course, the sulfur and other discharges from the burning of coal. The production and consumption of gas come off with only a slight reprimand, although there are possibilities of gas leakage, and, as a fossil fuel, gas contributes to those carbon dioxide and particulate effects that will either melt the ice caps or freeze us all

[7] Ibid., p. 92.

[8] E. J. Mishan, *The Costs of Economic Growth* (Praeger, 1967), pp. 171, 173.

[9] Council on Environmental Quality, *Environmental Quality*, First Annual Report (August 1970), p. 159: "The conflicts between the consumption we all want and the environmental ill effects we all wish to avoid is sharper for energy than perhaps any other aspect of natural resource use."

to death, no one knows which. Among primary energy sources, hydroelectric power would no doubt come out best were it not for the facts that sites appropriate for generation so frequently lie in scenic surroundings craved by nature lovers and that power has to be transmitted for long distances over unsightly transmission lines.

When we come to the conversion of primary energy resources into electric power, there are the questions of the location of power plants, undesirable emanations from the use of fossil fuels, transmission lines, and heat discharges into water. Nuclear power generation avoids contamination of the atmosphere, but there are dangers—and it is hoped that they are minimal—of radiation leakages; and heat discharges into water are some 50 percent above those of steam plants of similar capacity. Altogether, what energy production and consumption do to the environment presents a sorry picture.

At the same time, not only do energy requirements, overall, grow at about the same rate as GNP, but requirements for electrical energy occasionally have grown at nearly three times this rate. Furthermore, an expansion of the growth rate of electric power would seem to be required if other aspects of the pollution problem are to be handled. As recycling of materials becomes more necessary not only for reasons of efficiency but as one way of lessening the environmental problem of waste disposal, the draft on electrical energy supplies inevitably increases. As we dig into lower and lower grades of ore in the attempt to keep up with our insatiable requirements for goods, energy requirements in general and electrical energy requirements in particular are bound to expand. Nor are we talking about trivial needs when we consider a sustained 7 or 8 percent increase per year in requirements for electricity. As Joel Darmstadter has pointed out[10] twenty-four electric toothbrushes whirling continuously use no more power than a 60-watt bulb. And if one took the demands of all the exotic household uses for electric power and rolled them together, they would amount to nothing worth mentioning. What we are concerned with is power to move industrial machinery, to transport people in metropolitan areas, to air-condition buildings, to light and—increasingly—to heat houses, indeed, to support what are considered to be necessities in the kind of life we have become accustomed to lead. In a period of power shortages, one could wish that electric utilities would not find it so necessary to push vigorously for expansion of electric heating and other large household consumers of power. But, whether they do so or not, a 7 or 8 percent per annum growth in electricity requirements is definitely in the cards. And, as a member of the Federal Power Commission is quoted as saying, it is misleading "for President Nixon and others in Government to say that both rapid economic growth and unaltered environment are simultaneously possible."[11]

[10] See appendix.

[11] John A. Carver, Jr., in an address, "Potentials for an Energy Crisis," delivered to the New York Society of Security Analysts, January 28, 1971, *New York Times*, January 29, 1971.

120

The proposition that there is a conflict of serious magnitude between traditional goals of economic growth and preservation of the environment has been
well documented. Technology has led us into this problem and perhaps technology can lead us out. I leave that question to Dr. Seaborg. But whether it can
or not, technology will have to operate within a system of public rules and
regulations and an economy of incentives and disincentives that provides the right
signals and avoids the wrong ones. What we must aim toward if we are to achieve
a satisfactory reconciliation of the goals of growth and environmental preservation is a set of administrative, legal, and economic directives that meet the broad
approval of the electorate as expressed ultimately through political channels.
This is not a problem for science and technology, though the contributions of
scientists and technicians can be important; it is not a problem in economics,
though economists can be useful; nor is it a problem for administrators, though
their assistance is necessary. It is ultimately a question of finding out what the
people want and if what they want is feasible within technological, economic,
and administrative limits. And the ultimate answers can be found only in the
political arena.[12]

Having said that, let me draw back and nibble around the edges of a few of
the relevant questions as an economist see them, leaving it for wiser heads than
mine to grapple with the central issues. There would appear to be at least four
different channels of approach to the problem of introducing environmental
considerations into production and consumption decision making, all involving
interrelations among legislative, administrative, and judicial processes. The first
would involve an attempt to introduce considerations of social costs and benefits
into business and consumer calculations by changes in the pricing system. This,
of course, is an approach of considerable appeal to economists. If it were possible by changing the price signals to accomplish this objective, it would leave
producers and consumers free to make their own optimum adaptation to market
circumstances. Effluent charges and subsidies for the installation of pollution
control equipment have, in fact, been used in a number of situations. There are,
however, formidable difficulties of information and administration attached to
an attempt to push this technique very far.

Second, the production and distribution of certain polluting products, such
as DDT, can be prohibited or controlled by legislative fiat. Or certain techniques
of production can be prohibited, as probably should be done with coal strip
mining. Or, again, legislatures can attempt to set specific standards of tolerable

[12]One has to admit that what the people are likely to want, unless their values change
substantially, will be so heavily weighted in favor of economic growth that irreparable injury
may be done to the environment. This, indeed, is one of the theses propounded in a classical
essay on ecology: "Our ecological crisis is the product of an emerging, entirely novel,
democratic culture. The issue is whether a democratized world can survive its own implications. Presumably we cannot unless we rethink our axioms." (Lynn White, "The Historical
Roots of the Ecological Crisis." *Science*, March 10, 1967, p. 1204.)

pollution, as California is in the process of doing with automobile exhausts and as Congress is now attempting to do nationally.[13] Within limits, this is an effective procedure, but many environmental hazards escape the clear definition and management necessary for the formulation of legislative standards; in any case, this is a broad-brush approach that inevitably ignores differences in the situations in which those subject to the legislation find themselves.

Third, legislatures can express a broad intent and lay down a number of considerations that need to be taken into account in decisions affecting the environment and then leave it to administrative agencies to see that this intent and these considerations are heeded by persons, enterprises, and institutions affected by the law. This has been and is the favorite American procedure in dealing with environmental problems and currently it is under heavy attack. The Atomic Energy Commission is given authority to license nuclear power plants and to see to it that standards affecting radiation emissions are strictly observed. Recently, it has been given additional responsibilities for environmental protection under the National Environmental Policy Act and the Federal Water Quality Act. The Bureau of Reclamation and the Department of the Interior have the responsibility for taking environmental considerations into account in licensing operations on public lands. These organizations stubbed their toes in Santa Barbara and may be in the process of doing it again in Alaska. State public utility commissions are concerned with the siting of fossil fuel electric plants and, of course, there are dozens of other state and federal administrative agencies involved in interpreting legislative directives concerning environmental preservation. This type of administrative decision making is excessively prone to political pressures from interests wanting to make a dollar at the expense of the environment and, in particular, from interests the administrative agencies are supposed, under legislative authority, to hold in check.

It is charges of this sort that are mainly responsible for bringing the fourth procedure, an appeal to the courts against administrative decisions by concerned citizens, into the picture.[14] The secretary of the interior is now enjoined from proceeding with the Alaska pipeline. The Center for Law and Social Policy in Washington and other nonprofit entities have brought dozens of cases to court in recent years on environmental grounds, and many a power plant or processing firm has been held up pending the adjudication of such suits. One of my con-

---

[13] For a discussion of some of the problems involved in defining practical standards see Joe S. Bain, "The Technology, Economics and Industrial Strategy of Automobile Air Pollution Control," *Western Economic Journal*, vol. 8, no. 4 (December 1970), pp. 329–57.

[14] See Joseph L. Sax, *Defending the Environment: A Strategy for Citizen Action* (Knopf, 1971). Sax not only discusses many actual situations in which court action on the intervention of concerned citizens produced alterations in administrative plans and practices but suggests new interpretations of law designed to make such intervention more effective. He also drafts a proposed model statute facilitating court action in environmental cases for consideration by state legislatures.

servative colleagues asked me what would have happened to the economic development of the United States if legal actions of this sort and other Nader-like operations had plagued business decision making during the last century. I suspect it would have provided a sounder development in many respects than that we have seen. But there is no blinking the fact that in the process there would have been a considerable change in the combination of goods and services produced by the economy.

None of the four approaches, no matter how developed and refined, will be sufficient to assure an acceptable balance between the goals of economic growth and environmental preservation. All can be useful, but all have limitations. And it is unlikely they can be meshed into a system of incentives and restraints that, industry by industry and decision by decision, will produce a set of activities in which private cost-benefit calculations give way to social cost-benefit calculations. Moreover, each movement away from the calculus of private profitability toward a broader range of considerations will take place in a political context in which power groups oppose each other, values and ideologies are in conflict, and institutions and procedures shaped in a quite difficult environment of public-private relationships are called on to handle novel problems. We may expect the debate between the proponents of growth and the proponents of preservation to evoke all the irrational arguments that have characterized the debate on the Supersonic Transport or the Alaska pipeline. But to say this is merely to suggest that progress toward a political reconciliation of these conflicting goals will follow the course of any social development. The nature of the reconciliation will depend on the political strength of the opposing forces.

To date, despite the growing numbers of the environmentalists, political forces have been heavily weighted in favor of the economic and technological interests concerned with growth. Furthermore, there has been exaggeration, even hysteria, in the claims of various environmentalists that has not been of service to their cause. What is badly needed is a sober appraisal by a reputable authority of what is known and not known about the environmental effects of economic activities and of the trade-offs in these activities between production and preservation. I hope that Resources for the Future will take the lead in providing such an appraisal. But, even if and when this is done, I suspect that we shall discover how little is known of the relevant facts.

I am not concerned here with such obvious lacunae as ignorance of whether we have more to fear from the "greenhouse" effect of excessive discharges of carbon dioxide than from the "iceberg effect" of discharges of particulates into the upper atmosphere. We are astonishingly ignorant about much smaller matters. Let me give you an example. The State of Massachusetts decreed that by October 1, 1970, the sulfur content of residual fuel oil, which had been running at about 2.5 percent, should be reduced to 1 percent.[15] Consumers of

[15] Commonwealth of Massachusetts, Department of Public Health, Division of Environmental Health, Bureau of Air Use Management, Regulation 5 for the Control of Air Pollu-

fuel oil in the Boston area who had been paying $1.90 a barrel (admittedly an abnormally low price) found the price rising by stages to $4.30 a barrel. Obviously, the cost of sulfur removal was not the only factor involved, but it was important. The law also decreed that the permissible sulfur content should be reduced to 0.5 percent by October 1, 1971, and there have been suggestions that it be reduced to zero by 1975. Now, considering the fact that Boston is a seacoast city with prevailing westerly winds and that sulfur from fuel constitutes certainly less than 20 percent of the not very bothersome air pollution in the Boston area, one is entitled to doubt whether the benefit derived from this reduction of air pollution is worth the extra cost to fuel oil consumers. I do not know what the answer is, but I doubt very much whether the Massachusetts General Court did either.

The attainment of a sensible trade-off between growth and environmental preservation is currently hampered at every stage by ignorance--by lack of physical and chemical knowledge of the effects of various discharges on atmospheric changes or rates of change in water composition; by ignorance of the biological and entomological effects of various types and levels of pollution on human beings, plants, and animals; by ignorance, because of the lack of market tests, of what valuation people put on an improvement or worsening of levels of various types of pollution; and by ignorance of certain economic considerations that could tell us something about how various pollution measures would affect relative prices, outputs, and employment in particular industries and the location of business enterprises. We grope, not in complete darkness, but in a rather dismal sort of gloom. As I have emphasized, reconciliation of diverse energy goals takes place through a political process. But the kind of reconciliation that could emerge in the present state of our ignorance might involve either irreparable damage to the environment or, on the other hand, a sacrifice of growth possibilities to unreasonable and unnecessary environmental precautions. The kind of reconciliation we must aim toward is one arrived at by a political process of decision making based on technical knowledge of what the trade-offs between growth and environmental protection really amount to. It would still be a political reconciliation but one having some hope of being influenced by fact and rational analysis.

Let me offer two final observations. There are those who maintain that an expansion of output and investment along customary lines is essential to the maintenance of a high level of employment. But there seems to be no reason to believe, at least without further investigation, that the employment-creating effects of restoring the environment will be any less than those involved in polluting the environment. Furthermore, they will have approximately the same

---

tion in the Metropolitan Boston Air Pollution Control District. Adopted April 14, 1970, under the provisions of Section 142D, Chapter 111, General Laws, as inserted by Chapter 836 of the Acts of 1969.

effects on the rate of growth of GNP as it is conventionally measured. It is true we will not have as many final goods and services to consume. But those who take satisfaction in high GNP growth rates should have no cause for alarm.

There are also those who appear to believe that increasing concern for the environment would radically change the relationship between the public and private sectors of the economy. There might well be some change. But there would seem to be no reason to expect a large expansion of public ownership and control. Insofar as environmental considerations can be brought to bear by changes in the price system, private enterprise would continue to operate as it does now. No doubt legislative and administrative controls would frustrate certain courses of action. And in certain areas, it is possible that public-private collaboration of the type we are familiar with in space and defense activities would emerge. But, by and large, I see no reason why an economy in which growth and environmental protection are effectively reconciled would generate a relationship between public and private activities that would be drastically different from what we now have.

The Erehwon Machine: Possibilities for Reconciling Goals by Way of New Technology

GLENN T. SEABORG

Let me begin by describing the Erehwon Machine.[1]

Operating on natural, self-renewing sources of energy, it generates power with an efficiency approaching 100 percent and still makes beneficial use of its minute amount of waste heat. Anticipating changing public life-styles, it provides durable goods and efficient services exactly matching fluctuating demands and distributes these goods and services equitably to all people. It recalls all waste, reduces the waste to its elemental form, then recombines it as basic materials with needed new resources that the machine extracts from nature with a negligible environmental impact.

The Erehwon Machine is self-adjusting to a changing labor market; it provides retraining to workers as it upgrades itself and administers welfare to all it cannot employ. To the unemployed and unemployable, it offers satisfying leisure activities and psychological reorientation to a nonwork ethic. And in doing all this for man and nature, it still shows a profit to its stockholders and a favorable effect on the international balance of payments.

Glenn T. Seaborg, Chairman of the Atomic Energy Commission at the time this paper was written, is now University Professor of Chemistry at the University of California at Berkeley. Previously (1958–61), he was Chancellor of the university, where he has been a member of the faculty since 1939. He has served on the General Advisory Committee of the Atomic Energy Commission and on the President's Science Advisory Committee. In 1951 he was awarded the Nobel Prize for Chemistry (with E. M. McMillan) for work on the chemistry of transuranium elements. During World War II he headed the Metallurgical Laboratory group at the University of Chicago that devised the chemical extraction processes used in producing plutonium for the Manhattan Project. Dr. Seaborg was born in 1912 in Ishpeming, Michigan. He received his A.B. degree from the University of California at Los Angeles and his Ph.D. in chemistry from the University of California at Berkeley.

[1]With apologies to Samuel Butler.

Of course, you realize that "Erehwon" is "Nowhere" spelled backwards, and that is exactly where this machine, this whole industrial-economic system, exists today—nowhere. In describing such a Utopian system, perhaps I should have added that it would also control and redistribute population growth as efficiently, economically, and ethically as it carried out its other production and distribution functions. But I thought this might be stretching things a bit too far.

Seriously, I think much if not all of the task I have assigned to the Erehwon Machine is what most of us would like to see take place. Ideally, we want the beneficial social effects of economic growth with none of the detrimental environmental consequences. We want a just society with well-fed, well-housed people who are educated and enlightened enough to move easily between productivity and leisure. We want a modern civilization—a highly human one—that approaches a physical equilibrium but is creatively dynamic. In short, this is our new version of Utopia. The question is, why can't we have it? The fact is that we can have much of it over a reasonable period of time, if not all of it at once, and by a reasonable period of time I mean before many of the destructive forces at work today in our world reach overwhelming proportions.

I would like to contribute a few thoughts about technologies that, combined with a number of social outlooks and actions, might give us some of the desirable effects of that Erehwon Machine. The focus of my thoughts will be on energy technologies and other technologies closely associated with them.

I would like to begin with some general comments about the need for energy as related to economic growth and the environment—two subjects that many people believe must inevitably conflict and that some see as totally incompatible. This is a point of view with which I disagree. Let me explain why.

Although I usually distrust people who oversimplify, I will start with some simple observations. The first is that, essentially, we have here on earth the same amount of matter we have had since the dawn of history. The second is that only in recent times—relatively speaking, only the last few moments of history— have we gained the ability to change the form and location of matter to a significant degree through the growing use of an enormous amount of energy. And the third is that our current and growing problems—wars, social unrest, and massive pollution—seem to derive from the fact that, through the use of such energy, we have manipulated matter in ways and to an extent as to come into strong conflict with natural and, yes, moral laws. We have degraded many natural materials, making them economically if not technically too difficult to return to useful form. We have dislocated them in nature, thus disturbing her ecology, and we have distributed them badly in terms of human considerations.

The main reason that the continuation of all this is considered intolerable now is that we can finally visualize its limits; we can forecast in such unabated growth our own extinction. We now must rethink our entire outlook about the

relationship of energy and matter. And we must come up with a relatively new one that is positive, constructive, and based on values in tune with the closed-cycle, unified-mankind concepts that are no longer merely vague ideals but are rapidly becoming hard realities. There is evidence all around us that this type of thinking is dawning on every intelligent person, but most of us are still in a state of shock (future or otherwise) and are groping for ideas and a psychological base to reconcile ourselves to many of the profound changes that must lie ahead.

Let that pass for the simplification. Now let me turn to some specifics with which we are going to have to deal as we face our new realities. In doing so, I want to deal mainly with the following: the need for more energy; energy sources and the technologies for making their energy available; and how to release, apply, and distribute this energy in the most efficient, economic, and ecologically sound manner.

When one speaks these days of the need for more energy, one can almost see the hair rise on the backs of the necks of a great many environmentalists who see the destructive and misguided use of energy as the basis for our whole environmental dilemma. Why in the world would we advocate the need for more energy when its use today is responsible for the mess we are in? they question. But in raising this question, these environmentalists have overlooked many points and have made many dubious assumptions.

First, and generally speaking, they equate the availability of energy with its abusive and irrational use and draw a conclusion along the lines that energy is the root of all evil. Thus, they advocate reducing energy availability as a means of controlling man's transgressions and indiscretion. To me, this is a strange and misguided way of thinking, and, as I once pointed out, it is like saying, "If we did not have food we would not have indigestion." This borders almost on an immoral attitude if one takes a global view of things and sees that more than 2 billion of the world's people are still "energy starved," and that this lack has a direct bearing on their hunger for food as well as on their standard of living.

But there are many people who, seeing this and being generally concerned about the conditions of their fellow humans in other parts of the globe, have another fear. They are concerned that increased energy consumption by the world's underdeveloped nations will only be a means of sustaining a cancerous population growth and intensifying its environmental effects, hastening us toward an ecological Armageddon. This concern also, it seems to me, is based on limited thinking, or at least on thinking conditioned by historical trends and values that must and will change radically.

Today, the increased consumption of energy does not necessarily have to be environmentally destructive any more than advances in medical science must necessarily be responsible for an exploding population. Just as medical science has provided the technological means both for controlling population and for

prolonging life and improving health, so those sciences and technologies that provide for the release and application of energy can give us the means to control their environmental effects. What remains is more a problem of human values, a unity of will and a reordering of social priorities, than one of invention and engineering.

Let me examine this situation in terms of the United States, because our so-called affluent society is the best example of the growing conflicts between energy, economics, and the environment. The United States also is considered by many to be an overdeveloped country, because of the environmental impact of the production and services that maintain the American standard of living. In spite of this affluence and its effect, however, there are a substantial number of people in the United States who do not consider that they have arrived at *"our* standard of living" and are more concerned about their personal environment than the broader one many others think of. As Professor Philip Hauser of the University of Chicago indicated recently, in trying to balance the urgency of programs to take care of the concerns of our man-made environment against the concerns of our natural environment, there are many who believe we should put more emphasis on reducing the rats in our cities than on saving the bald eagle in the country. But I think most of us agree that we should and can do both.

Those who take the tack that we are an overdeveloped country (and they even use the designation ODC as opposed to UDC for "underdeveloped country") see the dire need for our "de-developing." And one way they suggest we do this is simply to reduce our use of energy. They often attack the concept of the gross national product (GNP) and, seeing that its rise has roughly correlated with our increased growth of total energy demand, draw the conclusions that such a relationship must continue to exist and to be environmentally destructive. Those who think this way do not fully understand the GNP, nor are they in touch with current developments in the relationship between energy and the environment.

First of all, they tend to associate the growth of the GNP only with the production of material things, hence, also with pollution, waste, congestion, the depletion of natural resources, and any other unpleasant effects they can associate with our material affluence. What they do not recognize is that the GNP represents both total goods and *services.* It includes teachers' salaries. It includes the cost of tickets to a symphony concert or a baseball game. It includes money going into medical research and health care and into the development and maintenance of parks and recreational facilities. And it includes the support of public libraries, art galleries, museums, the theater, and films. Depending on the values, will, and leadership of a country, the wealth of the GNP can shift radically between the production of private goods and public goods and between private services and social services. It can also be directed, as it is being directed in increasing measure now, toward environmental programs to reduce the public

"bads" of pollution and restore some of the quality of the environment and of life in general.

What is true in this way of the GNP is also true of energy and energy technologies. These technologies can support environmental efforts in pollution control, in recycle, in improved land management, in more livable urban communities, and in better transportation systems. Properly developed and directed, they can be used to emphasize quality and quantity and to provide more of the amenities of life to more people with relatively less harmful environmental impact.

Thus, an innovative and motivated society in an advanced nation does not have to "de-develop" to survive environmentally. It can use its wealth and energy to support a reasonably sized population at a reasonably decent standard of living and still maintain what we might call a high degree of favorable environmental interaction.

To give you some idea of how we might attempt to do this in terms of our energy use, let me pose and answer a number of questions that are most often asked or implied when a discussion of energy, the environment, and economics takes place.

The first question has to do with what we might call our "energy limits." If we assume that our society is intelligent enough, in the light of today's problems, not to use its energy blindly to support uncontrolled population growth or per capita consumption of resources based on uncontrolled avarice, what limits are we faced with related to (1) the release of energy to the environment, and (2) the amount of energy resources available to us?

Let's first consider the release of energy to the environment and begin with what some people have sought to pose as an ultimate limit—the thermal capacity of the earth's atmosphere as a whole. This does not appear to be a problem. Even if we make the outlandish assumption that there will be 20 billion people living on the earth, all using energy at *twice* the average per capita rate (kilowatts of thermal power) of a U.S. citizen, we would still raise the average temperature of the atmosphere only one-half of one degree Fahrenheit. This is true because of the rate at which our atmosphere rejects heat to space. So this total effect does not appear to be a matter of concern. Of course, this does not mean we should even consider attempting to support such a large number of people at such a level of energy consumption. Numerous insurmountable problems, physical and social, would crop up during such an attempt long before we reached those figures. But neither should we use the threat of those problems as an excuse to neglect our responsibility to the population that inevitably will be here in the coming decades.

Returning to the more realistic aspects of energy growth, we should focus our concern on thermal limitations at the local and regional level. This is a matter in which there is not only a substantial degree of concern but the be-

ginning of some important action. Heat can produce various effects locally—in bodies of water and in the atmosphere—that will create environmental changes. These changes must be better understood and controlled. Science and technology are seeking to do this, and I believe important progress is being made. Let me give you some examples.

Important studies have been and are being made of the thermal effects of the waste heat from power plants on several rivers and lakes. More than 300 such studies have been reported in the United States to date. Over half of these have been completed, and new studies are being proposed. The findings are providing a growing body of knowledge to help deal with the problems of thermal effects. One of the most extensive and interesting of these studies is that sponsored by Northeast Utilities on the effects of the Connecticut Yankee Atomic Power Plant on the Connecticut River. I urge you to read the account of this study[2] as an example of what is involved in this type of work.

The Atomic Energy Commission (AEC) has an important thermal-effects program that it is coordinating with other government agencies through participation in the activities of the President's Office of Science and Technology. The AEC has sponsored a steam temperature prediction system—designated Colheat—developed by Battelle Pacific Northwest Laboratory for investigation of the Columbia River. This system is being evaluated now on the Upper Mississippi Basin and the Ohio River Basin. Thermal effects studies are also being conducted by a number of AEC National Laboratories. In addition, a new research facility at the AEC Savannah River Plant should make a major contribution to the study of thermal effects.

Many who read accounts in the daily press of the environmental debates on thermal effects are not getting all the facts and are confused and unduly alarmed by what they read. Part of this confusion and alarm is due to the fact that distinctions are rarely made clear between the effects of a fossil-fueled plant and a nuclear plant, between immediate effects directly adjacent to the plant and overall effects on the entire body of water, between the effects of today's plants and projections of effects for decades hence (when technologies might be radically different), and even—as has happened in the past—between fish kills caused by correctable mechanical deficiencies of a plant and the release of heat that may attract certain fish to the area near the plant but not harm them.

It should be pointed out that technologies such as cooling towers, holding ponds, canals, and the diversion of waste warm water to beneficial applications are all possibilities to solve the problems of local thermal effects. And these are being used. A significant number of fossil-fueled plants and about one-quarter of all nuclear plants being built today will employ these cooling technologies, and improvements on such technologies are under continuing investigation. Natu-

[2]Daniel Merriman, "The Calefaction of a River," *Scientific American*, May 1970.

rally, these improvements tend to increase the cost of power, but this is a necessary part of our growing trade-off for a livable environment.

Cooling technologies that allow us to keep our natural bodies of water healthy do not, however, solve the whole problem of waste heat rejection. Such heat is ultimately released to the atmosphere and this accounts for what Dr. R. Philip Hammond of the Oak Ridge National Laboratory refers to as "heat islands." Because of local and regional geography and atmospheric conditions, heat does not always dissipate as rapidly as desirable, particularly where man's activities release large amounts over our cities and industrial and power complexes. Here again, we have technologies that can help us to understand the phenomena of these heat islands. Among the newest of these technologies are earth-orbiting satellites that carry infrared photography equipment and the use of computer simulation to study and project models of atmospheric conditions under various growth forecasts.

As a result of these and other techniques, we can institute and implement legislation—as we are beginning to do—to control local and regional power growth and the siting of power plants. But beyond this, the technological aspects of our Erehwon Machine must give way to even broader social aspects. Eventually, as we arrive at a substantially larger population and try to give all those people a decent standard of living, we are going to have to face questions involving the distribution of that population and its productive capacity, as well as its overall growth—and from more than just an energy standpoint. Otherwise, we will reach certain intolerable environmental limits.

I think this is a most serious long-term consideration for our future. On a global basis, the United States is not densely populated; some twenty-five nations have higher densities per square mile. But our local and regional population concentrations are heavy, and, because of the industry and energy supporting our living standards, our environmental impact is even more heavily concentrated. Merely sprawling out from these points of concentration, as we seem to have been doing, is not the answer. In fact, the way in which we have been doing this is destroying our cities and causing dangerous social problems.

Of course, technology can play a role, and it should be considered in our search for the right answers to these problems. For example, there are technologies under development or in the offing that will allow us to cluster large power plants in places where they would be environmentally acceptable; through ultra-high voltage lines, the plants could ship their power to distant industrial areas and cities. If such power plants were large nuclear breeder reactors, it might prove desirable to place them and their fuel recycling plants in "power parks" on sections of the seacoast reserved for such purposes, or even on man-made offshore islands. The same or a similar type of "power park," with the additional technology of cooling towers to recirculate most of its cooling water, could be located inland where only a small body of water or a river would be needed to

supply its "makeup" amount of water lost through evaporation. Another technology under investigation, the air-cooled closed-cycle gas turbine, might someday make it possible to cluster similar plants inland where water is not needed at all to produce steam or to act as a power system coolant.

In this and other ways, it would be possible to separate to some extent power production, industrial production, and urban areas and thus to reduce thermal concentrations and the effects of heat islands. Naturally this concept requires a capacity and resources for generating a huge amount of economic electricity, since to make it work effectively would require a shift to highly electrified industrial and urban systems, including transportation. But if this amount of electricity is generated cleanly, the reduction of air pollution could be another important plus for such a concept.

There are ways of combining technological and social innovations along these lines that we have not yet begun to explore seriously. But we should. This means, of course, that we may have to think of large-scale relocation of segments of population and industry. There must be leadership on the part of government in developing acceptable plans and incentives to carry out such a shift in population and industrial concentrations. In short, as a nation we must again be bold and innovative in outlook and spirit. The combination of environmental and economic problems we face today may force us to become pioneers again in this country in many ways.

The other aspect of the question on energy limits is that related to the availability of energy resources. Here again, the overall limit is not the overriding question. Theoretically, we can talk in terms of decades of known gas and oil supply and the potential of additional undiscovered reserves, including those in oil shales and tar sands. We can speak of a supply of coal in the earth lasting anywhere from a few centuries to 1,000 years. We can speculate on known uranium and thorium reserves and, through breeders, think of stretching such reserves through "burning the rocks." We can go on to calculate the inexhaustible energy that fusion would release from the heavy hydrogen in the oceans and the apparently endless supply of solar and tidal power.

But such exercises must be brought down to the level of hard realities in terms of courses of planning and action dictated by known and developing technologies, by environmental and economic considerations, and by time scales that involve human lives. In many cases, we will have to make decisions and set priorities that will require us to weigh all these factors against the sheer expediency of meeting more immediate power needs.

More than ever, energy will be needed to buy us time to refocus some of our thinking and to redirect some of our efforts toward the full realization of what seems to be a painfully evolving mankind. For example, though we should make enormous efforts toward controlling and leveling off world population, we have

to recognize the inevitable population that will arrive in the interim. At the very least, all these people must be fed, sheltered, clothed, and educated. To help feed them, an agricultural revolution—a "Green Revolution"—is already under way. But the high-yield crops of this revolution depend on intensive fertilization, and the greatest portion of the fertilizer will have to be man-made. It has been projected that by the end of this century three-quarters of the world's population will be depending on such man-made fertilizer; only one-sixth requires it today. This means that by the year 2000 we would need the production of some 50 million tons of fixed nitrogen annually. And I should point out that the annual production of 1 million tons of nitrogen fertilizer requires the initial production of at least 1 million tons of steel—to establish the basic industrial capacity to produce the fertilizer—and an additional annual energy expenditure equal to the burning of about 5 million tons of coal for its actual production.

This is only part of the energy cost of growing, harvesting, processing, and distributing the world's future food needs. And keeping people fed is only part of the coming challenge, so I will not reemphasize our total future energy needs—even with population control—by the year 2000.

But potentially, the energy reserves in all forms are available to us to be released through an orderly development of power technologies. This must be done in a way that includes consideration of the environmental impact of the technologies as well as consideration of the energy they make available to us.

Generally speaking, I think we are beginning to follow this pattern. For example, we in the United States know that even if there is a reasonable growth of nuclear power in the years ahead about 50 percent of our electricity needs will still be generated by coal at the end of this century. We also know, however, that during the next thirty years we will not be able to extract and burn the required billions of tons of coal in the ways we have been burning them up to now. It would be environmentally intolerable to our air and land and water. Therefore, through social action and technology we are going to improve that situation. Underground mining will be made safer, and strip mining will be controlled, if not completely eliminated. Methods of reducing the noxious effluents released from burning coal are being developed and tested today and will be applied and upgraded over the years. Improved unit train transport of coal will take place on a growing scale. The shipment of coal in slurry form through pipelines has been introduced and may grow. Alternatively, the number of mine-mouth power plants may increase, particularly if superconductive or very high-voltage power transmission become realities. As our supplies of oil and natural gas become tighter and more expensive, we will find it important to pursue the liquefaction and gasification of coal.

At the same time that we make and apply these technological advances in the use of coal, we will move ahead on the nuclear energy front. The twenty-five years of research and development that have gone into the light water reactors

being built and operated now will bring us a multiple payoff in the years ahead, both in reducing the burden that would have been put on the fossil fuels and the burden that would have been put on our environment if we used only those fuels. In spite of the current apprehensions some have expressed over the surge of nuclear power growth, I am convinced that these new plants will prove their safety, reliability, and environmental advantages as have their predecessors. In fact, they will improve in every way.

As these current nuclear plants take over a growing share of our increasing demands for electricity, we will see the successful development and commercial introduction of breeder reactors, particularly the Liquid Metal Fast Breeder Reactor (LMFBR), the type receiving our major support today. This nuclear technology is the next logical step in meeting our energy requirements, because through the breeding process it will allow us to stretch the world's known uranium supply from one lasting decades to one lasting centuries, even thousands of years. It will also give us many other advantages, both environmental and economic, among which will be a higher thermal efficiency for nuclear power, since breeder reactors using liquid metal coolants operate at higher temperatures. This, of course, would reduce the amount of waste heat rejected to the environment. The fact that such reactors will also operate at lower pressures will allow them to be almost hermetically sealed and thus to significantly reduce the release of radioactive effluents even below their present safe levels.

There is also the possibility of another type of breeder reactor that breeds new fuel by using slow neutrons to transmute thorium into fissionable uranium-233. Such a reactor, the Molten Salt Reactor, is under development at the Oak Ridge National Laboratory. It has reached the stage where it has been successfully operated on uranium-233. Another reactor under development that operates on the thorium-uranium-233 fuel cycle is the Light Water Breeder Reactor. Also the High Temperature Gas-Cooled Reactor, a "near breeder" that can use thorium as fuel, is gaining acceptance. Thorium is even more abundant in nature than uranium, and hence these breeding technologies open the possibility of another great source of fuel for the future.

The financial payoff of the breeders will be considerable. If we can introduce the commercial LMFBR in the mid-1980s—and we are still aiming for that timetable—the gross benefits to the United States from electrical energy savings in the thirty-five year period following could be more than $350 billion in terms of today's dollars.

We should also note that, as we make the transition from today's light water reactors to the breeders, the plutonium created in those light water reactors will serve as fuel for the breeders to follow, after which the breeders will produce their own fuel for the future. One aim of our fast breeder development program is to have reactors with a doubling time of seven to ten years—that is, breeders that, in operation during that time, can make enough new plutonium to fuel an

equal number of new reactors of the same size as well as to refuel themselves. This doubling time of seven to ten years, fortunately, is about the same time span during which our electricity demand also doubles.

Discussions of such nuclear growth inevitably bring up the question of the safe management of the nuclear materials involved—the handling, shipping, and storage of fuels and wastes, as well as the safe operation of the plants themselves. This question alone has been the subject of numerous forums and, more important, of more than a quarter of a century of research, development, testing, and formulation of regulations toward the safe management of nuclear technologies. It is impossible to discuss this now in detail, but I do want to make the point that during my own long association with the nuclear field I have not experienced anything that would lead me to believe that all aspects of nuclear power development, including the disposal of high-level waste, cannot be carried out safely and with far less risk than most people accept today in the course of their daily lives. I am not minimizing the hazards associated with nuclear energy, but I must emphasize that there is no segment of the nuclear industry that cannot be managed safely by the conscientious development, application, and regulation of our nuclear technologies. The excessive fear that has been fanned recently over nuclear power is simply not warranted. And we face far greater environmental problems, dangers to public health, and social disaster from the failure to have adequate power in the years ahead than we do from the much smaller risks associated with the manner in which we are pursuing nuclear power.

In the same orderly way that we make the transition from the use of coal to nuclear power, we will move into the era of controlled fusion. Contrary to what some people might think, controlled fusion will not spring fullblown from a laboratory breakthrough to a commercially acceptable power technology. It will have to go through various stages of development, including that of a full-scale demonstration plant—perhaps more than one type—to prove its reliability, safety, environmental acceptance, economic feasibility, and other factors to be considered at this time. Even with good planning and a priority effort, this may take a great number of years. So while we must work toward such a technology optimistically, we must also be realistic in not neglecting the continuing development of our other power technologies in the event that fusion meets unseen problems and delays. I do not think that those who urge us to bypass the breeder reactor for an all-out effort on fusion realize what a tragic mistake this could be. While the availability of large amounts of funds certainly can be helpful, funds are no guarantee of the success of such a difficult scientific and technological undertaking. In the decades ahead, when adequate power to meet social requirements will be essential, we cannot gamble on the full-scale use of a technology whose feasibility has yet to be demonstrated conclusively in a laboratory. This will be the ultimate technology to solve man's quest for a virtually unlimited source of energy.

In addition to its ability to draw on an inexhaustible energy source, controlled fusion will offer other advantages that will help us achieve our environmental and social goals. It may increase our thermal efficiency in power generation to as high as 60 percent, and advocates of one direct conversion system foresee the possibility of 90 percent. Since it will be inherently safer than fission power, it may from the very beginning allow the siting of large power plants near or directly inside urban areas.

There are some who believe that an unlimited and nonpolluting source of energy is best sought in harnessing the rays of the sun, the waters of the tides, or geothermal heat. The future possibilities of making use of such energy are being seriously investigated today. But indications are that, although they may prove useful for supplying limited amounts of energy locally or regionally, it will be a long time before they can be expected to make a major contribution to our total energy demands. For example, it has been estimated that the potential natural geothermal energy available in the United States is 30,000 megawatts, an amount less than one-twentieth of our anticipated 700,000-megawatt requirement for the year 1980, and this potential geothermal energy would be exhausted in less than a century if used to capacity. I do not point this out to discourage the development of geothermal energy. In fact, members of the AEC feel optimistic enough about this source of energy to be involved in a project to aid in its development. The AEC is collaborating with Battelle Pacific Northwest Laboratory and the American Oil Shale Corporation in a feasibility study to locate sources of thermal rock at depths below 5,000 feet and to utilize an atomic device to create deep underground cavities into which water can be piped and then returned in a closed-cycle system to generate steam-electric power. The potential energy such a technology might release could be large if this technology could be developed and utilized without impairing the environment.

The low intensity of solar energy means that it must be collected from a huge surface area of solar collectors on the earth and at a place where there are few cloudy days. Assuming that present technology could be scaled up to produce such an enormous system, about 15 square miles of solar collectors would be required to capture enough sunlight to generate 1,000 megawatts of electricity through the use of solar cells. In order to make such electricity available on a twenty-four hour basis, a scheme involving some storage system, such as pumped water storage, would be necessary. There are few areas of the country where such a combination can be worked out on a large enough scale to be feasible, much less economic.

The collection of solar energy in space via enormous fields of orbiting solar collectors has been proposed. Those huge satellites, properly spaced in synchronous orbits, would collect solar energy without day-night or cloud interference effects. Once collected and converted into electric energy, this energy would be transmitted to earth via laser or microwave. But such a scheme, while it may be

theoretically possible, is fraught with unknowns and cannot be considered as an early means of supplying our large quantities of much-needed electricity. Perhaps new research on solar energy will reveal technologies that eventually may allow us to convert the sun's boundless energy into electric power on a technically and economically feasible basis.

The harnessing of tidal power poses similar engineering difficulties. Its power is totally great, but it is also so diverse that it would require engineering projects too huge and costly to make even a significant fraction of this power economical.

I am not playing down these great natural sources of energy or discouraging continued investigation of means to apply them. I must stress, however, that we have to be harshly realistic about our power needs over the next thirty to fifty years, and perhaps longer, in order to meet the vital requirements of expected population growth. If, during this period, we have mastered population control, leveled off per capita resource consumption, and established a population-energy equilibrium, we may have the luxury of time to experiment with shifting to different energy sources and technologies.

When all the problems of our energy demands and their close relationship to environmental economic factors are presented, the question of increasing our efficiency and reducing our waste of power is inevitably raised. I believe we will be answering this question in a number of ways in the years ahead. Some of these answers will lie in technological progress. I mentioned before such items as the increased thermal efficiency of the breeder reactor and ultimately the much higher efficiencies that might be obtained by controlled fusion. The possibility that fusion plants could be located in or adjacent to urban or industrial areas also would allow for the opportunity of directly using the waste heat of the plants for space heating and process heat, thus tapping nearly all their available energy. In the meantime, energy sources will be used more efficiently through the application of new and different conversion technologies, such as fuel cells, the use of "topping cycles" (as with magnetohydrodynamics), gas turbines, and other conversion systems under investigation and in various stages of development.

The development of much more efficient electric transmission lines, made possible by cryogenics, could also facilitate the efficient use of large amounts of electric power. It may not be too far in the future when, through this technology of super-conductivity, we will see a single cable capable of providing the electricity for a city of several million—and carrying it all underground.

A different kind of efficiency will be achieved by the manner in which we apply our energy through other technological advances. The development of electric-powered mass transit is one example of this, since its greater movement of people per unit of energy, materials, or space can effect enormous savings of

resources and reduce our environmental impact. And the use of new synthetic fuel cells offers a future new dimension as a nearly pollution-free source of energy to power our vehicles.

The planning and design of our cities and our houses offer an infinite number of ways in which we can increase our efficiency and, contrary to some opinions, improve the quality of our lives as well. I believe we are going to see the rise of an entire generation of young scientists and engineers who will emphasize a new harmony between technology and the most human aspects of life as well as the considerations of the environment. They will use abundant energy with great imagination and ingenuity as the ultimate raw material to manipulate and manage the other natural resources with which we have been blessed. They will use it to recycle almost all waste and to store and keep on tap such recycle material not immediately needed. They will use it to extract, transport, and return to nature when necessary all materials in an acceptable form, in an acceptable amount, and in an acceptable place so that the natural environment will remain natural and will support the continued growth and evolution of all forms of life. And they will do this in a way that will allow economic growth to support a reasonable living standard for all people.

In short, they will see to it that energy technologies serve as integral parts of the Erehwon Machine—that they are always available in the amount and form needed but are never factors that dictate the human and social goals and values of the system. Energy, as necessary as it is, and abundant energy, as important as it could be, is not the key factor in determining whether we will turn the Nowhere Machine into one that is somewhere—here, it is hoped. This energy and the tools to apply it can be available to us if we make the effort to reach out for them. And we should do so, learning to use these tools with skill and confidence. But more important is the synergistic mixture of knowledge, insight, will, and leadership needed to make this great experiment called modern civilization a going and lasting success. These are the resources for the future we must emphasize if our other resources are to enrich rather than enslave us. I believe we are now beginning to do that. And the years ahead should see us mastering a technological system finely matched with well-conceived and balanced economic and environmental needs. This is the way we should and must go to reconcile our new-found power with our age-old hopes. This is the way to the good society— and eventually to that global society in which we can all live in harmony with each other and with the good earth that sustains us.

New Goals for Society?

KENNETH E. BOULDING

The thing in pollution we most need to know
Is, where does it come from and where does it go?
One major idea in the pot must be tossed,
That things may be missing, but never are lost.
Most chemical elements cannot be changed.
They can't be destroyed, they are just rearranged.
So clean water and air, and, indeed, your clean shirt,
Are obtained by the wise segregation of dirt.
So if our research is to bear healthy fruit,
The critical question is what *to pollute.*
One policy matter is clear; the polluter
Should not be allowed to become a commuter.
And as long as industrial systems have bowels
The boss should reside in the nest that he fouls.
Economists argue that all the world lacks is
A suitable system of effluent taxes.
They forget that if people pollute with impunity
This must be a symptom of lack of community.
But this means producing a mild kind of love
So let's hope the eagle gives birth to a dove.

Kenneth E. Boulding is Professor of Economics and Program Director of the Program of Research on General Social and Economic Dynamics, Institute of Behavioral Science, University of Colorado. Previously, he was Professor of Economics at the University of Michi-

The idea that society could have goals of any sort is a fairly modern one. I am not familiar with any intensive study of the history of the idea, and it is far beyond the scope of this paper to produce one. The rise of social self-consciousness and the idea that society itself might have an image of the future into which it could proceed is unfamiliar in classical civilization. For the Greeks, the future was in the hands of essentially random fates, and the idea that the society could decide what it was going to be like in 100 years would have been thought of as outrageous hubris, certain to call down almost immediate retribution from the gods.

In the Old Testament one finds a concept of a conditional future: Obey the Law and prosper; disobey the Law and be clobbered—and even this idea suffered substantial modification as a result of disappointments. Josiah was a good king and was clobbered; Manasseh was a bad one and prospered. The Babylonian captivities spiritualized the Jews' concept of social causation, and the Greek and Roman conquests pushed it toward eschatology and the messianic hope, a concept that also was dominant in early Christianity, where the individual goal was salvation and the social goal was simply to wait until the end. We see this view surviving vigorously to our own day in the Seventh-Day Adventists and similar cultures.

The idea that society in the secular sense might have patterns in time that could be detected, and hence have an image of its own future that might be realized, can perhaps be traced back to Machiavelli, but the idea of society as a developing process, with regularities that can be detected and a future that can be projected must be attributed to Adam Smith and classical economics. The "magnificent dynamic," as Baumol[1] calls it, the great scheme of secular processes by which a society accumulates knowledge, population, and capital and moves toward the stationary state, is as dramatic and magnificent in its own way as the great scheme of salvation in Christianity as we see it in Dante or Milton. Marx, however, is perhaps the first writer who seized upon the idea of a social dynamic, in this case a modified Hegelian dialectic, and turned it into a rhetoric for social change. The Marxist image, curiously enough, is perhaps closer to Christian eschatology than it is to Adam Smith, for it has a Garden of Eden in Primitive Communism, a "fall" in the invention of private property and primary

gan (1949–67) and at Iowa State College (1947–49), having taught earlier at McGill, Fisk, and Colgate Universities. He was Co-Director of the Center for Research on Conflict Resolution, University of Michigan (1961–64), Research Director (1964), and Director (1965–66). He is President of the Association for the Study of the Grants Economy and in the past served as President of the American Economic Association and of the Peace Research Society (International), and as Vice-President of the International Studies Association and of the American Association for the Advancement of Science. Mr. Boulding was born in 1910 in Liverpool, England. He received his B.A. and M.A. degrees from Oxford University.

[1] William J. Baumol, *Economic Dynamics* (3rd ed., Macmillan, 1970).

accumulation, "sin" in the expropriation of surplus value by private property owners, a "last judgment" in the Revolution and the expropriation of the expropriators, and the Kingdom of Heaven on Earth in the Communist society to follow.

By contrast, Adam Smith, Ricardo, and Malthus are more deterministic and more pessimistic, though the very formulation of the iron laws of the dismal science held open the possibility of breaking them. Thus, Malthus's dismal theorem that if the only checks on population growth were starvation and misery, then the population would grow until it was miserable and starved, can be expressed in the cheerful form that if something other than starvation and misery can be found to check population growth, the population does not have to grow until it is miserable and starves. All the classical economists were well aware of this potential cheerfulness underneath the gloom. To be cheerful, however, one has to understand the iron necessities of social life and social relationships, and that understanding has to be widespread enough for even political decision makers to understand it and act accordingly.

The development of images of the social future and of social self-consciousness, however, does not necessarily mean that society and those who make decisions on its behalf set goals, especially ultimate goals, for society to achieve. We really know very little about the future, and the further we look into the future the vaguer it gets. Even a self-conscious society, therefore, does not really proceed toward well-defined goals; it tries rather to proceed from day to day in a direction it perceives as "up"—"up," for some strange reason, meaning "better." This is perhaps why most of the social goals literature, such as that produced by President Eisenhower's Commission on National Goals,[2] for example, tends to have a slightly unreal and otherworldly quality. This is true even in the socialist countries. If one tries to talk to Communists about what they mean by Communism, which is supposed to be the ultimate goal toward which they are tending, they also become very fuzzy and unreal. No description of heaven, whether in another world or in this one, has ever sounded very convincing. There are very good reasons for this. Any statement of ultimate goals inevitably involves a projection of the growth of human knowledge, and this by definition is impossible, for if we could project knowledge we would know it now.

Another reason for rejecting the concept of social goals as inadequate is that the path that can be taken toward goals is itself subject to evaluation. Means are not evaluatively neutral. In some respects, means are more subject to evaluation than ends, and the doctrine that the ends justify the means is justly abhorred. I recall writing a verse inspired by Ward's study, *Goals of Economic Life*,[3] that

---

[2] *Goals for Americans*, The Report of the President's Commission on National Goals and Chapters Submitted for the Consideration of the Commission, Administered by the American Assembly, Columbia University (Prentice-Hall, 1960).

[3] Alfred Dudley Ward, ed., *Goals of Economic Life* (Harper, 1953).

went: "Oh where does economics tend, when end is means and means is end?" The whole distinction between ends and means becomes extremely difficult to maintain, when in a sense all ends are approximate and are means to something else. Even in the rituals of the Planning, Programming, and Budgeting System, the ends that are defined are usually quite arbitrary and are in fact always means to something else. There is a great deal in the Kantian ethic that every person should be treated as an ends rather than as a means. Even though it is never really possible to carry this out fully in practice, extreme violations of this principle, such as the Communists have sometimes practiced, destroy the legitimacy of the very ends of those who are so careless and indifferent to the means. Belief in an overriding social goal that justified any and every means was precisely what destroyed the legitimacy of the Communist party in the United States and is now very rapidly destroying the legitimacy of an aggressive American foreign policy.

It brings us closer to realism when we abandon the "social goals" concept and concentrate simply on what might be called a "dynamic evaluation function," which is simply a way of trying to describe "which way is up." To those eagle-eyed soaring souls who want to base every action on some splendid glimpse of a distant glorious future, this may seem like chickening out. The awful truth is that most of us are chickens, not eagles, and we could even take some evangelical solace in Newman's great hymn: "Keep Thou my feet;/ I do not ask to see the distant scene:/ one step enough for me." Even the kindly light that enables us to see the next step, however, is often remarkably dim, and in many social systems we do not really know whether we are going up or down.

What is implied here, of course, is a social welfare function, which we might perhaps better call an evaluative function, such as $V = f(a, b, c,$ etc.$)$. All we need for V is a set of ordinal numbers so that the higher numbers indicate a better state of the world, but what is inside the bracket is nothing less than the universe, or at least that part of it that most immediately concerns us. The difficulty here is that no general evaluative index, such as V, exists. That is, there is no single social indicator of which it can be said "the bigger the better" unequivocally.

If indeed we are to take the doctrine of the Aristotelian mean seriously, then all particular relationships between the indicators of the universe within the bracket of the function and the value indicator V will be nonlinear and will exhibit a maximum so that when an indicator is small, an increase in it will be "good," that is, will increase V, but as it gets larger it will reach a certain point where the impact on V is zero, and beyond that point an increase in the indicator diminishes V and is "bad." This could well be true even of something like the gross national product (GNP) per capita, or of any other measure of wealth. When the people are poor, it is obviously good if they become richer; but if the

rich get richer they may merely become corrupted—an undesirable result that will cause V to decline with an increase in riches. Similarly, with an index like the expectation of life—when this is very low, an increase is clearly good; when it reaches, let us say, seventy or eighty, it is by no means clear that an increase in expectation of life is a good thing. It may easily become a bad thing. This essential nonlinearity of the social evaluation function makes these evaluations very difficult and opens up all sorts of possibilities of disagreement. This is particularly true of the more subtle qualities of a society, such as individual freedom, if we could index them. At what point, for instance, does freedom become license? At what point does equality become leveling? At what point does justice need to be turned into mercy, and so on?

Another source of difficulty in the development of social evaluation functions is the difficulty of estimating the interrelationships among the various items of the argument—a, b, c, and so on. Because of the enormous interrelatedness of the social system, it is very hard for any one of these items to go up without something else going down. The famous economic principle that none of the best things in life are free applies also to the social evaluation function in the sense that an increase in almost anything that is regarded as good, that is, an increase in it increases V, is likely to be accompanied by an increase in something else that is "bad," which decreases V, or a decrease in something else that is good, which also decreases V. Almost the whole pollution-environmental problem is summed up in the proposition that all goods are generally produced jointly with bads.

As we increase electric power, which is good, we also increase air pollution, destroy the beauty of the landscape with overhead wires, and use up irreplaceable fossil fuels, all of which are bad, but we diminish more polluting forms of power, which is good. The total evaluation thus becomes very difficult, partly because of psychological censoring processes that suppress information about bads and partly because of failures of the price system to put negative prices on negative commodities. There is thus a constant tendency to overestimate the goods and to underestimate the bads in these joint processes, and hence to indulge in processes of production that produce too many bads per good. Almost the only answer to this problem is to increase the visibility of the bads by better social indicators and by what might almost be called "Naderometers," or visible fuss.

There is no adequate name for decisions that involve and affect large numbers of people. Perhaps we might call them "macro decisions." It does not seem quite correct to call them "political decisions," because many decisions that affect large numbers of people, such as those made by the directors of large corporations, are not political in the ordinary sense of the word, yet they may affect more people than do the decisions of government bodies. A very important aspect of social dynamics is the process by which the evaluative functions of

powerful decision makers are created and changed, for all decisions are made by evaluating alternative futures, according to some evaluation function.

The law and the prophets of decision theory can be summed up in the simple proposition that everybody does what he thinks is best at the time; then the question arises, however, the best for whom? There is a real distinction between "private" decisions, which are believed to be best for a particular individual, organization, or segment of society, and "public" decisions, which are supposed to be guided by what is best for society as a whole. There is, of course, an enormous literature, especially in economics, on the question of the circumstances under which what is best for the part is also best for the whole. The general conclusion found in this literature might be described as the law of parametric invariance. The simplest example of this is the economist's theory of perfect competition, in which each individual finds that all the exchange ratios with which he is faced cannot be affected by his own behavior. Even the economist's theory of natural liberty, however, soon becomes riddled with exceptions, particularly when we introduce threats, malevolence and benevolence, community, interdependence of utilities, and so on, so that a general theory of correspondence between public and private decisions still seems a long way off.

In any theory of social process, however, we must recognize that there is an enormous process of influencing the evaluation functions of powerful people who make macro decisions, whether these decisions are private or political. This may take place through persuasion, a process that goes on continuously in all organizations and also between organizations—in intimate chat, in committee discussions, in lobbying, in the mass media, and so on. When the processes of persuasion do not produce unanimity, social rituals, such as voting, may have to be invoked in order to achieve political decisions. If we define a ritual as an arbitrary procedure approved by everybody in the group concerned, it does not seem to be stretching the use of the word to use it to describe voting procedures—the majority rule, the two-thirds voting rule, or even nonvoting procedures, such as the choice of the occupants of political roles by lot, as in ancient Greece, or by hereditary succession. The great social significance of ritual is that it is usually easier to reach unanimity on ritualistic procedures than it is on substantive issues, and that hence the ritualistic procedures can be used to resolve conflicts where there is no agreement on substantive issues.

We by no means have exhausted the processes that are involved in acting on the welfare functions of powerful people. Threat processes are certainly important and are an element in persuasion. A man who commands a powerful bloc of votes that he can withdraw is apt to have a more persuasive rhetoric than one who does not. It must also be recognized that threats in the absence of a proper rhetorical matrix can easily backfire or produce counterthreat rather than submission. The exchange system, likewise, is significant in these processes. At its crudest, this is bribery and corruption, and a good many powerful people in

history have been persuaded to change their evaluation functions by payments under the table.

It has been pointed out also by political analysts, such as David Easton,[4] that more subtle and legitimate exchange processes are also usually at work— such things as logrolling and the generalized exchange of political favors for support. In a society like the United States, which has a powerful voting ritual that commands almost universal acceptance, a critical factor in achieving political power is the identification of that cluster of evaluation functions that will command a majority of the electorate. This may easily result in curious inconsistencies or even intransitivities in the evaluation function, for instance, of the president, simply because the easiest way to get a majority of votes is to have a lot of people voting for one for different reasons. Hence, a candidate whose evaluation function is very clear and definite is less likely to be successful than one who creates a generalized impression of benign personality. A language that is blessed with enough ambiguity, so that it can mean a lot of different things to different people, can also be a powerful resolver of conflict.

These political considerations are taking me considerably beyond the original scope of this paper, and I must return to consider the problem of the impact of ultimate goals, or at least the vision of these goals as held by a significant number of significant people, and of the present evaluation functions that, as I have argued, really govern present behavior. I threw social goals out of the window in order to make way for the social evaluation function. Now I can sneak them in again by the back door. Certainly it cannot be denied that the prevailing vision of the future, either social or personal, has a profound effect on the evaluation function of the present.

Thus, if the prevailing image of the future is that of an otherworldly paradise, which all the great world religions have fostered in some of their phases, the general impact is to deny all social goals except that of toleration of the religion and support of the existing order. For certain kinds of religions, Marx's accusation that religion is an opiate of the people has some validity. There are times, however, when the prevailing ideology, whether religious or secular, becomes expansionist and comes to have an image of the future in which the existing structure spreads beyond its present boundaries. Expansionism is a persistent yet still very puzzling aspect of human history, as reflected in missionary religions and also in political imperialism. Nobody understands why some cultures become expansionistic and some do not. What is still more puzzling is why expansionism collapses, as it often does, very suddenly. It is within present lifetimes that British audiences, for instance, were singing Elgar's "Land of Hope and Glory," with its incredible couplet: "Wider, still and wider, may thy bounds be set,/ God who made Thee mighty, make Thee mightier yet"—a sentiment that

[4]David Easton, *A Systems Analysis of Political Life* (Wiley, 1965).

could only draw embarrassment from a modern British audience. Christianity, Islam, and Buddhism, likewise, have had periods of great expansionism and missionary endeavor and periods of withdrawal and support of the status quo.

Expansionism, however, is not the same thing as an image of future social change. Presumably the participants in all rebellions and uprisings have had some such image in mind. But as a major factor in social change itself, persuasive images of future social change became significant only after the eighteenth century. It is curious that even in the eighteenth century the image of the past, especially the ancient history of the Greeks and Romans, was frequently used to create and to legitimate expectations of the future, as in the American and the French Revolutions. The tremendous impact of Marxism on the world has unquestionably been because Marxism provided an image of social change as a legitimation of revolution and of treason against established orders. Revolutions, however, because of the randomness of the forces they unleash, almost inevitably produce changes that are very different from those in the minds of the original founders. Indeed, I have argued that revolutions have to be interpreted as disturbances in the course of the development of social evolutionary phyla, which frequently divert these phyla from their original potential.

More significant than revolutions, therefore, are the nonrevolutionary images of social change, such as those of the British Fabians and the American Institutionalists—even, one should add, the Prohibitionists—which had a very profound effect on policies and the evaluation functions of whole decades of subsequent decision makers. To a considerable extent the Fabians at the turn of the century wrote the history of Britain for the subsequent fifty years.

The effect of a vision of ultimate goals on immediate evaluation functions and decisions is by no means always benign. The disaster of the first collectivization of agriculture in the Soviet Union in the 1930s was a clear example of certain very long-run ultimate goals taking precedence over any kind of immediate pragmatic solution of problems. In the case of the United States, the disaster of Vietnam may well be the result of certain long-run images of the international system, derived from past experiences, such as Munich, which may not be at all applicable in the present situation. It is all too easy to keep one's eyes on the stars and then fall into the ditch. Nevertheless, it is also true that without vision the people perish; hence the development of ultimate goals and images of future society, which are not only persuasive and dramatic but realistic as well, is a very high priority for human survival.

We are now witnessing a fundamental shift that might be described without exaggeration as one of cataclysmic proportions in man's image of his own future. I have described this as a shift from "the great plane" to "the spaceship earth." Until very recently, man has inhabited, psychologically, a virtually unlimited flat earth. There has always been somewhere to go over the horizon, some boundary to the known world beyond which there were further worlds to explore. Now

this long period of human expansion has suddenly come to an end, actually, in my own lifetime. Even when I was a boy, there were still white places on the map of the globe where no man had ever been. Today there are none. The space enterprise has, if anything, accentuated the smallness of the earth and the loneliness of man. This beautiful blue and white ball is clearly the only decent piece of real estate in a very long way and we are stuck with it. We have had a period of enormous expansion in the last 200 years, in which, for instance, the growth of human knowledge has almost certainly increased natural resources much faster than man has used them up. Nevertheless, there is now a brooding sense that this cannot go on forever, or indeed for very long as historical time is counted, and that within, say, 100 years, or at most 500 years, a very radical change has to be made in man's technology and in all probability in his social system, his culture, and in his image of himself as he makes the transition into the small, tight, closed, crowded, limited spaceship earth, which will almost certainly have to rely on inputs of solar energy for its power and will have to recycle virtually all materials for its goods. We are moving toward the end of the linear economy that goes from mines and wells to dumps and pollution. The circle must be made complete. All the excreta of man's activities must be transformed, and this by inputs of solar power, into goods again.

This image of the future has a grim air of physical necessity about it. We are living in just so big a house and there are only so many things that can be done with it. The psychological impact of this shift has barely begun to be felt. I think many of what look like pathological aspects of the current youth culture may be a symptom of further changes to come. Young people, after all, are more sensitive to the future than oldsters, simply because they are going to live in it longer. My own personal concern about the twenty-first century is strictly abstract, since I will be quite surprised if I reach that century, whereas young people today will live well into it.

Closely connected with this vision of a spaceship earth is a slowly gathering realization that perhaps the really great age of change is now over, that economic growth, or at least its technical basis, is slowing down and is likely to slow down even further. I have been teasing audiences by saying that I thought the great age of change was my grandfather's life. When I look back on my childhood in the 1920s, the world does not seem terribly different; there were automobiles, electricity, the beginnings of the radio, telephone, the movies, and with one or two exceptions, like television, plastics, and antibiotics, what I have seen in my lifetime is more of the same. By contrast, my grandfather, looking back in 1920 on his childhood in 1860, looked back on a wholly different world—without electricity, without automobiles, without airplanes, without movies, without telephones, without anything that we think of as constituting modern life, and his life as a boy was certainly not very much different from that of his grandfather or his grandfather or his grandfather.

In the United States since 1967 we have seen a very sharp decline in the rate of increase of gross productivity, that is, GNP in real terms divided by the total employed labor force, including the armed services (table 1). We have had periods like this in the past so that it is hard to tell whether this is a temporary phenomenon or the beginnings of a long-run trend, but it certainly suggests why

Table 1. Rate of Increase of Gross Labor Productivity in the United States, 1961–1970

Year	Gross labor productivity change from previous year (*percent*)
1961	1.90
1962	4.70
1963	2.59
1964	3.19
1965	3.81
1966	3.43
1967	0.21
1968	2.58
1969	0.35
1970	−0.88

we managed to have both unemployment and inflation in 1970, with the economy geared to increases in money income to take advantage of expected increases in productivity that did not materialize. Even over the last forty years economic growth in the United States has not been spectacular. It took thirty years to increase real per capita disposable income by 50 percent. This might underestimate welfare somewhat, since it does not take account of public goods, but even on the most optimistic assumptions, we are certainly not much more than twice as rich as our grandfathers. Furthermore, many of the factors that have permitted increasing incomes in the last thirty years are not repeatable. One of these is the remarkable release of manpower from the increase in productivity of agriculture, which has now brought agriculture down to 6 percent of the labor force so that even if agricultural productivity doubles in the next generation only 3 percent of the labor force would be released for other things. As productivity in particular occupations increases, the proportion of the economy in industries that are improving declines, and the proportion in productivity-stagnant industries, such as education, government, medicine, and so on, increases. It seems highly probable, therefore, that there will be a substantial decline in the rate of increase in gross productivity in the next few decades.

A sharp decline in the rate of population growth is also very much in the works for the United States and indeed for the whole temperate zone. Fertility in the United States has declined so dramatically from 1961 that a little further decline will bring Americans to a net reproductive ratio of 1. It seems, therefore,

that the United States is much closer to what might be called ZPPG, that is, Zero Population and Productivity Growth, than anyone could have conceived ten or twenty years ago.

It is a fundamental principle of futurology that all projections are wrong, including mine, and certain events, of course, could postpone the coming of the spaceship earth and could lead to a longer period of productivity growth, though not perhaps of population growth. I have been able to think of only three changes, all of which seem to have rather low probability, that could drastically change the picture. These are artificial life, as a result of the developments of molecular biology; artificial intelligence, as a result of the development of computers—or even a breakthrough on the understanding of natural intelligence and human learning; and the gravity shield (a substance or process that would block the force of gravity), which would drastically change the whole power picture. None of these, however, seem at all probable in the next 50 or 100 years, with the possible exception of the first.

The image of the future outlined here is bound to have a profound effect on the evaluation function of all kinds of decision makers, an effect that will increase as we move further into the future. It implies a high value on modesty rather than grandeur. There is no room for "great societies" in the spaceship. It implies conservationism to the point of conservatism rather than expansionism. It implies a high value on taking things easy, on conflict management. There is no place in the spaceship for men on white horses and very little room for horsing around. We cannot afford to have war, revolution, or dialectical processes. Everything must be directed toward the preservation of precarious order rather than experimentation with new forms. We have to stress equality rather than incentives, simply in order to minimize uncertainty and conflict. It is important to realize that the case for equality may not rest at all on the concepts of social justice. Equality, indeed, denies at least one principle of social justice— that distribution should be in rough proportion to desert—for under an equalitarian regime the deserving get less than they deserve and the undeserving get more, assuming at least something like a normal distribution of deservingness. Nevertheless, there may be a case for equality that rests not at all on social justice but on the sheer demand of the system for stability. A just society that provided incentives for virtue might simply prove to be too unstable.

If all this sounds rather depressing, it is intended to be. Economists have never been very cheerful about the stationary state, and a permanent, planetwide stationary state, from which there seemed to be no possible means of escape, might be a very depressing prospect indeed. What is even more depressing is that a stationary state (ZPPG) might not even be stable, simply because of the intensification of conflicts within it.

In the progressive state, conflicts can be resolved fairly easily by progress itself. The poor can get richer without the rich getting poorer. In the stationary

state, if the poor are to get richer, then the rich must get poorer, and what is even more frightening, if the rich are to get richer, they can only do so by increasing their exploitation of the poor, and since the rich may be the most powerful, they may have strong incentives to do this. Thus, the banished specter of exploitation, which progress made obsolete, is reintroduced into the world. The dialectical processes to which a stationary state would be exposed would thereby become much more acute and might easily destroy the state's precarious equilibrium, in war, revolution, social upheaval, the decay of all legitimacies, and a Hobbesian nightmare of retrogression in the war of all against all. As Adam Smith said prophetically, the declining state is melancholy.[5]

As long as I am being pessimistic, I might as well go the whole way. Let me suggest, therefore, that the romantic socialism of the Mao–Castro variety, which seems at the moment to both the capitalist world and the "business socialist" camp of the Soviet Union and Eastern Europe to be an embarrassing blemish on the face of at least a moderately rational earth, may turn out to be more significant than we think, as a legitimation of economic stagnation. These societies still make some sort of pretense that they are engaged in economic development. A genuinely equalitarian society, however, in which reward is completely divorced from performance of any kind is extremely unlikely to have very much increase in productivity. It will be like Adam Smith's Oxford University, which was a society remarkably equalitarian among the Fellows, in which rewards were completely divorced from productivity; which, being celibate, certainly had zero or negative population growth; which had zero productivity growth; and which therefore should be the beau ideal of any thorough-paced ecologically minded advocate of Consciousness Three. One can even visualize the scientists lingering in these future stable societies like the despised clerics of C. P. Snow's Cambridge, as the unhappy practitioners of a departed religion of truth in a society devoted entirely to propaganda and agreeable illusion. In a mood that was not intended to be congratulatory, I once defined Maoist economics as the substitution of euphoria for commodities. In the stationary state, one has a haunting feeling that this trick might be highly valuable.

I cannot bear to end on a note of unrelieved gloom, and even the practitioner of the dismal science knows that every dismal theorem can be restated in a more cheerful form. My natural glandular optimism, therefore, always reasserts itself in moments like these. I do have considerable optimism about what might be called the "middle run" of the next 100 years, if we are lucky. The chance of nuclear war I think is quite low, although large enough to be very uncomfortable. There are distinct signs that sheer social self-consciousness is beginning to solve the population problem, for even Communists, Catholics, Fundamentalists,

[5]"The progressive state is in reality the cheerful and the hearty state to all the different orders of the society. The stationary is dull; the declining melancholy." Adam Smith, *The Wealth of Nations* (Modern Library, 1937), p. 81.

and Traditionalists will be forced to come to terms with the blunt logic of Malthusian arithmetic. Many of our immediate environmental problems are soluble, I think, in the sense that the particular environments of urban areas, for instance, can be noticeably improved—they have been in many places—with the aid of relatively simple social devices that give negative commodities negative prices. The resource exhaustion problem is very unpredictable because of the unpredictability of human knowledge. Still, we use such a fantastically small proportion of our current input of solar energy, it would be very surprising if this could not be vastly improved, and we have put so little thought into large-scale recycling that it would be surprising if this also could not be enormously improved. We are not operating here within tight limits of human capacity but within very wide limits.

The ultimate question of whether a stationary state would be bearable, or even stable, depends a great deal on the human capacity for social invention. One might even have an optimistic image of the present period of human expansion as a kind of adolescence of the human race, in which man has to devote a large proportion of his energy and information to sheer physical growth. Hence, we could regard the stationary state as a kind of maturity in which physical growth is no longer necessary and in which, therefore, human energies can be devoted to qualitative growth—knowledge, spirit, art, and love. One might even romantically regard the twenty-first century as symbolizing the achievement of this maturity. Fortunately for us, we have to leave most of these problems to our descendants. All we can really do is to wish them well, to leave them a little elbow room, and to guide our current evaluation functions somewhere toward the minimax of being on the safe side.

APPENDIX

Energy Consumption: Trends and Patterns

JOEL DARMSTADTER

For a better understanding of the problems taken up at the RFF Forum on Energy, Economic Growth, and the Environment, it seemed desirable to have available an underpinning of basic information pertaining to the historic, present, and prospective role of energy in the U.S. economy and throughout the world. The purpose of this paper, which focuses particularly on the United States, was to assemble such material in a way that would help to illuminate subjects dealt with by the participants of the forum.

Five major topics are covered. First, there is a review of long-term and recent trends in U.S. energy consumption as they are reflected in broad statistical aggregates. But in order to depict in somewhat greater detail the trends and patterns of energy use that are characteristic of an advanced economy, the role played by energy within particular sectors and activities of the American economy is reviewed as well. The relationship between energy and GNP growth and the key role of the electricity sector are also given in some quantitative detail. Second, in a more sweeping manner, worldwide trends in energy consumption are considered, with particular attention given to historical and cross-sectoral comparisons. Third, the matter of the projected growth of energy in the United States over the next three decades is taken up. Here, the emphasis is on illus-

Joel Darmstadter is a Senior Research Associate with Resources for the Future. He is the principal author of *Energy in the World Economy* (1971) and a contributor to a number of other RFF studies. Prior to joining RFF in 1966, he was an economist on the staff of the National Planning Association. He was born in 1928 in Mannheim, Germany. Mr. Darmstadter received his B.A. degree from George Washington University and his M.A. from the New School for Social Research.

trating the effect of certain alternative assumptions regarding the expected growth of total energy and its constituent forms. But such assumptions will by no means exhaust the range of probable or desirable developments, for, as the environmental and social consequences of the prospective trends are evaluated by those more strictly concerned with these aspects, it may well be that equally (or more) valid and quite different assumptions might be appropriate for additional consideration. The fourth part of the paper is a broad treatment of the future energy outlook on a worldwide basis. The fifth and final part is a brief discussion of some of the environmental aspects of the growth in U.S. and worldwide energy demand.

THE U.S. HISTORICAL RECORD

Long-Term Trends in Major Aggregates

Expressed in quantity of heat contained, the consumption of energy resources in the United States in 1970 amounted to some 69 quadrillion British thermal units (Btu).[1] This level of consumption was far in excess of the amount of energy consumed by all the countries of Western Europe, although their combined population is 75 percent above that of the United States. A somewhat less abstract impression is gained if heat value in Btu, which for analytical reasons is the preferred formulation, is expressed in terms of its underlying 1970 resource components: 527 million short tons of coal, used largely in the generation of electricity; 22 trillion cubic feet of natural gas; nearly 5.5 billion barrels of oil products; 245 billion kilowatt-hours (kwh) of electricity generated by falling water and about 19 billion kwh by nuclear energy—in addition to the 1.4 trillion kwh based on fossil fuel generation and covered in the statistics above on coal, oil, and gas.

The quantitative dimensions, within the economy, of the industries that are responsible for producing, processing, delivering, and marketing these resources to the point at which they heat and light homes, power factories, fuel the private and industrial transport system, and satisfy a variety of other demands cannot be unambiguously specified. While the energy-producing and conversion sectors per se (principally coal mines, crude petroleum and natural gas production, pipelines, oil refineries, and electric and gas utilities) constitute only a modest proportion of the nation's gross national product (GNP)[2]—and partly this is a

[1] Energy consumption, or use, here refers to the combined resource inputs (coal, oil, natural gas, hydro, and nuclear electricity) expressed in Btu and irrespective of whether such resources are ultimately utilized in the form of fuels and power, on the one hand, or as raw materials (e.g., in the chemical industry) on the other. For hydro and nuclear, the Btu equivalent of the electricity generated is computed on the basis of primary energy inputs at fossil-fueled generating stations at prevailing rates of efficiency. In practice, about 95 percent of energy resource inputs go to fuels and power use.

[2] Not much more than 5 percent, as measured by the value added of these industries.

consequence of the abundance of low-cost U.S. energy resources—other measures, reflecting energy-related activities, signify considerably greater relative importance. For example, these same energy industries, which, moreover, exclude some sectors involved in the energy field (e.g., water and rail transport), in some years account for as much as one-fifth of the nation's capital investment spending. And energy supplies constitute a far more significant input to certain economic activities than to others.[3]

The long-term growth of total energy use in the United States has been closely parallel to the nation's overall economic expansion, even though, as shown later, the two trends have not always proceeded in lockstep. The twentieth century record in its entirety is one showing a 3.2 percent yearly growth rate for aggregate consumption of primary energy resources, compared with an only slightly higher one of 3.3 percent for a constant dollar GNP. On a per capita basis, the long-run growth rate of energy comes to 1.7 percent per annum; GNP per capita, to 1.8 percent. For the more recent fifty-year (1920–70) period shown in table 1, a wider gap in growth rates prevailed: energy consumption grew at the annual average rate of 2.5 percent; GNP, at 3.3 percent. The respective per capita figures were 1.2 percent and 2 percent. These trends are reflected in the persistent long-term decline in the ratio of Btu of energy consumed for each dollar (in constant prices) of GNP—down from 141,000 Btu in 1920 to 95,000 Btu in 1970. As table 1 indicates, however, a reversal of this energy-GNP trend occurred during the 1960s, and much interest centers on the meaning and implications for the future of this apparent turnabout. This point will be discussed further a little later.

Steadily rising shares—from 8 percent in 1920 to 25 percent in 1970—of total energy resources have been devoted to the production of electricity (see the percentage share, table 2).[4] Hence, electricity consumption, with a long-term

---

[3] The variability of the role of energy in different industrial activities is illustrated by the following selected figures for 1966, showing the ratio of dollar purchases of fuels and electricity per $100 in output:

	Dollars
All manufacturing	1.40
Primary nonferrous metals	5.50
Hydraulic cement	15.40
Basic chemicals	6.00
Steel rolling and finishing (incl. blast furnaces)	4.10
Machinery	0.65
Printing and publishing	0.50

Source: U.S. Bureau of the Census, *Annual Survey of Manufacturers, 1966* (1969).

[4] The continually rising percentages of table 2 reflect, moreover, a downward bias since, with rising thermal efficiency, progressively lower quantities of primary energy have been needed to produce a given amount of electric power. For example, if the nation's electric power output in 1969 (reflecting an efficiency factor of about 10,500 Btu per kwh) would have had to be produced at the 1940 efficiency rate (or 16,400 Btu per kwh), some 24

Table 1. Total U.S. Energy and Electricity Consumption, Gross National Product, and Population, Selected Years, 1920-1970

Year	Total energy consumption (trillion Btu)	Electricity consumption (billion kwh)	GNP 1958 (billion dollars)	Population (million)	Per capita			Per $1 of GNP	
					Energy consumption (million Btu)	Electricity consumption (kwh)	GNP (1958 dollars)	Energy consumption (thousand Btu)	Electricity consumption (kwh)
1920	19,782	57.5	140.0	106.5	185.8	540	1,315	141.3	0.41
1930	22,288	116.2	183.5	123.1	181.1	944	1,490	121.5	0.63
1940	23,908	182.0	227.2	132.6	180.3	1,376	1,720	105.2	0.80
1950	34,154	390.5	355.3	152.3	224.3	2,564	2,342	96.1	1.10
1960	44,960	848.7	487.7	180.7	248.8	4,967	2,699	92.2	1.74
1965	53,785	1,157.4	617.8	194.6	276.4	5,948	3,175	87.1	1.87
1970	68,810	1,648.3	724.1	205.4	335.0	8,025	3,525	95.0	2.28

NOTES AND SOURCES: Total energy consumption, 1920-40, from U.S. Bureau of the Census, *Historical Statistics of the United States, Colonial Times to 1957* (1960); 1950-60, from Warren E. Morrison and Charles L. Reading, *An Energy Model of the United States, Featuring Energy Balances for the Years 1947 to 1965 and Projections and Forecasts to the Years 1980 and 2000*, U.S. Department of the Interior, Bureau of Mines Information Circular 8384 (1968); 1965, from U.S. Bureau of Mines, *Minerals Yearbook, 1969* (1970); 1970, from U.S. Bureau of Mines, news release, March 9, 1971.

The data on electricity consumption represent net generation by privately and publicly owned utilities as well as other generation (e.g., industrial firms' own electricity production), and, in addition, include net imports of power. The 1920-65 data are from the U.S. Bureau of

the Census and the FPC, shown in Edison Electric Institute, *Statistical Yearbook of the Electric Utility Industry for 1969* (New York: EEI, 1970), and *Historical Statistics of the Electric Utility Industry* (New York: EEI, 1963). Figure for 1970 is preliminary estimate.

GNP for 1920, from U.S. Bureau of the Census, *Long-Term Economic Growth, 1860-1965* (1966); 1930-65, from U.S. Department of Commerce data shown in *Economic Report of the President, January 1971*; 1970 figure, from U.S. Department of Commerce, *Survey of Current Business*, May 1971.

Population for 1920-65, from U.S. Bureau of the Census, *Statistical Abstract of the United States, 1970* (1970); for 1970, from *Economic Report of the President, January 1971*.

Table 2. Total U.S. Energy Consumption, by Source and Form of Use, Selected Years, 1920–1970

| | Consumption by source[a] | | | | | Consumption by form of use | | | |
| | | | | | | Fuel and power | | | |
Year	Coal	Natural gas	Petroleum	Hydro and nuclear	Total	Electricity	Other	Total	As raw material
					(trillion Btu)				
1920	15,504	827	2,676	775	19,782	1,663	—	—	—
1930	13,639	1,969	5,898	785	22,288	1,965	—	—	—
1940	12,535	2,726	7,781	917	23,908	2,458	—	—	—
1950	12,914	6,150	13,489	1,601	34,154	5,142	27,570	32,712	1,442
1960	10,414	12,699	20,067	1,780	44,960	8,387	34,328	42,715	2,245
1965	12,358	16,098	23,241	2,088	53,785	11,104	40,036	51,140	2,645
1970	13,792	22,546	29,617	2,855	68,810	16,967	47,943	64,910	3,900
					(percent)				
1920	78.4	4.2	13.5	3.9	100.0	8.4	—	—	—
1930	61.2	8.8	26.5	3.5	100.0	8.8	—	—	—
1940	52.4	11.4	32.4	3.8	100.0	10.3	—	—	—
1950	37.8	18.0	39.5	4.7	100.0	15.1	80.7	95.8	4.2
1960	23.2	28.2	44.6	4.0	100.0	18.7	76.3	95.0	5.0
1965	23.0	29.9	43.2	3.9	100.0	20.6	74.4	95.1	4.9
1970	20.0	32.8	43.0	4.1	100.0	24.7	69.7	94.3	5.7

NOTE: Dashes indicate "not available."

[a] Coal includes bituminous, anthracite, and lignite. Petroleum includes natural gas liquids. The nuclear component (not shown separately) amounted to 6 trillion Btu in 1960, 39 trillion Btu in 1965, and 208 trillion Btu (or 0.3 percent of total energy consumption) in 1970.

SOURCES: Same as those for total energy consumption in table 1, except that data on energy consumed in electric generation were based, for 1920, on data in U.S. Bureau of the Census, *Historical Statistics of the United States* (1960); and for 1930–40 were obtained on the basis of data shown in Edison Electric Institute, *Historical Statistics of the Electric Utility Industry* (New York: EEI, 1963). The EEI series on total net electric generation (expressed in kwh) was multiplied by the EEI estimate of the heat rate (Btu per kwh) for all boiler fuels; the result was added to the hydro figures shown above.

average annual growth rate of about 7 percent, has expanded at a pace far greater than either total energy consumption or GNP and much faster still, obviously, than the long-term population growth rate of 1 to 2 percent in the United States. Indeed, viewing the growth of electricity consumption for the period, say, since 1950 (7.5 percent yearly) as the product of a 1.5 percent per annum growth in population and a 6 percent growth in electricity consumption per capita, it turns out that only about one-fifth of total electricity growth is attributable to population increase and as much as 80 percent to growing levels of per capita use. As a corollary calculation, one can say that a halt to population growth, everything else being equal, might scarcely have affected the rising volume of electric power use; while an unchanged volume of electric power use since 1950 would, in order to accommodate rising per capita standards, have required a 1970 population level of around 50 million—the figure for the year 1880.

The Changing Importance of Different Primary Energy Sources

Major shifts have taken place in the relative contribution to total consumption of the major primary energy resources—coal, natural gas, oil, hydro, and most recently (and as yet insignificant within this overall perspective), nuclear sources.[5] The major long-term shifts are spelled out in table 2.

The dominance of coal in the various U.S. energy markets (households, industry, transport, and commerce) persisted well into the 1920s, even though by then its supremacy in the nation's fuel and power base was beginning to be challenged—particularly by the growth of automotive transport and, hence, the inroads of gasoline. Various circumstances sheltered the position of coal. The steam locomotive was still preeminent, while in merchant shipping, oil-fired vessels had only recently begun to displace coal-burning ships. Coal was the preponderant fuel in thermal electricity generation, and it had a virtually complete grip on space and process heating. In fact, not until after World War II did coal relinquish its 50 percent-and-over share of the nation's energy consumption. By 1970 it accounted for a fifth of nationwide energy consumption.

During the past two decades, the use of natural gas has made the most rapid strides among the primary energy sources. With an average growth rate of over 7 percent, the natural gas share of overall energy consumption rose from around 14 percent after World War II to one-third by 1970. Oil already occupied a one-third share during and immediately after World War II; its postwar growth

---

quadrillion Btu of primary energy (rather than the actual 1969 level of 17 quadrillion Btu) would have been required, and one-third of all energy consumption would have been accounted for by the electricity sector, as against the approximately one-fourth that actually prevailed.

[5] Note that, in this context, fossil-fueled electricity—being treated as a secondary energy form—is excluded from consideration.

was therefore more modest. Reaching a share of about 45 percent in 1960, its subsequent percentage place has been one of relative stability. The hydro share—scarcely ever above 4.5 percent of total energy consumption—rose during the first fifty years of the century but leveled off in the past two decades, since the practical potential for developing new hydroelectric sites in the country is limited.

The Changing Importance of Different Sectors of Consumption

Available statistics make it possible to distinguish among four major energy-consuming sectors of the economy (table 3). It is evident in the table that, compared with the sharply increasing relative importance of the electric utility sector as a consumer of primary energy resources, distributional changes evident over the postwar period were modest for the most part. Households and commercial users together increased their share of nationwide energy consumption slightly, while the transport sector reduced its share. The decline in the industrial share—a fall from 36 percent in 1950 to about 30 percent in 1970—was more marked. Thus, while the respective sectoral shares in recent years were close to their level of two decades earlier—particularly for households and commerce and for transportation—the proportion for electric utilities had risen from 15 percent in 1950 to 25 percent in 1970.

A somewhat different perspective emerges when input into power generation is apportioned among final consumers rather than as a separate end-use sector. This adjustment, made in table 3, shows the industrial sector to remain the largest customer; its slightly declining shares since 1950 are now more modest than when industrial electricity purchases were excluded. Because transportation is effectively out of the electric power market, it slips markedly below the household and commercial sector in its share of energy consumption, retaining, however, its only slightly declining postwar relative position in total energy markets. The household and commercial segment, on the other hand, now reflecting its large and rapidly rising demand for electric power, both lifts its share substantially for any given year and shows modestly rising shares.

But the end-use breakdown of table 3 should be recognized as exceedingly broad, with each identifiable sector covering a multitude of different activities. "Defense uses, agriculture, and use of energy materials for non-energy purposes, are all included in one or the other of the three specifically designated economic segments. Compounded with ambiguities in the data as originally collected and classified, these categorizations should not be looked at as more than rough suggestions of change. . . ."[6] For clues to some underlying factors obscured by these sectoral aggregates, it is useful to look at the behavior of specific energy sources within each of the end-use sectors. This is taken up next.

[6] Resources for the Future, *U.S. Energy Policies: An Agenda for Research*, Staff Report (Resources for the Future, 1968), p. 14.

Table 3. U.S. Energy Consumption, Shares of Major Consuming Sectors, Selected Years, 1950–1970

Year	Electric utilities treated as consuming sector					Electric utility energy consumption allocated to ultimate consumers of electricity[b]				Total energy consumption
	Households and commercial	Industrial	Transportation	Electric utilities	Total[a]	Households and commercial	Industrial	Transportation	Total[a]	
	(--- percent ---)									(trillion Btu)
1950	22.2	36.1	25.2	15.1	100.0	29.5	43.5	25.5	100.0	34,154
1955	21.6	35.3	24.6	16.7	100.0	29.2	44.3	24.8	100.0	39,956
1960	22.7	33.1	24.1	18.7	100.0	31.8	42.5	24.2	100.0	44,960
1965	22.1	32.6	23.6	20.6	100.0	33.2	42.0	23.7	100.0	53,785
1970	20.5	30.7	23.9	24.7	100.0	34.3	41.5	24.0	100.0	68,810

NOTE: See also the notes to table 4, which provide further definitional remarks.

[a] Including a small amount of "miscellaneous and unaccounted for," not shown separately.

[b] That is, the primary energy input into the electric utility sector,

e.g., 5,142 trillion Btu in 1950 (see table 2), is apportioned according to sectoral purchases of kilowatt-hours of utility output and is then added to each sector's direct (nonelectric) fuel consumption shown in the first four columns above.

SOURCE: Same as those for total energy consumption in table 1.

Shifts Among Energy Sources in Different
Sectors of Consumption

The way in which each fuel source has positioned itself in the broad energy markets of the U.S. economy during the past two decades is shown in table 4. This table represents the standard aggregative statistical framework developed by the U.S. Bureau of Mines for examining the sectoral disposition of energy resources. To probe somewhat beneath these rather unwieldy totals, it is useful to refer to the three-part summary presentation shown in table 5, where the 1950, 1960, and 1970 absolutes of table 4 have been translated into percentages, once again reverting to the treatment of electric utilities as a consuming sector and omitting the utilities' electric sales to their customers because, except for hydro and nuclear, these sales represent secondary energy based on the primary fuels (coal, oil, and gas), and it is the trend of these fuels that is of primary interest here.

From the top panel (A) of these summary data, it is seen that—based on this broad classification scheme—petroleum consumption in the transportation sector, which accounts for nearly a quarter of nationwide energy consumption, represents the single most important sectoral purchase of an energy resource in 1970. Just after World War II, in 1950, petroleum consumed in the transportation sector had also been very important, representing 20 percent of U.S. energy consumption of all types, though in that year industrial consumption of coal ranked a close second with 17 percent. Among other numerically important consumption flows in 1970, coal deliveries to the utility sector represented 11 percent of the nation's energy consumption; natural gas consumption by industry, 15 percent; and natural gas consumption by the household and commercial sector, 11 percent. Along with the 23 percent accounted for by petroleum deliveries to the transport sector, these flows aggregated to 60 percent of nationwide energy consumption in 1970.

The middle panel (B) of table 5 shows the changing importance of the different consuming sectors for each energy source. For coal, the virtual disappearance of the household and commercial and the transportation markets was compensated by the electric utility sector, but only to a limited extent since the absolute volume of coal consumed was falling (see table 4). The industrial market, essentially iron and steel, continues to represent an important share of total coal consumption. Electric utilities and the household and commercial sectors both increased their relative importance to natural gas. The 1970 distribution of sectoral deliveries of petroleum was rather similar to that of 1950, the most striking change being the relative increase in deliveries to utilities between 1960 and 1970, a consequence of a shift within the past few years toward environmentally less objectionable fuels.

The bottom panel (C) discloses striking shifts in shares of the different energy sources in given markets—for example, the decline of coal from nearly

Table 4. Total U.S. Consumption of Energy Resources, by Source and Consuming Sector, 1950, 1960, 1970

(*trillion Btu*)

Consuming sector[b]	Primary energy source[a]					Utility electricity[f]	Total sector inputs of primary energy and utility electricity[g]
	Coal[c]	Natural gas	Petroleum[d]	Hydro and nuclear[e]	Total sector inputs of primary energy		
	(1)	(2)	(3)	(4)	(5)	(6)	(7)
Household and commercial:							
1950	2,912	1,642	3,038	—	7,593	546	8,139
1960	1,023	4,268	4,923	—	10,214	1,262	11,476
1970	399	7,350	6,349	—	14,098	2,904	17,002
Industrial:							
1950	5,957	3,728	2,642	—	12,326	559	12,885
1960	4,898	6,287	3,682	—	14,867	1,306	16,172
1970	5,560	10,500	5,069	—	21,129	2,275	23,404
Transportation:							
1950	1,701	130	6,785	—	8,616	24	8,640
1960	91	359	10,372	—	10,822	18	10,840
1970	9	671	15,756	—	16,436	18	16,454
Electric utilities:							
1950	2,228	651	662	1,601	5,142	1,129	—
1960	4,257	1,785	564	1,780	8,387	2,586	—
1970	7,824	4,025	2,263	2,855	16,967	5,197	—
Miscellaneous and unaccounted for:							
1950	115	0	362	—	477	—	—
1960	145	0	526	—	671	—	—

Total primary energy inputs:								
1950	12,914	6,150	13,489	1,601	34,154	—	—	—
1960	10,414	12,699	20,067	1,780	44,960	—	—	—
1970	13,792	22,546	29,617	2,855	68,810	—	—	—

NOTE: Dashes indicate "not applicable."

[a] Represents the energy content of all primary energy sources, both domestic and net imported, and their derivatives (e.g., gasoline) at the time they are incorporated into the indicated consuming sectors of the economy and irrespective of whether used for fuel and power or other nonenergy purposes. (Strictly speaking, fossil fuel-based electricity is a derivative energy source—analogous to gasoline—but it is represented statistically as being incorporated at the fuel-input stage, prior to conversion.)

[b] Energy consumption arising from the operation of household passenger cars is included in the transportation sector, which also includes commercial transport services, bunkers, and military. Nontransport government energy consumption is distributed largely between the household and commercial sector (e.g., lighting of government buildings) and the industry sector (e.g., electricity purchases for the Atomic Energy Commission nuclear enrichment plants).

[c] Largely bituminous coal, but also including anthracite and lignite.

[d] Including natural gas liquids.

[e] Includes net imports of electric power, however fueled. The nuclear component applies only to 1960 (6 trillion Btu) and 1970 (208 trillion Btu). Hydro- and nuclear-based electricity are not distributable by consuming sectors, because only aggregate electric energy purchases from utilities (col. 6) can be allocated to end uses. Thus, hydro and nuclear electricity—converted to theoretical fossil fuel inputs, using the prevailing fuel-per-kwh requirements at central electric stations—are assigned entirely to the electric utility sector.

[f] Represents utility electricity delivered to the indicated consuming sectors, computed at 3,412 Btu per kwh, the direct calorific value of electricity. The sum of this column, shown under electric utilities, falls short of the total primary energy inputs into the electric utility sector by the amount of conversion losses experienced by fossil fuels and those ascribed theoretically to hydro and nuclear. The column excludes power generated by *nonutility* plants. Correspondingly, fuel inputs for nonutility power is excluded from the electric utility sector. Such nonutility power and its primary fuel requirements are included within the other consuming sectors.

[g] Represents sectoral energy resource inputs, including direct fuels and electricity furnished by utilities. The sum of this column (not shown) plus electricity conversion losses (the difference between columns 5 and 6 in the electric utility sector) plus the miscellaneous and unaccounted-for totals equals the grand total of column 5.

[h] Owing to subsequent revision of less detailed statistical series, this figure differs slightly from the corresponding total shown in other tables.

SOURCES: Same as those for total energy consumption in table 1.

Table 5. Total U.S. Consumption of Energy, by Source and Consuming Sector, 1950, 1960, and 1970

	Coal	Natural gas	Petroleum	Hydro and nuclear	Total
A. Percent distribution of total energy consumption, by sector and source					
Household and commercial:					
1950	8.5	4.8	8.9	a	22.2
1960	2.3	9.5	10.9	a	22.7
1970	0.6	10.7	9.2	a	20.5
Industrial:					
1950	17.4	10.9	7.7	a	36.1
1960	10.9	14.0	8.2	a	33.1
1970	8.1	15.3	7.4	a	30.7
Transportation:					
1950	5.0	0.4	19.9	a	25.2
1960	0.2	0.8	23.1	a	24.1
1970	—	1.0	22.9	a	23.9
Electric utilities:					
1950	6.5	1.9	1.9	4.7	15.1
1960	9.5	4.0	1.3	4.0	18.7
1970	11.4	5.8	3.3	4.1	24.7
Total energy:[b]					
1950	37.8	18.0	39.5	4.7	100.0
1960	23.2	28.2	44.6	4.0	100.0
1970	20.0	32.8	43.0	4.1	100.0
B. Percent distribution of energy sources, by sector					
Household and commercial:					
1950	22.5	26.7	22.5	a	22.2
1960	9.8	33.6	24.5	a	22.7
1970	2.9	32.6	21.4	a	20.5
Industrial:					
1950	46.1	60.6	19.6	a	36.1
1960	47.0	49.5	18.3	a	33.1
1970	40.3	46.6	17.1	a	30.7
Transportation:					
1950	13.2	2.1	50.3	a	25.2
1960	0.9	2.8	51.7	a	24.1
1970	0.1	3.0	53.2	a	23.9
Electric utilities:					
1950	17.3	10.6	4.9	100.0	15.1
1960	40.9	14.1	2.8	100.0	18.7
1970	56.7	17.9	7.6	100.0	24.7
Total energy:[b]					
1950	100.0	100.0	100.0	100.0	100.0
1960	100.0	100.0	100.0	100.0	100.0
1970	100.0	100.0	100.0	100.0	100.0
C. Percent distribution of sectors, by energy source[c]					
Household and commercial:					
1950	38.4	21.6	40.0	a	100.0
1960	10.0	41.8	48.2	a	100.0
1970	2.8	52.1	45.0	a	100.0

Table 5. (Continued)

	Coal	Natural gas	Petroleum	Hydro and nuclear	Total
Industrial:					
1950	48.3	30.2	21.4	a	100.0
1960	32.9	42.3	24.8	a	100.0
1970	26.3	49.7	24.0	a	100.0
Transportation:					
1950	19.7	1.5	78.7	a	100.0
1960	0.8	3.3	95.8	a	100.0
1970	0.1	4.1	95.9	a	100.0
Electric utilities:					
1950	43.3	12.7	12.9	31.1	100.0
1960	50.8	21.3	6.7	21.2	100.0
1970	46.1	23.7	13.3	16.8	100.0
Total energy:[b]					
1950	37.8	18.0	39.5	4.7	100.0
1960	23.2	28.2	44.6	4.0	100.0
1970	20.0	32.8	43.0	4.1	100.0

[a]Not shown, since only aggregate electric energy deliveries can be allocated to end uses. See table 4.

[b]For convenience, and because of the small magnitudes involved, the "miscellaneous and unaccounted for" category is not shown.

[c]It should be remembered that the percentage shares of panel C show only the distribution of sectoral purchases of *fossil* fuels. If their respective electricity utility purchases are added to the household and commercial and the industrial sectors, the following percentages result for 1970:

	Coal	Natural gas	Petroleum	Utility electricity	Total
Household and commercial	2.3	43.2	37.3	17.1	100.0
Industrial	23.8	44.9	21.7	9.7	100.0

SOURCE: Table 4.

two-fifths of household and commercial energy consumption in 1950 to a mere 3 percent in 1970, and, conversely, the rise of natural gas to over 50 percent in 1970 from 22 percent in 1950. Comfort heat is, of course, the main source of demand for these fuels in the household and commercial sector. In the industrial sector, natural gas gained at the relative expense of coal, though in this market coal retains an important share due to its continuing importance in steelmaking. In transport, the trend could not be more dramatic: largely because of the disappearance of steam railroads, which right after World War II gave coal over one-third of the transportation market, coal declined from 20 percent of the market in 1950 to the point where petroleum enjoyed a virtually captive market, with a 96 percent share in 1970. In the electric utility sector, the shares for both coal (43 percent in 1950, 46 percent in 1970) and oil (13 percent in both years) remained very much the same, with a rising natural gas share (from 13 to 24 percent) offsetting the declining hydroelectric proportion. This offset was, of

course, statistical—in the sense that the rising utility share taken by natural gas would not otherwise have largely gone to hydro. It must also be noted that these terminal-year comparisons are slightly misleading, since they obscure some ups and downs during the period. Thus, the use of coal by the utility sector was somewhat higher in 1960, while that of oil was quite a bit lower. Shifts since then reflect in part the rising demand for low-sulfur fuel oil at the expense of coal.

A Closer Look at Energy Consumption
and Economic Growth

Economic history attests to the critical role played by the consumption of inanimate energy in advancing the material well-being of mankind. The Industrial Revolution and the growth of industry in the nineteenth century are almost synonymous with the significant contribution of coal to the development of the iron and steel industry, to railways, and to factory mechanization. In the twentieth century, electrification and motorized transport served to modify the process and in many ways helped step up tangible economic progress.

In the United States, as elsewhere, growth in the aggregate demand for inanimate energy supplies bears a close relationship to growth of the economy in general. But while there is a broad parallelism between economic growth and energy growth, it is important to pin down the relationship as precisely as possible, given the compounding effect of even a narrow spread in growth rates. Whether a 4 percent rate of growth in GNP means a 3.5 or 4.5 percent rate of growth in energy consumption could spell a difference in U. S. energy use in the year 2000 equal to this country's total annual level of consumption within the past few years. From the standpoint of both environmental impacts and resource use, there is more than academic curiosity over this point, which has been the subject of considerable discussion in the past year or so.

Although more research is needed to shed light on the correlation between economic growth and energy consumption, one's judgment may be guided by some broad suggestive evidence from the past. During the forty-year period of intensive industrialization occurring in the United States between 1880 and 1920, the annual growth of energy consumption averaged 5.6 percent, substantially exceeding annual GNP growth of 3.4 percent. By contrast, over the ensuing four decades, U.S. energy consumption growth steadily fell below GNP growth, the annual figures for the period 1920–60 averaging out to 2.1 percent and 3.2 percent, respectively. In both periods, of course, energy and GNP each grew more rapidly than population, yielding per capita growth for both indicators.

Sorting out the factors at work in the contrasting trends for these two periods of American history is a complicated business and cannot be done here, but some summary observations are worth making. The steeper rise of energy

consumption than of GNP in the closing decades of the nineteenth century and in the early part of the twentieth century almost certainly reflects the disproportionately fast growth of manufacturing in the economy—a sector requiring far higher energy input per unit of activity than the agricultural component, which had dominated the economy in the past. This phenomenon is at work at present in developing parts of the world where consumption of energy rises at rates considerably in excess of output in general, unlike the situation in most of the advanced countries.

The forces making for relatively slower growth in energy consumption than in GNP in the United States after World War I—or, to put it differently, for progressively less energy used per constant dollar of GNP—are more difficult to unscramble, but at least several distinct elements appear to have played a role.[7] An important contributing factor was the rapid rise of electrification, which greatly enhanced the efficiency of factory operations formerly dependent on, and constrained by, the limitations on plant layout imposed by the coal-burning factory steam engine. And this occurred in spite of the fact that the generation of a kilowatt-hour of electricity required many times the caloric output of the electricity produced. This disadvantage was moderated in a very important respect, however: the thermal efficiency of electricity generation improved substantially over the years. In 1925 it took over 2 pounds of coal to produce 1 kwh of electricity; by the 1960s it took less than 1 pound. Another important instance of improved energy conversion later in this period was the replacement of steam locomotives by more efficient diesel engines.

Against this historical backdrop of long-term developments, the decade just ended can be seen in perspective, with the recognition that observations based on ten years should not carry an undue amount of interpretive weight. Between 1960 and 1965 things continued pretty much as they had in preceding decades; U.S. energy consumption increased at the average annual rate of 3.6 percent, while GNP increased by 4.8 percent. Energy consumption per dollar of GNP (expressed in constant 1958 prices) continued its prior downward path, falling from 92,000 Btu to 87,000 Btu. But then a sharp reversal occurred. Between 1965 and 1970 energy consumption rose by 5 percent yearly, and GNP rose by 3.2 percent, or from a level of 87,000 Btu per dollar to one of 95,000 Btu per dollar—a level left behind in the early 1950s and, until 1970, never again recorded. (In 1970 alone, energy consumption rose by over 4.5 percent, while GNP actually declined.)

The figures in table 6 provide some insight into the anatomy of this acceleration in U.S. energy consumption during the 1960–70 decade. Column 7, showing how the 1.4 percentage point increase (from the 3.6 percent annual rate

[7]For a more elaborate treatment, see Sam H. Schurr, Bruce C. Netschert, and others, *Energy in the American Economy, 1850–1975* (Johns Hopkins Press for Resources for the Future, 1960), especially chap. 4.

Table 6. Contributions of Different Components to Changes in U.S. Energy Consumption, 1960-1965 and 1965-1970

(percent)

End-use sector and type of energy consumed	(1) 1960 share of total U.S. energy consumption	1960-1965		(4) 1965 share of total U.S. energy consumption	1965-1970		(7) Change between 1960-65 and 1965-70 in the contribution of different components (col. 6 − col. 3)
		(2) Average annual rate of change	(3) Contribution to average annual rate of change in total energy consumption[a] (col. 1 × col. 2)		(5) Average annual rate of change	(6) Contribution to average annual rate of change in total energy consumption[a] (col. 4 × col. 5)	
Households and commercial:							
Fossil fuels	22.7	3.05	0.69	22.1	3.51	0.78	0.09
Electricity	2.8	9.08	0.25	3.6	8.31	0.30	0.05
Industry:							
Fossil fuels	33.1	3.37	1.12	32.6	3.78	1.23	0.11
Electricity	2.9	4.58	0.13	3.0	6.84	0.21	0.08
Transportation:							
Fossil fuels	24.1	3.28	0.79	23.6	5.27	1.24	0.45
Electricity conversion losses	12.9	5.29	0.68	14.0	9.42	1.32	0.64
Total energy	100.0	3.65	3.65	100.0	5.05	5.05	1.40
In fuel and power uses	95.0	3.67	3.49	94.9	4.88	4.63	1.14
In nonenergy uses	5.0	3.33	0.17	5.1	8.07	0.41	0.24

NOTE: Components of columns 1, 3, 4, and 7 do not quite add to totals, because of rounding and because of omission of electricity consumption under transportation (a statistically insignificant sector) and a minor "miscellaneous and unallocable" component.

[a] Weighted by relative contribution to nationwide energy consumption in 1960 and 1965, respectively, as shown in columns 1 and 4.

SOURCES: U.S. Bureau of Mines, *Minerals Yearbook*, for selected years, and various USBM releases.

during 1960–65 to the 5 percent rate for 1965–70) was distributed, is of particular interest. A major thrust (a 0.64 percentage point portion, or 45 percent of the increment) came from "electricity conversion losses." This item refers to the thermal losses associated with electricity conversion at power plants.[8] Contrary to the long-term historical experience of electric-generating efficiency exhibiting persistent improvement, during the 1965–70 years such improvement stopped. Indeed, there was a decline: electric-generating efficiency was 32.5 percent in 1965, around 30 percent in 1970. (Since most new electric plants operate with efficiencies much closer to 40 percent, this decline might have been due to excessive use of old plant for peaking purposes.) Note that, in itself, electric power use by the household-commercial and industrial sectors, though exceedingly high, did not drastically change between the two periods,[9] and thus did not materially contribute to the *accelerated* rate of growth in energy consumption.

The transportation sector was the next most important contributor to the stepped-up energy growth rate, accounting for one-third of the increment of 1.4 percentage points. In the case of transport, almost solely involving oil consumption, the significant contribution resulted from the twofold fact that there was a fairly substantial increase in the consumption growth rate (from 3.3 percent per annum to 5.3 percent) and that this sector holds great weight within the nation's total energy use.

Although the overwhelming portion of basic energy resources are consumed in fuel and power uses, in recent years their use in nonenergy applications (e.g., as raw materials for the petrochemical industry) has tended to rise. The last line of table 6 shows that energy sources so used grew at the rate of 3.3 percent during 1960–65 but rose to 8.1 percent during 1965–70. From column 7, it can be calculated that this acceleration contributed about 17 percent to the increment in growth rates in total energy consumption between the two periods, although the weight of the nonenergy sector in overall energy consumption, and even in its contribution to the overall 5 percent 1965–70 growth rate was far below this. (Nonenergy applications are largely contained within fossil fuel consumption in the industry sector.)

Conjecture about the meaning of some of these rather distinct recent changes in U.S. energy consumption and their implications for the future will be given later in the discussion of projections.

The Key Role of Electricity

A relentlessly high growth rate coupled with major environmental ramifications have made electricity a focal point in public discussion on energy matters.

---

[8] Other energy-using sectors of the economy are, of course, also subject to efficiency losses not indicated in the table, e.g., automotive power plants.

[9] For all sectors combined, the average annual rate went from 6.7 percent to only 7.2 percent.

It is therefore desirable to single out electricity for particular, though limited, consideration. Sectoral trends in electric utility sales are shown in table 7.

In spite of the attention that has been directed to household demand for electricity, the table shows that it is the commercial sector of the economy (office buildings, shopping centers, public facilities, and the like) whose electricity consumption growth has been relatively the most rapid, even though the purchases of that sector are still substantially exceeded in absolute levels by residential and industrial customers. Still, residential customers have expanded

Table 7. U.S. Electric Utility Sales, 1960–1969

Year	Billion kwh				Percent of total			
	Residential	Commercial	Industrial	Total	Residential	Commercial	Industrial	Total
1960	195.6	114.4	344.1	681.2	28.7	16.8	50.5	100.0
1961	208.2	134.4	346.6	718.6	29.0	18.7	48.2	100.0
1962	225.5	143.6	373.0	773.7	29.1	18.6	48.2	100.0
1963	240.7	165.9	387.4	828.2	29.1	20.0	46.8	100.0
1964	261.0	182.9	408.3	887.5	29.4	20.6	46.0	100.0
1965	279.8	201.4	432.2	950.4	29.4	21.2	45.5	100.0
1966	305.4	225.1	463.8	1,035.6	29.5	21.7	44.8	100.0
1967	330.2	241.7	484.7	1,103.5	29.9	21.9	43.9	100.0
1968	366.2	264.2	517.3	1,198.4	30.6	22.0	43.2	100.0
1969	402.0	290.0	557.3	1,303.8	30.8	22.2	42.7	100.0

NOTE: Growth rates based on the figures in table 7 show these annual averages for the period 1960–69:

	Percent
Residential	8.3
Commercial	10.9
Industrial	5.5
Total sales	7.5

Per residential customer, sales went up from 3,851 kwh in 1960 to an estimated 6,550 kwh in 1969—or by approximately 6 percent per year (the difference from the 8.3 percent total growth being essentially due to the growth of customers).

SOURCE: *Electrical World* data shown in *The Economy, Energy, and the Environment*, prepared by the Legislative Reference Service for the Joint Economic Committee, 91 Cong. 2 sess. (1970), p. 73. The 1969 breakdown is estimated. A sectorally unallocable "other" component is not shown above. Also, to the extent comparison is possible, the *Electrical World* data are not precisely comparable to the figures in table 4.

their electric power use faster than the economy as a whole, and show by far the largest absolute growth, and since the growth of that market has been so widely singled out in discussions of the environmental consequences of electricity, it is useful to take a closer look at those components of household electricity consumption that can be said to have provided particular thrust to this growth. For example, the following table indicates the way in which the 195 billion kwh of

residential electricity purchases in 1960 were apportioned among different household uses[10] (asterisks signify that gas constitutes an alternative energy source):

	Billion kwh	Percent of total
Lighting	43	22
Ranges*	21	11
Water heaters*	45	23
Air conditioners*	8	4
Space heating*	12	6
Refrigerators and TV sets	28	14
Home freezers	9	5
Clothes dryers*	9	5
All other	20	10
	195	100

It is interesting to see that eight separately identifiable sources of electricity demand within the home accounted for 90 percent of residential consumption in 1960. That is, in spite of what one often hears about the proliferating range of frivolous household electrical gadgets, these gadgets could not possibly have contributed a great deal to electricity consumption in 1960. Of course, one person's necessity is another's luxury; and over time, luxuries become necessities. What is important to establish is that in 1960 the preponderant share of household electric power demand originated in what had, by then, come to be viewed as fairly basic uses and excluded many of the items commonly singled out as typifying the runaway craze for domestic electrification: toothbrushes, shoeshine kits, slicing knives, vibrators, and so on. (In the course of this research, the existence of an electric spaghetti fork came to light.) Moreover, it is likely that the overwhelming portion of the "all other" category in the preceding tabulations consisted of such resistance appliances—otherwise unidentified in the tabulations—as roasters, broilers, grills, and irons, as well as such lesser-wattage but nevertheless "basic" items as clothes washers and radio-phonographs.

What, then, explains the continued surge of household electricity consumption during the most recent decade? Although no systematic data were at hand

[10]Hans H. Landsberg, Leonard L. Fischman, and Joseph L. Fisher, *Resources in America's Future: Patterns of Requirements and Availabilities, 1960–2000* (Johns Hopkins Press for Resources for the Future, 1963), tables in chap. 10 appendix. The "all other" category was increased slightly in order to conform Landsberg's overall total of 193 billion more closely to the figure of 195.6 billion shown in table 7.

at the time of writing, sufficient figures to permit some tentative judgments were available. In this connection, it is useful to recall the extent to which American households in 1960 were or were not equipped with such items as were cataloged in the above tabulation (whether powered by electricity or other energy sources). For example, the "saturation factor" (i.e., the percentage of American households possessing the item in question) for central air conditioning was only 1 percent, that for room air conditioning, 14 percent. Some 60 percent had water heaters, of which about half were electric. A bit over 20 percent had freezers, a bit under 20 percent had clothes dryers—70 percent of the latter were electric. Although the overwhelming proportion of American homes were centrally heated, less than 1 percent had electric heat. And while 87 percent possessed some kind of TV set, the proportion having color could not have been much over 1 percent, if that.[11] The potentiality for a growing electricity demand arising from quite conventional needs was therefore present.

Indeed, in trying to account for the increment of slightly more than 200 billion kwh in household electricity consumption between 1960 and 1969 (i.e., from 196 billion kwh to 402 billion kwh in table 7), it is found, first, that roughly 32 billion kwh (or 16 percent) of incremental growth was due to air conditioning alone.[12] In a recent congressional report it is noted that "some utilities found during the summer of 1969 that as much as 25 to 35 percent of their peak loads were attributable to air conditioning or other weather related needs."[13]

Another major stimulus has come from the installation of electric heat—principally in new homes. In recent years this has been the fastest growing component of residential sales, the 1960 figure of 0.9 million electrically heated homes having jumped to nearly 3.5 million by the end of 1968.[14] If, as a rough approximation, kilowatt-hours absorbed by electric heating are multiplied by a corresponding factor of 3.5, then 36 billion kwh of the 1969 nationwide total of 402 billion can be ascribed to residential space heating in that year—up from 12 billion in 1960, the 24 billion increment accounting for another 12 percent of

[11] Presumed from the fact that only 2.9 percent had color sets in 1965 (*Merchandising Week* data, in U.S. Bureau of the Census, *Statistical Abstract of the United States, 1970* [1970], p. 687).

[12] Based on 8 billion kwh in 1960 (from Landsberg, Fischman, and Fisher, *Resources*, p. 747) and an estimated 40 billion kwh in 1969. The latter figure was based on a *Merchandising Week* estimate (shown in U.S. Bureau of the Census, *Statistical Abstract, 1970*) on ownership of window units and on Air Conditioning and Refrigeration Institute figures (oral communication) on central air conditioning. Landsberg's projected kwh estimate for each type of unit per household was then applied.

[13] *The Economy, Energy, and the Environment,* prepared by the Legislative Reference Service for the Joint Economic Committee, 91 Cong. 2 sess. (1970), p. 73.

[14] Ibid.

1960-69 growth. Thus, 28 percent of household electricity expansion during the period 1960-69 can be traced solely to air conditioning and space heating. Put another way, compared with the total residential electricity growth rate of 8.3 percent per year, air conditioning and space heating combined went up by 14 percent and all other uses by about 7 percent. As a result, in 1969 air conditioning and space heating occupied twice their relative 1960 share in residential electric power consumption.

Statistics enabling the distribution of the balance of 1960-69 residential growth among different uses are lacking. However, some ideas can be gotten by looking at the following changes in the percentage of U.S. households owning electrical appliances:[15]

	1960	1969
Blenders	7.5	25.9
Coffeemakers	53.4	82.9
Dishwashers	6.3	20.8
Disposals	9.5	20.5
Clothes dryers (incl. gas)	17.8	38.8
Freezers	22.1	28.5
Frypans	40.7	53.4
Irons	88.6	99.5
Mixers	53.4	80.5
TV, black & white	89.9	98.5
TV, color	2.9 (1965 figure)	35.7
Clothes washers	83.1	90.8
Refrigerators	98.0	99.8
Toasters	70.4	89.3

As suggested earlier, the items among these that may be presumed to have provided particular stimulus to growing household electricity use are those—with heating elements—drawing substantial current. The lowly toothbrush—frequently the symbolic villain in our despair over relentless power growth—may prove something or other about man's hedonism. But it has not contributed to power shortages.[16]

[15]*Merchandising Week* data in U.S. Bureau of the Census, *Statistical Abstract, 1970*, p. 687.

[16]An electric toothbrush draws 2 watts of current. Thus, a household could have thirty toothbrushes whirring simultaneously throughout a 24-hour day without exceeding the current drawn by a single 60-watt bulb lit at all times. The wattage rating and average annual

SOME INTERNATIONAL COMPARISONS

Growth of Total and Per Capita Energy Consumption

Some broad indicators of worldwide and regional trends[17] in total and per capita energy consumption appear in tables 8 to 12.[18] The growth of total world energy consumption from 44 quadrillion Btu in 1925 to 190 quadrillion Btu in 1968 (see table 8) is the same thing, calorically, as going from a level of 1.6 billion metric tons of coal, or about 1.1 billion metric tons of oil, in 1925 to a level of approximately 7 billion metric tons of coal, or 4.5 billion metric tons of oil, in 1968. Actually, the preponderant worldwide energy source in 1925 had been coal, while the leading component in 1968 was oil. Some period growth rates, reflecting this expansion of world energy consumption, are as follows (average annual percentage rates of change):

| | Energy consumption | |
	Total	Per capita
1925–50	2.2	1.1
1950–60	4.9	3.1
1960–68	5.5	3.5
1925–68	3.4	2.0

---

consumption for home heating as well as kwh for selected household appliances appear below (in a compilation by the Potomac Electric Power Company, Washington, D.C.):

	Average watts	Estimated annual kwh per home
Air conditioner (window)	1,300	1,265
Clothes dryer	4,800	1,100
Frying pan	1,170	190
Food freezer	300	1,560
Range	11,720	1,225
Refrigerator-freezer (14 cu. ft.)	330	1,330
Heat pump (medium-sized home)	9,600	17,000
Broiler	1,375	140
Vibrator	40	2
Radio	80	90
Shaver	15	2
Sewing machine	75	10
Clock	2	18

[17] This discussion is based to a considerable extent on information in Joel Darmstadter and associates, *Energy in the World Economy: A Statistical Review of Trends in Output, Trade, and Consumption Since 1925* (Johns Hopkins Press for Resources for the Future, 1971).

[18] As in the preceding discussion concerning the United States, world energy consumption is here defined to comprise coal, natural gas, hydro and nuclear power, as well as

Table 8. World Energy Consumption and Population, Selected Years, 1925–1968

Year	Total energy consumption (*trillion Btu*)	Population (*million*)	Energy consumption per capita (*million Btu*)
1925	44,249	1,890.1	23.4
1950	76,823	2,504.5	30.7
1955	99,658	2,725.6	36.6
1960	124,046	2,989.9	41.5
1965	160,722	3,281.2	49.0
1968	189,737	3,484.5	54.5

NOTES AND SOURCES: This table represents the addition of data for the United States and for the rest of the world. U.S. data are from table 1 or from sources cited there. Rest-of-world data for the period 1925–65 were adapted from Joel Darmstadter and associates, *Energy in the World Economy: A Statistical Review of Trends in Output, Trade, and Consumption Since 1925* (Johns Hopkins Press for Resources for the Future, 1971).

For purposes of this table and succeeding tables, the scope of the rest-of-world total energy-consumption measure (shown in the RFF study cited above) was broadened in three ways: (1) to include the consumption of bunker fuels; (2) to include nuclear energy for years when applicable (1960 and beyond) and for areas for which data shown in U.N., *Statistical Yearbook*, were available (for the U.S.S.R., none were); and (3) to calculate primary electricity (hydro, nuclear, geothermal), not by the heat value produced, but rather by the estimated (higher) fuel inputs required at fossil-fueled thermal electric power stations. Also, data expressed in coal equivalents in the RFF study were converted into Btu at the rate of 27.3 million Btu per metric ton of coal equivalent. The U.S. data, which, for overlapping years, are derived from table 1 or are based on its sources, already embody each of these characteristics.

Rest-of-world data for 1968 were derived by linking 1965–68 figures shown in U.N., *World Energy Supplies*, Statistical Papers, Series J, no. 13 (New York, 1970) to 1965 figures adapted from *Energy in the World Economy*.

"Energy" includes the so-called commercial fossil fuels and primary electricity; it excludes firewood, animal wastes, and most other noncommercial fuels.

If there is an inherent accelerating trend in the growth of international energy consumption, these figures should not necessarily be viewed as corroborative, for the slow growth during the first twenty-five years occurred during a period marked by worldwide depression and terminating when war-induced industrial dislocation still persisted. (Indeed, the period 1925–29—preceding the Great Depression—had annual growth rates in total and per capita energy consumption of nearly 4.5 percent and 2 percent, respectively.) Still, the rather fast pace of expansion in energy use has prevailed for nearly two decades, and according to numerous analyses is not judged likely to abate soon.

negligible amounts of geothermal power. The so-called noncommercial fuels—e.g., firewood and animal and vegetal wastes—are mostly excluded even though in such countries as India, they continue to represent as much as 30 percent or even 50 percent of total energy use. But even in such countries, the use of noncommercial fuels is dwindling, and for the world as a whole these fuels probably do not account for more than 5 percent. Because of the substitution of commercial for noncommercial fuels, growth rates based on commercial energy forms only (as in this paper) may be somewhat overstated for certain less-developed regions. The conspicuously low efficiency with which noncommercial fuels are commonly used, however, makes their omissions a less serious matter than might be thought.

Changing Regional Shares of World Energy Consumption

Some rather striking post-World War II geographic shifts have accompanied the growth in total world energy utilization. In a number of areas, these shifts represented a continuation of trends that were in progress even earlier. For example, the Soviet Union's share of world energy consumption stood at under 2 percent in 1925; just before World War II it was up to 10 percent, and from its early postwar share of around 11 percent, it rose to approximately 15 percent in 1968.

The figures in tables 9 and 10 point to rising shares occurring elsewhere in the world in the past several decades: the other Communist countries, Latin America, Africa, and Asia all exhibit long-term increases in their relative standing. The postwar rise of Asia reflects in part the growing share of the region's developing countries; but to an even greater extent it reflects the phenomenal momentum of energy growth in Japan, whose annual postwar growth rates of between 10 and 15 percent have been sustained to the most recent years for which figures are available.

A principal offset to these long-term increases in regional shares of worldwide energy consumption has been the declining relative position of North America. Although North America retains its leading world share, with the United States occupying the top-ranking country share, its proportion of world energy consumption (which had been as high as 50 percent in the mid-twenties) fell from 45 percent in 1950 to approximately one-third in 1968. The relatively slight decline of Western Europe's share of world energy consumption since 1950 reflects the fact that in 1950 the area was still in the midst of postwar recovery; in 1925, its world share had been around 35 percent.

Regional Trends in Per Capita Energy Consumption

These distributional shifts in total energy consumption among different parts of the world have also been accompanied by disparate trends in the growth of per capita energy consumption. As shown in the last column of table 10, numerous regions of the world have exceeded—by a substantial margin in some cases—the per capita energy growth of North America and Western Europe, both during the long-range time span since the 1920s and during the briefer post-World War II period highlighted in the table.

Nevertheless, regional differences in per capita energy use, while narrowing, remain dramatically wide, as can be seen in table 9. In 1968 U.S. per capita energy consumption of 310 million Btu and that of Canada, which was only slightly lower, were more than two and one-half times the level of the next ranking regions—Oceania, the Soviet Union, and Western Europe, all of which recorded per capita figures in the vicinity of 120 million Btu. And the more extreme disparity is reflected in the fact that North American per capita con-

Table 9. World Energy Consumption and Population, by Major Regions, 1950, 1960, 1968

Region	1950			1960			1968		
	Total consumption (trillion Btu)	Population (million)	Consumption per capita (million Btu)	Total consumption (trillion Btu)	Population (million)	Consumption per capita (million Btu)	Total consumption (trillion Btu)	Population (million)	Consumption per capita (million Btu)
North America[a]	36,860	166.1	221.9	48,701	198.7	245.1	68,594	220.0	309.9
Canada	2,707	13.7	197.6	3,885	17.9	217.0	6,162	20.8	296.3
United States	34,153	152.3	224.3	44,816	180.7	248.0	62,432	201.2	310.3
Western Europe[b]	17,483	302.4	57.8	26,066	326.5	79.8	41,584	350.6	118.6
Oceania	890	12.2	73.0	1,398	15.4	90.8	2,240	18.3	122.4
Latin America	2,397	161.9	14.8	4,939	212.4	23.3	8,034	267.4	30.0
Asia (excl. Communist)	3,804	805.4	4.7	8,228	970.6	8.5	16,757	1,182.7	14.2
Japan	1,739	82.9	21.0	3,672	93.2	39.4	8,691	101.1	86.0
Other Asia	2,063	722.5	2.9	4,556	877.4	5.2	8,066	1,081.6	7.5
Africa	1,297	217.0	6.0	2,162	276.0	7.8	3,343	336.5	9.9
U.S.S.R. and Comm. Eastern Europe	12,842	269.8	47.6	25,973	312.9	83.0	39,843	341.9	116.5
U.S.S.R.	8,427	180.0	46.8	17,898	214.4	83.5	28,628	237.8	120.4
Eastern Europe[b]	4,414	89.7	49.2	8,075	98.5	82.0	11,215	104.1	107.7
Communist Asia	1,250	569.8	2.2	6,579	677.5	9.7	9,342	765.2	12.2
World	76,823	2,504.5	30.7	124,046	2,989.9	41.5	189,737	3,484.5	54.5

[a]In some of the regional tables, "North America" may exceed very slightly the sum of Canada and the United States because of statistically minor territorial inclusions, e.g., Greenland.

[b]Yugoslavia is included in Western Europe throughout these tables.

SOURCES: See table 8, whose notes are also applicable here.

Table 10. World Energy Consumption and Population, by Major Region, Percentage Distribution, 1950, 1960, 1968, and Average Annual Percentage Rates of Change, 1960-1968

| | Percentage distribution | | | | | | Average annual percentage rates of change, 1960-68 | | |
| | 1950 | | 1960 | | 1968 | | | | |
	Energy consumption	Population	Energy consumption	Population	Energy consumption	Population	Energy consumption	Population	Energy consumption per capita
North America	48.0	6.6	39.3	6.6	36.2	6.4	4.4	1.4	2.9
Canada	3.5	0.5	3.1	0.6	3.2	0.6	5.9	1.9	4.0
United States	44.5	6.1	36.1	6.0	32.9	5.8	4.2	1.3	2.8
Western Europe	22.8	12.1	21.0	10.9	21.9	10.1	6.0	0.9	5.1
Oceania	1.2	0.5	1.1	0.5	1.2	0.5	6.1	2.2	3.8
Latin America	3.1	6.5	4.0	7.1	4.2	7.7	6.3	2.9	3.2
Asia (excl. Communist)	5.0	32.2	6.6	32.5	8.8	33.9	9.3	2.5	6.6
Japan	2.3	3.3	3.0	3.1	4.6	2.9	11.4	1.0	10.3
Other Asia	2.7	28.9	3.7	29.4	4.3	31.0	7.4	2.7	4.7
Africa	1.7	8.7	1.7	9.2	1.8	9.7	5.6	2.5	3.0
U.S.S.R. and Comm. Eastern Europe	16.7	10.8	20.9	10.5	21.0	9.8	5.5	1.1	4.3
U.S.S.R.	11.0	7.2	14.4	7.2	15.1	6.8	6.1	1.3	4.7
Eastern Europe	5.7	3.6	6.5	3.3	5.9	3.0	4.2	0.7	3.5
Communist Asia	1.6	22.8	5.3	22.7	4.9	22.0	4.5	1.5	2.9
World	100.0	100.0	100.0	100.0	100.0	100.0	5.5	1.9	3.5

SOURCE: Calculated from figures in table 8, whose notes are also applicable here.

sumption was between thirty to forty times the levels prevailing in Africa and the developing portions of Asia.

If North America's level of per capita energy consumption in 1925 (roughly 175 million Btu) had remained unchanged throughout the period 1925–68, it would still have been some 45 percent above the next highest areas tabulated for the year 1968. A simple computational exercise—one meant to illustrate rather than to forecast—dramatizes these regional trends and disparities: it would take another decade at per capita energy growth of close to 10 percent annually even for a booming Japan to reach North America's 1925 per capita level of consumption. It would take Africa about sixty years with an annual per capita growth rate of at least 5 percent (a probably ambitious target) to achieve North America's figure of the mid-1920s. To be sure, trends and levels in per capita energy consumption are not synonymous with per capita income or GNP; nor are the latter measures, in turn, truly reflective of living standards, however defined. (As will be shown below, the disproportionately high per capita energy levels of numerous Communist countries are characteristic of the industrial structure in these nations as well as, in certain cases, an inefficient use of energy resources.) Nonetheless, there is unquestionably a sufficiently close connection between levels of per capita energy consumption and general economic development to permit one to point to the simple calculation for Africa as yet another sign that substantial improvement in living standards in the years ahead will be difficult.

International Energy-GNP Comparisons

This is an appropriate juncture at which to examine some of the historical and comparative international statistics bearing on the relationship between energy consumption, on the one hand, and overall economic activity (as measured by GNP), on the other. Some pertinent country data have been assembled in table 11.

In the earlier discussion of the United States, it was pointed out that, as a general proposition, a close connection between energy and economic development was unassailable, even though in its more specific aspects the relationship was seen to be far from systematic. The same observation holds for the world as a whole—both cross-sectionally and historically. The higher a nation's income or output is on the current international scale, the higher, in general, is its level of energy consumption; as its GNP rises over time, so does its energy consumption—in close, even if not proportionate, conformity.

Although the connection between energy consumption and GNP may be more or less self-evident, the chain of causation between these two factors is less distinct, for there are clearly two-directional forces at work. For example, some amount of electric-generating capacity is obviously required in order to support a modern industrialized economy or one on the move toward such a stage. This

Table 11. Miscellaneous Data Relating to Energy Consumption, Gross National Product, and Population, 37 Selected Countries, 1950-1968

Country	1968 per capita		Average annual percentage rates of change					Ratio of energy growth rate to GNP growth rate		Energy consumption per $1 of GNP, 1968 (thous. Btu)
	Energy consumption (mill. Btu)	GNP ($U.S., current prices)	1950-1960		1960-1968			1950-1960	1960-1968	
			Total energy consumption	Total real GNP	Total energy consumption	Total real GNP	Population			
Canada	296.3	3,157	3.6	4.0	5.9	5.2	1.9	0.90	1.13	94.0
United States	310.3	4,290	2.8	3.2	4.2	4.7	1.3	0.88	0.89	72.3
Belgium-Luxembourg	166.9	2,386	2.2	2.9	5.3	4.4	0.6	0.76	1.20	69.9
France	110.1	2,617	4.2	4.6	5.0	5.4	1.1	0.91	0.93	42.1
West Germany	138.9	2,597	4.7	7.9	4.6	4.3	1.0	0.59	1.07	53.5
Italy	81.2	1,591	9.8	5.8	8.8	5.3	0.9	1.69	1.66	51.0
Netherlands	146.2	2,217	4.4	4.7	7.7	4.7	1.3	0.94	1.64	65.9
Austria	89.3	1,651	4.9	6.1	3.2	3.9	0.5	0.80	0.82	54.1
Denmark	137.0	2,710	4.2	2.8	7.4	4.2	0.8	1.50	1.76	50.5
Norway	229.1	2,451	3.4	3.6	6.1	5.1	0.8	0.94	1.20	93.4
Portugal	22.2	521	6.8	3.6	5.9	6.3	0.6	1.89	0.94	42.6
Sweden	206.1	2,949	5.0	3.4	6.3	4.4	0.7	1.47	1.43	69.9
Switzerland	113.5	2,705	5.2	4.5	6.2	4.4	1.7	1.16	1.41	42.0
United Kingdom	149.9	2,327	1.4	2.6	1.4	3.1	0.6	0.54	0.45	64.4
Greece	38.8	1,001	9.6	5.8	11.3	7.4	0.7	1.66	1.53	38.7
Ireland	89.7	1,167	2.2	1.8	5.4	3.5	0.3	1.22	1.54	76.8
Spain	48.8	856	4.8	5.0	7.1	7.1	0.9	0.96	1.00	57.1
Yugoslavia[a]	35.8	841	7.6	5.4	5.4	6.8	1.2	1.41	0.79	42.6
Australia	156.1	2,218	4.6	3.9	6.1	4.6	2.0	1.18	1.33	70.4
New Zealand	104.0	2,203	3.5	—	4.3	3.6	1.9	—	1.19	47.2

Bulgaria[a]	67.1	1,000	12.4	6.8	14.9	6.6	0.8	1.82	2.26	67.1
Czechoslovakia[a]	158.4	1,797	5.9	5.0	3.2	2.4	0.7	1.18	1.33	88.1
East Germany[a]	148.5	1,762	5.0	6.0	3.3	3.3	-0.1	0.83	0.61	84.3
Hungary[a]	83.4	1,284	8.7	5.0	3.8	4.7	0.3	1.74	0.81	64.9
Poland[a]	101.1	1,133	5.9	4.8	3.6	5.2	1.1	1.23	0.69	89.2
Romania[a]	60.4	936	9.7	6.2	8.9	6.2	0.7	1.56	1.44	64.6
U.S.S.R.[a]	120.4	1,767	7.8	6.2	6.1	6.0	1.3	1.26	1.02	68.1
Mexico	33.8	558	8.0	6.1	5.5	3.6	1.3	1.31	0.86	60.6
Venezuela	103.9	999	14.3	8.2	4.9	4.8	3.5	1.74	1.02	104.0
Puerto Rico	79.0	1,426	–	–	10.5	7.8	1.8	–	1.35	55.4
Argentina	43.5	791	5.4	3.0	2.9	1.7	1.7	1.80	1.72	55.0
Chile	36.6	559	4.5	3.6	6.5	4.4	2.5	1.25	1.48	65.5
Israel	74.1	1,615	10.6	9.0	12.5	8.4	3.3	1.18	1.49	45.9
Turkey	14.0	328	6.0	5.8	11.7	5.4	2.4	1.03	2.17	42.8
Japan	86.0	1,830	7.5	9.5	11.4	10.4	1.0	0.79	1.10	47.0
Taiwan	25.1	301	11.2	8.0	8.7	10.0	3.0	1.40	0.87	81.7
South Africa	87.2	735	4.8	4.1	4.5	6.2	0.9	1.17	0.73	118.7

NOTE: Dashes indicate "not available."

[a]For these countries, 1967 figures are used instead of 1968.

SOURCES: Energy and population data are based on sources cited in table 8.

GNP data for the period 1950–65 based on Joel Darmstadter and associates, *Energy in the World Economy: A Statistical Review of Trends in Output, Trade, and Consumption Since 1925* (Johns Hopkins Press for Resources for the Future, 1971) were linked to constant-price GNP growth rates for the period 1965–68 or 1965–67 as obtained from the following sources: U.S.S.R., from *The Military Budget and National Economic Priorities*, Hearings before the Subcommittee on Economy in Government of the Joint Economic Committee, 91 Cong. 1 sess. (1969), p. 912; Yugoslavia and other East European countries, from *Economic Developments in Countries of Eastern Europe*, A Compendium of papers submitted to the Subcommittee on Foreign Economic Policy of the Joint Economic Committee, 91 Cong. 2 sess. (1970), pp. 49–50; Puerto Rico, from U.S. Bureau of the Census, *Statistical Abstract of the United States, 1970* (1970), p. 798 (current-dollar Puerto Rican GNP was then deflated, using the U.S. implicit GNP deflator); and all other countries, from Agency for International Development, *Gross National Product—Growth Rates and Trend Data*, Document RC–W-138 (April 25, 1969).

For the Communist countries, Canada, Japan, and the more industrialized Western European nations (with the exception of Sweden and Switzerland) the per capita GNP estimates reflect approximate purchasing power equivalents. Elsewhere, official exchange rates were used to construct U.S. dollar estimates. For further notes, see Darmstadter, *Energy in the World Economy.*

"input" of energy may, for example, take the form of an increase in motorized capital equipment, endowing each worker with more horsepower with which to increase his productivity.

Conversely, advancing living standards involve new wants whose fulfillment is made possible by fuels and power. One need only note the role of the private passenger car, of comfort heat and air conditioning, of air travel, and of countless other products and services to appreciate the claims on energy arising from high and growing levels of personal income.

Thus, the first two columns of table 11 show a generally close cross-sectional relationship between per capita GNP and per capita energy consumption.[19] Any graphic representation of such data invariably shows a close fit to the left-to-right, upward-sloping regression line and is associated with a high (nearly 0.9) and significant correlation coefficient. Of the thirteen top-ranking nations in terms of per capita GNP, eleven are also among the top thirteen in terms of energy consumption per capita; of the eight lowest-ranking in GNP per capita, seven are also in the bottom standing in energy use per capita.

There are nonetheless sufficient exceptions (and a few outright anomalies) to warrant a somewhat closer look at the data. A good way of analyzing these less typical cases is by means of the ratios showing energy consumption per unit of GNP—a measure of the "energy intensiveness" of an economy. These data appear in the last column of table 11, and they show a good deal of variation among the thirty-seven countries listed. A substantial group of countries have higher ratios than the United States with its indicated ratio of 72,000 Btu per dollar of GNP in 1968. Among these countries are Canada, Norway, Czechoslovakia, East Germany, Poland, Venezuela, South Africa, and—for reasons that mystify[20]—Ireland and Taiwan.

In at least a number of cases, variable energy-GNP ratios are most plausibly related to variations in industrial structure. In predominantly agricultural economies the energy-GNP ratio is likely to be rather low, but in countries where the "industry mix" is heavily characterized by activities with relatively large energy requirements, such as metallurgy or mining (e.g., Canada and Norway), chemicals (East Germany), or petroleum refining (Venezuela), energy per unit of output tends to be high. Thus, compared with, say, Denmark, Canada consumes a far greater amount of energy per capita than would be explained by the relatively slight per capita income differences between these two nations. This arises because—partly as a result of low-cost hydroelectric energy—Canada, much more than Denmark, has an energy-intensive industry mix oriented to such

[19] The exchange-rate problem as well as other conceptual and statistical difficulties make international GNP comparisons a hazardous undertaking, particularly where such comparisons involve measurements for socialist and less-developed economies. This precludes reliable analysis, especially where only modest country-by-country differences exist. (See notes to table 11.)

[20] Although deficient statistics of GNP and/or energy consumption may be involved. In the case of Ireland, it could also relate to widespread availability of low-cost peat.

activities as metallurgy, electroprocess industries, chemicals, pulp and paper, and mining. To some extent, this characterization also fits Norway.[21]

Among other explanatory factors, differences in the thermal efficiency with which fuels are converted in different sectors of the economy will also have some effect on national energy-GNP ratios. For example, in terms of Btu requirements per kwh of electricity, Czechoslovakia's power plants are only 80 percent as efficient as those of West Germany. And, of course, the electric power sector, though a prominent part of the national economy, is not the only one subject to varying thermal efficiencies among countries.

In addition to the cross-sectional statistics for the year 1968, table 11 also presents post-World War II growth rates in energy consumption and in real GNP and shows as well the ratio of those respective rates of change—sometimes labeled the "energy-GNP elasticity coefficient." (Elasticity of over 1.0 implies energy consumption growth in excess of GNP growth; elasticity of under 1.0, energy consumption growth less than that in GNP.)

During the period 1960–68, twenty-six of the thirty-seven countries recorded energy growth rates above 5 percent per year; twelve out of the thirty-seven countries exceeded a rate of 7 percent a year: Italy, Holland, Denmark, Greece, Spain, Bulgaria, Poland, Puerto Rico, Israel, Turkey, Japan, and Taiwan. A large group of the fastest-growing energy-consuming countries tended, during the last decade, to exhibit elasticities (shown in the next-to-last column of table 11) in excess of 1.0—that is, reflecting faster growth in energy consumption than in GNP. Where this phenomenon accompanied a marked transformation of the economy away from agriculture toward manufacturing (as in the case of Italy), or where a country in relatively early stages of development was still undergoing a transition from primitive to commercial energy forms (as in Greece, where firewood was still an important energy source in the 1950s), such a statistical result makes a good deal of sense. Yet, understanding on this score is sufficiently bare to foreclose further generalizations.

Shifts Among Different Energy Sources

Because the environmental implications of future energy growth derive not only from the aggregate levels that may be consumed but also from the role of the different energy sources, it may be well to dwell in a limited way on the latter aspect. By way of historical background, the data contained in table 12 indicate the principal compositional shifts among the different energy resources between 1950 and 1968 in various parts of the world. For the world as a whole,

[21]It should again be noted that the Btu value ascribed to hydro represents the hypothetical amount of energy that would have been required—given prevailing efficiency factors—at fossil-fueled power plants to produce an equivalent amount of thermal electricity. As a result of this measurement convention, which for a number of reasons is the preferred one, the total energy consumption of hydro-oriented countries (such as Norway and Canada) tends to be considerably higher than it would be under the alternative practice of valuing hydro at the inherent calorific content of the electricity generated.

Table 12. World Energy Consumption, by Source and Major Region, 1950 and 1968

	1950					1968				
	Coal[a]	Oil[b]	Natural gas	Hydro[c]	Total	Coal[a]	Oil[b]	Natural gas	Hydro and nuclear[c]	Total
				(trillion Btu)						
North America	14,013	14,264	6,226	2,357	36,860	13,968	29,734	21,032	3,860	68,594
Canada	1,100	775	76	756	2,707	639	2,682	1,468	1,373	6,162
United States	12,913	13,489	6,150	1,601	34,153	13,329	27,052	19,564	2,487	62,432
Western Europe	13,533	2,506	49	1,395	17,483	13,541	21,535	1,566	4,942	41,584
Oceania	581	243	0	66	890	958	1,086	0	196	2,240
Latin America	235	1,747	199	216	2,397	414	5,501	1,475	644	8,034
Asia (excl. Communist)	2,026	1,084	52	642	3,804	4,475	10,428	714	1,140	16,757
Japan	1,076	87	3	573	1,739	2,259	5,615	88	729	8,691
Other Asia	950	996	49	68	2,063	2,216	4,813	626	411	8,066
Africa	797	478	0	22	1,297	1,531	1,583	46	183	3,343
U.S.S.R. and Communist Eastern Europe	10,453	1,870	298	221	12,842	20,840	10,876	6,977	1,150	39,843
U.S.S.R.	6,369	1,660	207	191	8,427	12,294	9,167	6,140	1,027	28,628
Eastern Europe	4,084	210	87	33	4,414	8,546	1,709	837	123	11,215
Communist Asia	1,160	11	0	79	1,250	8,443	669	—	230	9,342
World	42,798	22,203	6,824	4,998	76,823	64,170	81,412	31,810	12,345	189,737

(percent of each region's total energy consumption)

North America	38.0	38.7	16.7	6.4	100.0	20.4	43.3	30.7	5.6	100.0
Canada	40.6	28.6	2.8	27.9	100.0	10.4	43.5	23.8	22.3	100.0
United States	37.8	39.5	18.0	4.7	100.0	21.3	43.3	31.3	4.0	100.0
Western Europe	77.4	14.3	0.3	8.0	100.0	32.6	51.8	3.8	11.9	100.0
Oceania	65.3	27.3	0	7.4	100.0	42.8	48.5	0	8.7	100.0
Latin America	9.8	72.9	8.3	9.0	100.0	5.2	68.5	18.4	8.0	100.0
Asia (excl. Communist)	53.3	28.5	1.4	16.9	100.0	26.7	62.2	4.3	6.8	100.0
Japan	61.9	5.0	0.2	32.9	100.0	26.0	64.6	1.0	8.4	100.0
Other Asia	46.0	48.3	2.4	3.3	100.0	27.5	59.7	7.8	5.1	100.0
Africa	61.4	36.9	0	1.7	100.0	45.8	47.4	1.4	5.5	100.0
U.S.S.R. and Communist Eastern Europe	81.4	14.6	2.3	1.7	100.0	52.3	27.3	17.5	2.9	100.0
U.S.S.R.	75.6	19.7	2.5	2.3	100.0	42.9	32.0	21.4	3.6	100.0
Eastern Europe	92.5	4.8	2.0	0.7	100.0	76.2	15.2	7.5	1.1	100.0
Communist Asia	92.8	0.9	0	6.3	100.0	90.4	7.2	–	2.5	100.0
World	55.7	28.9	8.9	6.5	100.0	33.8	42.9	16.8	6.5	100.0

NOTE: Dashes indicate "not available."

a Principally bituminous coal, but also includes anthracite, a variety of low-quality coals, and lignite.

b Including, where known, natural gas liquids.

c Also includes small quantities of geothermal electricity. The nuclear portion of this column for 1968 was (in trillion Btu): Canada, 8; United States, 130; Western Europe, 355; Japan, 11; Eastern Europe, less than 0.5 trillion; and U.S.S.R., unavailable. This column also includes net regional imports of electricity.

SOURCE: See table 8, whose notes are also applicable here.

a sharp relative decline of coal during this period was accompanied by marked relative increases in both oil and gas. The two accounted for 38 percent of worldwide energy consumption in 1950 and 60 percent in 1968; concurrently, coal experienced a relative decline, from 56 percent to 34 percent. The hydro-electric share, including a minute nuclear component in 1968, remained unchanged at 6.5 percent.[22] Translated into physical units of measure, those 1968 shares stack up as follows:

	Percent of worldwide energy consumption	Quadrillion Btu	Physical units
Coal	33.8	64.2	2.3 billion metric tons
Oil	42.9	81.4	2 billion metric tons (or nearly 40 million barrels per day)
Natural gas	16.8	31.8	875 billion cubic meters
Hydro & nuclear	6.5	12.3	1,200 billion kwh[23]
Total	100.0	189.7	

To a greater or lesser extent, similar changes—at least the shift from coal to oil and gas—occurred in principal regions of the world. In no area did the share of coal fail to decline. In each area, the share of natural gas was higher in 1968 than in 1950, which was true also of oil consumption in each area, with the exception of Latin America, for in that region (where oil had already contributed to 73 percent of energy consumption in 1950) the oil proportion dropped somewhat, while that for gas rose sharply. Only in two regions—the group of Communist East European countries and Communist Asia—did coal continue to contribute more than half of total energy consumption in 1968. Changes in the hydro share in the total energy picture of the different regions have been less systematic. In some areas, particularly in those where, as in the case of Japan, the number of potential waterpower sites is dwindling, the hydroelectric contribution to total energy use has declined dramatically. In other areas, where considerable potential remains to be exploited—e.g., Africa and the rest of non-Communist Asia—the hydroelectric share has risen. As the data show, those opposite trends have netted out, leaving the worldwide hydro share unchanged as a result.

Other striking changes are evident in table 12. In Western Europe, coal consumption remained virtually unchanged *absolutely*; as a result, the share of

[22]The hydro (including nuclear) share is figured at the Btu input equivalent that would have been required at fossil-fueled stations to produce the same amount of electricity.

[23]Of which 50 billion kwh represent nuclear power. The figure of 1,200 billion kwh also includes 9 billion kwh of geothermal electricity.

coal declined in less than two decades from over three-fourths to under one-third. Concurrently, oil and gas went from 15 percent to 56 percent. Japan's energy pattern disclosed similarly dramatic shifts. The Soviet picture is high-lighted by a big postwar rise in the share of natural gas—from 2 percent to 21 percent. The changing U.S. pattern was far less remarkable, for the vanguard role of the United States in world oil and gas resulted in important shares for these fuels in the country's total energy consumption far earlier than in most other regions. Thus, the proportion of oil in U.S. energy consumption rose only modestly between 1950 and 1968, the sharply declining relative position of coal (with, incidentally, only slight long-term absolute growth) being principally con-pensated for by natural gas.

In short, the figures show an erosion of the position of coal in much of the world—an erosion that had already begun prior to World War II but that has gathered momentum since then. The underlying reasons can be identified. After World War II the technical feasibility of pipeline gas transport became estab-lished. World crude oil supplies were boosted by major Middle Eastern and African discoveries. Vast gas fields were discovered in the Soviet Union, and more recently substantial finds were made in the Netherlands and the North Sea. In cases of fuel substitutability, even where oil or gas did not immediately display the direct cost advantages over coal that would sooner or later occur, they did offer numerous attributes of convenience, transportability, and com-bustibility that frequently tended to compensate for a higher price. In areas that lacked significant indigenous resources of either coal or petroleum, the heavy transportation costs (relative to energy content) of imported coal were an added incentive for switching to liquid fuels. And, of course, oil itself provided stim-ulus to particular industries and to new technical developments, such as the growth of automotive transport and railroad dieselization. Expanding markets for oil, in turn, served to bring about relative price improvements through scale economies that would then enhance the attractiveness of oil still further. Thus, even though coal in 1968 retained a one-third share of world energy consump-tion, having continued in recent years to be a dominant fuel in electric power stations, its position—under the impact of these enumerated developments—was bound to lose supremacy.

PROSPECTIVE TRENDS IN U.S. ENERGY CONSUMPTION

Highlights and Major Assumptions of a "Standard" Projection

As a point of departure, a "standard," or medium-range, projection of U.S. energy consumption over the next three decades will be examined.[24] A summary of the projection appears in table 13. The data represent a composite adaptation

---

[24]The projection is labeled "standard" because it shows that course of events judged to be the most reasonable one to assume, given the need for a *single* set of numbers. (Alterna-

Table 13. U.S. Consumption of Energy Resources: Total Consumption, Consumption in Electric Generation, and Consumption in Other Sectors, 1969, and Standard Projection, 1980–2000

	Total energy inputs						Utility electricity generated and distributed[a]	
	Coal	Natural gas	Petroleum	Hydro	Nuclear	Total gross energy inputs		
	(----------------------------- *trillion Btu* -----------------------------)						(*billion kwh*)	(*trillion Btu*)
Total energy inputs:								
1969	13,538	21,322	28,419	2,635	141	66,055	—	—
1980	17,935	27,329	37,266	3,145	9,470	95,145	—	—
1990	16,728	35,005	48,337	3,956	30,660	134,687	—	—
2000	26,185	47,097	59,671	5,498	51,563	190,014	—	—
In sectors other than electric utility generation:								
1969	6,082	17,710	26,816	—	—	50,608	—	—
1980	6,221	22,478	35,117	—	—	63,816	—	—
1990	2,774	29,424	46,253	—	—	78,452	—	—
2000	2,000	37,570	56,739	—	—	96,308	—	—
In electric utility generation:								
1969	7,456	3,612	1,603	2,635	141	15,447	1,442	4,920
1980	11,714	4,851	2,149	3,145	9,470	31,329	3,110	10,613
1990	13,954	5,581	2,084	3,956	30,660	56,235	5,920	20,198
2000	24,185	9,527	2,932	5,498	51,563	93,706	10,802	36,858

NOTES AND SOURCES: The table is a condensed version of the more complete sectoral and energy-source breakdown for historical years in table 4. Dashes indicate "not applicable."

The projections are adaptations based on several sources. The kwh data on electric generation through 1990 are based on preliminary materials from the FPC's 1970 *National Power Survey*, unpublished at the time of this writing. However, the share of total electricity assumed for nuclear power represents and Atomic Energy Commission projection, adopted by the FPC. For the decade 1990–2000, it was assumed that electric power consumption would decelerate from the 1980–90 annual rate of 6.6 percent to 6.2 percent.

For the sources of energy used to generate the projected levels of electricity, as well as for projected data on the nonutility sectors of energy demand, the author relied to a considerable extent on a preliminary and unpublished updating of an earlier study, Warren E. Morrison and Charles L. Reading, *An Energy Model of the United States, Featuring Energy Balances for the Years 1947 to 1965 and Projections and Forecasts to the Years 1980 and 2000*, U.S. Bureau of Mines Information Circular 8384 (1968). In adapting information from this document and from the USBM revisions, the author made a number of modifications to ensure a reasonable measure of consistency with the FPC electric power projections.

[a]The breakdown by major consuming sectors of electric utility deliveries follows:

	Billion kwh	Trillion btu
Household and commercial		
1969	786	2,681
1980	1,852	6,318
1990	3,316	11,314
2000	5,855	19,977
Industrial		
1969	650	2,219
1980	1,245	4,248
1990	2,580	8,802
2000	4,915	16,771
Transportation		
1969	6	20
1980	14	47
1990	24	81
2000	32	110

of long-term energy projections prepared by two U.S. government agencies deeply involved in energy matters—the Bureau of Mines and the Federal Power Commission (FPC).

For the period 1969–2000, growth of nationwide energy consumption in the United States is projected at the average annual rate of 3.5 percent—slightly above its long-term historic rate (since 1900) of 3.2 percent, though below the average figure of 4.3 percent recorded during the 1960s. The consumption of electric power alone (see table 14) is expected to continue rising far more rapidly. The average rate of increase to the year 2000 works out to 6.7 percent per year, with a somewhat higher rate during the current decade and deceleration to about 6.2 percent per annum during the last decade of the century.

As with total energy, the projected electricity growth rate falls somewhat below its rate of increase in recent years. The fact, however, that the consumption of electric power will continue to rise at a rate exceeding that for energy in its entirety means, of course, that the historical expansion in the share of primary energy consumption going into electricity will persist for the remainder of the twentieth century. As can be quickly calculated from table 14, the nearly one-fourth of primary energy consumption going into electric power generation in 1969 is expected to rise to one-third by 1980, to over 40 percent by 1990, and to essentially one-half by the year 2000. Some leveling off by that time may stem from the assumption that the types of energy demand that can be met in the form of electricity will, in the absence of technological breakthroughs (e.g., electric vehicles recharged by utility electricity), gradually slow their rate of growth—a tendency perhaps reinforced by future price increases for electricity, which many persons deem likely as a consequence of environmental and other factors.[25]

What are some of the additional basic assumptions underlying these projections? Both the FPC and the Bureau of Mines experts premise their forecasts on rates of increase of 4 percent per annum in GNP, 1.6 percent per year in population,[26] and 1.9 percent in the number of households. These rates of growth are assumed not to vary significantly from one decade to another over the next thirty years. It will be seen that the projected GNP rate exceeds the 3.5

---

tive assumptions are taken up later.) This applies particularly to the figures for the expected growth of electricity consumption derived from FPC studies. The FPC figures reflect the demographic, economic, and technological assumptions that guide the nation's utilities in planning future expansion of generating capacity to meet expected growth in electric power demand.

[25] The projected proportion of energy resources going into electric power would level off more were it not for the "standard" assumption that we can expect only modest overall improvements in the efficiency of electric generation.

[26] Even before examining alternative possibilities, it might be noted that an annual 1.6 percent population growth assumption is perhaps high, in light of recent U.S. experience. (Population growth averaged 1.3 percent yearly during 1960–69, 1.1 percent during

Table 14. U.S. Electric Utility Industry: Installed Generating Capacity Net Generation, and Equivalent Energy Resource Inputs, 1969 and Projected to 1980, 1990, and 2000

	Installed generating capacity (*megawatts*)	Net generation[a] (*billion kwh*)	Energy resource inputs[b] (*trillion Btu*)
1969: Fuel-burning plants	251,563	1,178.0	12,670
Nuclear plants	3,980	16.3	141
Hydropower plants[c]	57,069	250.1	2,635
Total	312,612	1,444.4	15,466
1980: Fuel-burning plants	396,000	1,890.8	18,714
Nuclear plants	147,000	902.0	9,470
Hydropower plants[c]	125,000	317.6	3,145
Total	668,000	3,110.4	31,329
1990: Fuel-burning plants	559,000	2,445.0	21,619
Nuclear plants	500,000	3,066.0	30,660
Hydropower plants[c]	201,000	408.5	3,956
Total	1,260,945	5,919.5	56,235
2000: Fuel-burning plants	984,270	4,311.1	36,644
Nuclear plants	955,550	5,859.4	51,563
Hydropower plants[c]	288,580	632.0	5,498
Total	2,228,400	10,802.5	93,706

[a]The plant factors used to translate generating capacity into net generation are as follows for 1969 and 2000:

	1969 actual	2000 projected
	(----------*percent*----------)	
Fuel-burning plants	53	50
Nuclear plants	47	70
Hydropower plants	50	25
Total	53	55

[b]Obtained by applying to net generation figures the average historical and projected heat rates for fuel-burning plants and theoretical heat rates for hydropower and nuclear plants, based on average Btu rate of fossil fuels per kwh at central electric stations. The implicit nationwide heat rate thus derived was 10,712 Btu/kwh in 1969 and is projected to fall to 8,670 Btu/kwh by 2000.

[c]Comprising conventional hydro and pumped storage, but also including small quantities of internal combustion and gas turbines.

SOURCES: See table 13.

1965–69.) Indeed, the FPC and Bureau of Mines 1.6 percent figure corresponds to a now outdated Bureau of the Census projection, which at the time represented the second highest of a range of Census population growth rate estimates, the highest being a 2 percent growth rate. In the more recent Census projection, the *highest* assumed growth rate is only 1.4 percent, while the second highest among four alternatives works out to a bit under 1.3 percent. If one were to assume that future population growth would somewhat more closely match recent trends, the effect on the projected rate of growth in energy consumption might be (via a somewhat lower GNP) to reduce that figure from 3.5 to, say, 3.2 percent, assuming that lower population growth would not affect per capita GNP growth.

percent growth foreseen for energy consumption, signifying a reversion to the relationship between energy and GNP that had persisted for much of the period since the 1920s but which, as noted earlier, was arrested around the mid-1960s. In their more specific aspects, the energy projections summarized in table 13 are "surprise-free" in most respects, novel in some others.

The major sectors of demand are all projected to contribute proportionally to future electricity growth—as they have in the past. Growth in residential electricity consumption—not identified separately in table 13—is expected to parallel overall electricity growth, that is, at an annual rate of 6.7 percent for the time span 1969-2000, as noted earlier. This implies a per capita growth of 5 percent yearly, or per household (essentially, residential customer) of 4.7 percent yearly. The average residential customer's electricity consumption would grow from 6,550 kwh in 1969 to 27,200 kwh in 2000. The FPC is not explicit— no one can be—on all types of residential demands reflected in this figure. Obviously, saturation factors far short of 100 percent today, e.g., color TV, could easily denote complete saturation by the year 2000 (generating largely a replacement and "multiple ownership" demand), while other still unanticipated needs and still undeveloped products remain to be established. The FPC is specific with regard to future expansions in electrically heated homes. The commission expects 40-50 percent of new residential construction during 1970-90 to involve electric heating, up from about 15 percent in the latter part of the 1960-70 decade. In this respect, the FPC cited the environmental virtues of replacing fossil-fueled residential furnaces by efficient central station electric generation embodying the latest anti-pollution devices. Finally, the figures in table 13 reflect a significant rise in the electric power share of energy requirements by industry.

Fundamental changes are in prospect in the mix of energy sources used to generate electricity. As can be seen from table 14, nuclear energy is expected to be the dominant source of electricity in the United States by 1990. The extent to which this nuclear power forecast is tied to a precise timetable for development and operation of advanced reactors and breeders is not specified by the FPC, although it may reasonably be assumed that there is a necessary connection.[27] Energy inputs into electric generation are estimated to rise to 94 quadrillion Btu by the year 2000; the inputs amounted to 15 quadrillion Btu in 1969. (The implicit annual rate of increase—6.1 percent—falls somewhat below the projected 6.7 percent growth for utility electric generation, owing to a modest

[27]Indeed, in a recent speech dealing with forecasts of nuclear generating capacity to the year 2000, Glenn T. Seaborg, then chairman of the Atomic Energy Commission, stated that about two-thirds of the nuclear capacity in 2000 is expected to be represented by fast breeder reactors, with light water and advanced reactors splitting the balance. (" The Plutonium Economy of the Future" [speech given at the Fourth International Conference on Plutonium and Other Actinides, Santa Fe, N.M., October 5, 1970].)

improvement factor expected in the thermal efficiency of conversion. If such an improvement materializes, as assumed, it would spell a resumption—albeit slight by past standards—of electric generation efficiency advances. As noted earlier, such advances have been notably absent in the last few years.) The percentage distribution of resource inputs into utility electric generation is as follows (based on absolute figures in table 13):

	Coal	Natural gas	Petroleum	Hydro-power	Nuclear	Total
1969	48.3	23.4	10.4	17.1	0.9	100.0
2000	25.8	10.2	3.1	5.9	55.0	100.0

Overall energy consumption is likewise assumed to undergo a sharp shift in its constituent fuel mix. To some extent, of course, this follows from the rising weight of electricity in total energy, both because of new uses for electricity and the substitution of electricity for direct fuel use, all accompanied by shifts in the fuels mix in the generation of electricity just mentioned. Shifts are also foreseen in nonelectric sectors of the economy (e.g., a marked decline in the relative importance of coal in industrial activity).[28] The percentage distribution of overall energy consumption (from table 13) is as follows:

	Coal	Natural Gas	Petroleum	Hydro-power	Nuclear	Total
1969	20.5	32.3	43.0	4.0	0.2	100.0
2000	13.8	24.8	31.4	2.9	27.1	100.0

The Projected Change in the Energy-GNP Relationship

As noted, in the standard projection, energy growth is somewhat below GNP growth, as has been the case for the greater part of the twentieth century. This represents the conventional approach to projecting energy consumption in the context of overall economic activity, and not only for the United States, but for numerous other highly industrialized nations as well. In this approach, even where sectoral, rather than merely aggregative relationships are examined, it is presupposed that factors operative throughout much of the present century (and some have been mentioned) would continue to exert a heavy weight on the growth of energy needs. It is also implicitly assumed that growth of an increasingly service-oriented society might entail proportionately fewer energy inputs. Yet, as noted in earlier parts of the discussion, energy consumption growth has outstripped the increase in GNP since about 1965 in a sufficiently striking

[28] In this standard forecast, no significant role is assigned to coal gasification or liquefaction—either of which could dramatically change the picture described here.

fashion to surprise those involved in projecting future energy requirements. While it is possible that what we have been witnessing in recent years—and table 6 may be instructive in this connection—may be a transitory phenomenon, it is also worth pondering whether there are here the seeds of a more enduring phenomenon.

One should at least allow for the possibility that there is a short-term aspect to the recent experience. Earlier post-World War II retardations in the nation's economic growth (particularly the recessions of 1954 and 1958) did not produce anywhere near a corresponding retardation in energy growth. Thus, it is conceivable that the demand for energy has become insensitive to short-term fluctuations in economic activity and that, with a resumption of full-employment growth of the economy, more traditional relationships will reappear.

Behavior of the transportation sector in the past few years presents something of a puzzle. As table 6 shows, this sector's 5.3 percent annual growth in energy demand during 1965 – 70 was an important factor in overall energy growth and was far above growth in any preceding five-year postwar period. Does this reflect the fact that patterns of suburbanization and the ways in which the American people spend their leisure time will increasingly cause transport requirements to grow rapidly relative to total economic growth? Was it related to the disproportionately rapid growth of high-powered cars? On the other hand, what part have the transportation-fuel needs associated with the Vietnam war played in this development? The subject requires further study.

What other economic aspects point to energy needs expanding either persistently faster or slower than the economy as a whole in the years ahead? The electric power branch of the energy industry is likely to exert a propulsive, rather than a moderating, impact in this respect. Of the total consumption of primary energy resources in this country, 25 percent now go into the utility sector for generation of electricity (up from under 20 percent in 1960). The well-publicized decadal doubling of electricity, amounting to a 7 percent annual growth rate, as yet shows no serious sign of abating. Sharply rising demands for air conditioning and electric residential heating have played a large role in mounting electricity needs during the 1960s, and air conditioning, at least, will no doubt continue to do so. In time, of course, saturation points are likely to be approached, both with respect to the acquisition of electrical appliances not formerly owned and the conversion to electricity (in homes as well as industry) in uses formerly dependent on fuels used directly. On the basis of FPC projections cited in table 14, however, such a state of affairs is still some time off. Even between 1980 and 1990 the FPC projects electric generation to increase at a rate of 6.6 percent per year. At that point—in the last decade of the century—the share of nationwide primary energy consumption accounted for by the electric utility sector would probably begin to approach one-half.

Growth in the use of electricity as a source of comfort heating is almost certain to lead to a faster growth of energy than the direct use of fuels in the home furnace, by virtue of the thermal losses in generating electric energy. This trend, however, may abort for a number of reasons, including the adoption of environmentally induced policies designed to discourage this development.

Beyond this, the growth of electricity is of critical importance because of the uncertain outlook for changes in electric-generating efficiency—that is, the "heat rate," which measures the Btu requirements to generate a kwh of electricity. Historically, as noted, there has been a persistent fall in the heat rate. For the postwar years as a whole, the heat rate declined by 1.4 percent annually; for 1955–65 only slightly less at 1.2 percent. Had the latter rate of improvement been sustained into 1970, overall energy consumption, due to lower input requirements by the utility sector, would have grown by only about 4.5 percent instead of the recorded figure of 5 percent. To be sure, this still would have exceeded GNP growth. The FPC, in its 1970 *National Power Survey*, foresaw for the future half the historic heat rate improvement (i.e., a decline of about 0.7 percent per year). The difference between even that relatively modest figure and *no* improvement is significant, however. While the FPC–Bureau of Mines composite projections given in tables 13 and 14 show that a postulated 4 percent rate of GNP growth is associated with a 3.5 percent rate for energy consumption and a 7 percent growth rate for electricity, with *no* further heat rate improvement (and other things remaining the same), energy requirements would grow just about as fast as GNP. Ultimately, of course, progressive improvements in thermal efficiency approach limits set by the thermodynamic principles associated with the nature of the equipment and the energy conversion process; but, since even today the actual efficiency approaches 40 percent in some plants, while the prevailing national average continues to be much closer to 30 percent, that constraint does not figure in calculations—at least from a technological point of view—for, say, two to three decades.

Whether, apart from electricity needs in particular, the pattern of economic life will evolve in a way that, compared with the past, is energy-intensive, energy-saving, or essentially neutral from an energy point of view is a question that again is obviously unanswerable. One prevalent viewpoint is that an economy shifting toward services and leisure-time activities would tend to slacken its energy needs. But as one thinks about the numerous services and activities associated with an affluent society (for example, airplane and automobile vacation trips and at least some of the more energy-demanding household conveniences) that notion may not withstand critical scrutiny.

Again, some insight might be gained from study of the past. In an intensive study covering the period 1939–54, Alan M. Strout sought to determine whether, at a given overall economic growth rate, shifting patterns of consump-

tion in the U.S. economy (i.e., toward more services and leisure) tended, on balance, to raise or lessen the demand for energy.[29] Using input-output analysis, Strout found that during this period—when the GNP increased by 92 percent—total energy use, expressed in Btu, grew by only 66 percent. Strout's major effort lay in breaking down this growth in energy, according to the relative importance of three factors: total growth in GNP, changes in the composition of final output (i.e., the familiar "bill of goods" in input-output parlance), and changes in input-output technical coefficients largely reflecting efficiency improvements, including those in the energy sector. Strout found that changes in the output mix between 1939 and 1954, holding technology constant, would have raised the level of energy consumption by 106 percent (as opposed to the actual increase of 66 percent); while, with technology changing, an unchanged (i.e., 1939) pattern of final demand would have increased energy consumption 53 percent.[30] In other words, changing final demand patterns between the two years were in the direction of more energy-intensive goods and services. Only because of technological change did energy use in fact grow less than GNP. Technological progress within the energy sector, such as improved thermal efficiency in electric generation, and in energy-using sectors (e.g., the effect of the replacement of steam by diesel railways) played a key part in this development.[31]

The study is, of course, now too dated to stand as the definitive word. On the other hand, nothing that has been reviewed here contradicts that finding. It would be prudent, therefore, not to rely on the growth of activities other than manufacturing—even the growth of leisure—to lead to a significant lowering of the growth of energy consumption relative to national output. If reduction in the rate of growth of energy consumption is conceived to be important, society may well have to devise means for bringing it about, either through price disincentives resulting from the internalization of its social costs or through other approaches. If, as a result of such factors, one had best assume that energy consumption growth will conform essentially to the growth pace of the nationwide economy, the projected energy consumption levels shown in table 13 might represent a point near the lower, rather than the midpoint, range of probability.

Some Alternative Possibilities

Considering the uncertainty surrounding the energy-GNP relationship, it follows that even if the future growth of the national economy could be pinpointed

[29] Alan M. Strout, "Technological Change and United States Energy Consumption, 1939–1954" (Ph.D. dissertation, University of Chicago, 1966).

[30] Ibid., table 33, pp. 144–45.

[31] Those acquainted with input-output will appreciate that output mix change and technical coefficient change cannot be precisely separated, largely because of aggregation problems.

fairly precisely, there would still be a great deal that would be unknown about what this would portend for energy use. With the assumed independent variables (such as GNP, population, and industrial production) *themselves* subject to considerable uncertainty, the course of future energy consumption may be still more problematical.

Thus, based on the projected 3.5 percent annual growth rate of energy consumption and an assumed rate of 4 percent in GNP growth and 1.6 percent in population, total energy consumption was projected as rising from 66 quadrillion Btu in 1969 to a level of 190 quadrillion by 2000—a nearly threefold increase. In the latest Bureau of the Census population projections,[32] the highest rate postulated to 2000 is "only" 1.4 percent per year (321 million people by 2000), while the midpoint in the Census range of four alternatives works out to 1.2 percent (291 million people). If a 1.2 percent rate of growth, conforming to the fertility experience of recent years, were to materialize and were ultimately to slow down the rate of labor force growth, it might mean a GNP growth rate of, say, 3.7–3.8 percent. Under relationships otherwise prevailing in the standard forecast, energy growth might then be reduced to 3.2 percent, suggesting a level of consumption by 2000 of 175 quadrillion Btu instead of 190 quadrillion. This presupposes no effect on rates of increase in output per man (productivity)—itself in part sustained, of course, by continued growth of energy supplies per worker.

Note how, under these assumptions, a 25 percent reduction in the population growth rate yields a less than 10 percent reduction in the energy growth rate—the reason being, of course, that neither GNP per person nor energy per person is, by assumption, regarded as being affected thereby. The point would be even more dramatically illustrated with respect to electricity. For if the same share of total energy would go to electric utility generation in the reduced growth consumption case as in the standard forecast (see table 14), it would mean electric power output of 9.7 trillion kwh instead of the 10.8 trillion kwh shown in table 13, or an average annual growth rate of 6.3 percent rather than 6.7 percent (only a 6 percent reduction in the growth rate). The example underscores what has by now perhaps become a labored point: that growth in total electric power demand is to a considerable extent the intractable consequence of factors (per capita consumption, economic growth, tastes, and so on)[33] going well beyond demographic explanations.

Of course, it is quite conceivable that GNP growth may be held in check even more, not only because of low population growth, but also because of decelerated growth in output per capita, brought on by a slower-than-expected

[32] See U.S. Bureau of the Census, *Statistical Abstract, 1970*, p. 6.

[33] One might note that successive models of a given appliance are frequently improved in a way requiring higher wattage.

productivity advance. This is not the place to speculate upon the variety of elements bringing about such a situation; these could include changed values and policies (both public and private) that would subordinate growth, at least as traditionally reckoned, to other considerations.[34] In any case, a 3 percent GNP growth rate over the long run, comprising 1.2 percent yearly population growth coupled with an increase of 1.8 percent in GNP per head (the postwar rate averaged out to 2.3 percent) is not that difficult to imagine. In that event, energy consumption growth of, say, 2.6 percent per annum would lead to a level of 146 quadrillion Btu in energy consumption by 2000 and, given the other projected relationships, electric power deliveries of 8.3 trillion kwh, representing a growth rate of 5.8 percent per annum.

Let us, for symmetry, work through the implications of a faster-than-4 percent GNP growth rate. A 4.5 percent average annual increase in GNP (comprising a 2.8 percent growth rate in output per head and 1.7 percent in population—today probably regarded as a high rate) would produce by the year 2000:

1. Energy consumption of 216 quadrillion Btu, representing yearly growth of 3.9 percent.
2. Electricity consumption of 12.3 trillion kwh, representing yearly growth of 7.2 percent.

The preceding growth-rate alternatives are summarized below:

	Energy consumption in 2000	
Case	Quadrillion BTU	Average annual percentage growth rate from 1969
Standard, or medium-range, projection; assuming 4 percent GNP growth rate	190	3.5
Somewhat lower (3.7-3.8 percent GNP growth rate) economic growth assumption	175	3.2
Low (3 percent) GNP growth rate	146	2.6
High (4.5 percent) GNP growth rate	216	3.9

[34] Slower productivity advance could presumably result from slower growth in energy supplies provided each worker.

Another group of alternatives relates both to the effect of various assumed developments in technology and efficiency and to the form in which energy is desired by ultimate consumers. (Here energy flows are considered at a *given* level of GNP—i.e., the assumed 4 percent growth rate.) "Form" means essentially electrical energy versus fuels consumed directly (e.g., electrically heated homes versus gas-fired furnaces).[35] The reader will appreciate that the form in which energy is provided is partially dependent on the technological advances assumed. That is, the circumstances under which vastly higher proportions of primary energy would be in the form of electricity would also be those under which great forward strides in technology would make such a development economically feasible. This is apparent from the different possibilities that were considered and that are summarized in table 15. Except for cases 2 and 3, which may be viewed within a context of continued evolutionary change, the different situations whose effect on levels of energy consumption is explored in the table are based on the supposition that there will be either some major breakthrough in the technology and economics of energy conversion (e.g., the gas-fired fuel cell) or some fairly radical departure from evolving trends and patterns—perhaps an all-electric economy based on conventional electricity generation techniques.

The variations in the projected quantity of primary energy resources consumed by the year 2000 within this range of alternatives are not insignificant. The highest amount estimated, in case 7, is over 80 percent above that for case 6, the lowest energy-consuming model hypothesized. This high model is 27 percent above the standard case, while the low model is 30 percent below.

PROSPECTIVE TRENDS IN WORLDWIDE ENERGY CONSUMPTION

For a projection of the estimated growth in world energy consumption over the next 10- and 30-year periods, a number of different forecasts and analyses have been taken into account, and, as in the earlier case of the U.S. standard projection, a composite picture of what might be regarded as the medium-range worldwide outlook has been made. The principal sources that were consulted

---

[35] The third form (energy resources—essentially petroleum—desired for raw material nonfuel and nonpower uses), while gradually increasing as a share of nationwide energy consumption, is not likely to vary its growth in a manner greatly altering the quantity of primary energy sources consumed from the levels that would prevail otherwise. Rather surprisingly, in fact, in Warren E. Morrison and Charles L. Readling, *An Energy Model of the United States, Featuring Energy Balances for the Years 1947 to 1965 and Projections and Forecasts to the Years 1980 and 2000*, U.S. Bureau of Mines Information Circular 8384 (1968), pp. 114–15, the share of total energy consumption for the year 2000 ascribed to nonfuel and power uses is barely higher than that in 1969. As a projected share of U.S. petroleum consumption *alone*, however, it rises from 10 percent in recent years to 17 percent. It is possible, however, that a growing volume of energy sources used as raw materials may have significant environmental repercussions, relating to the use and disposition of products in which they are embodied.

Table 15. Projected Energy Consumption Levels and Growth Rates Under Alternative Technological Assumptions

Case	Energy consumption in 2000 under assumed 4 percent GNP growth rate	
	Quadrillion Btu	Average annual percentage growth rate from 1969
1. Standard or medium-range projection	190	3.5
2. Rapid improvements in electric generating efficiency (1.5 percent annual decline in heat rate)	170	3.1
3. No change in electric generating efficiency (1969 heat rate prevails)	210	3.9
4. Single fuel (natural gas) economy; transportation sector features electric vehicles recharged by utilities	205	3.8
5. Single fuel (natural gas) economy; all-electric transportation sector as in preceding case; energy inputs into central power stations via hydrocarbon-air fuel cells	186½	3.4
6. No purchased utility electricity; sectoral needs (including fuel cell-powered vehicles) supplied by natural gas-fired hydrocarbon-air fuel cells	133	2.3
7. All-electric economy, based on utility power plants, fueled by conventional sources, hydro, and nuclear	241	4.3
8. All-electric economy, based on utility power plants, fueled by natural-gas hydrocarbon-air fuel cells; transportation sector features battery electric vehicle system recharged by utility power	211	3.8
9. All-electric, all-coal economy with MHD technology of centrally operated utility power plants	190	3.5

and the broad underlying assumptions are described in some detail in the notes to table 16.

One basic premise is that worldwide population growth will continue to hover around 2 percent per annum, with some deceleration assumed toward the end of the century. If, as with the U.S. projections, this produces a somewhat exaggerated picture of future energy demand, in the context of data assembled for the purpose of evaluating environmental consequences, erring on the side of overstating rather than understating future consumption might be entirely prudent.

Total world energy consumption is projected at slightly over 5 percent per year during the next decade, with a 4.5 percent rate assumed thereafter. (The

rate during the 1960s was approximately 5.5 percent per year.) Electricity consumption is assumed to continue increasing very fast around the world—sufficiently so that by the year 2000 the average electricity consumption per capita in areas outside the United States would approximate the U.S. per capita level achieved in the late 1950s. Overall energy consumption per capita outside the United States, however, would only approach the U.S. level at the beginning of the present century. A bit over one-third of primary energy consumption outside the United States would be destined to go into electric generation; a share of nearly 50 percent is projected for the United States. This suggests that any concern over the possibility of having overstated future worldwide energy growth may be misplaced, the more important issue being whether even this projected level is compatible with reasonable social stability throughout the world.

No attempt has been made here, however, to project the geographic distribution of world energy consumption all the way to the end of the century. Some idea about the general drift of regional changes may be gotten from table 17, in which energy consumption is projected for major parts of the world to 1980.[36] Not surprisingly, rising shares of worldwide energy consumption are most markedly indicated for the developing areas, while modestly declining proportions seem likely for the most advanced areas.

What are the prospects for the different energy sources for the remainder of the twentieth century? Table 16 shows that a further substantial reduction in the proportion of coal in world energy consumption is assumed; at least that is the case barring a large-scale conversion of coal to pipeline gas and gasoline—a development whose technological feasibility has been demonstrated but whose economics remain in doubt.[37] On the basis of a range of estimates contstructed by the U.N. Economic Commission for Europe,[38] the percentage importance of coal is projected to fall particularly sharply during the next decade—from one-third of world energy consumption in 1968 to one-fifth by 1980. Beyond 1980 the projected decline in the share of coal in total energy is dampened, and, in fact, coal is assumed to revert to a phase of reasonable absolute growth because of practical limits to the extent to which coal can continue to be replaced. For example, steelmaking will probably be an important market for coal for years to come.

[36] The table was adapted from a study in which attention was directed to future trends in energy and GNP in specific regions. (See Sam H. Schurr, Paul T. Homan, and associates, *Middle Eastern Oil and the Western World: Prospects and Problems* [New York: American Elsevier, 1971].)

[37] In any comprehensive projection effort, which this paper does not purport to be, the analyst should, however, consider as a serious scenario the possibility that coal gasification will be economically feasible long before the year 2000 in the United States and may likely be in operation in other countries of the world by that time.

[38] U.N., *Symposium on the Future Role of Coal in the National and World Economies*, Warsaw, September 1969, ST/ECE/COAL/47 (March 9, 1970), pp. 19–21.

Table 16. Energy Consumption, Electricity Consumption, and Population: Projections of Selected Data, United States and World, 1968, 1980, 2000

A. United States

	Unit	1968		1980		2000	
Energy consumption							
Coal	Percent and trillion Btu	21.3%	13,329	18.8%	17,935	13.8%	26,185
Oil	Percent and trillion Btu	43.3	27,052	39.2	37,266	31.4	59,671
Natural gas	Percent and trillion Btu	31.3	19,564	28.7	27,329	24.8	47,097
Hydro	Percent and trillion Btu	3.8	2,357	3.3	3,145	2.9	5,498
Nuclear	Percent and trillion Btu	0.2	130	10.0	9,470	27.1	51,563
Total	Percent and trillion Btu	100.0	62,432	100.0	95,145	100.0	190,014
Population	Million	201.2		243.4		334.4	
Energy consumption per capita	Million Btu	310.3		390.9		568.2	
Electric generating capacity	Mw	310,125		668,000		2,228,400	
Of which: nuclear	Percent and Mw	0.9%	2,817	22.0%	147,000	42.9%	955,550
Electric generation	Billion Kwh	1,434.9		3,110.4		10,802.5	
Of which: nuclear	Percent and billion Kwh	0.9%	12.5	29.0%	902.0	54.2%	5,859.4
Electric generation per capita	Kwh	7,133		12,790		32,300	
Resource input equivalent of electric generation	Trillion Btu	14,494		31,329		93,706	
Share of energy consumption	Percent	23.2%		32.9%		49.3%	

Table 16.) (Continued)

	Unit	1968		1980		2000	
		B. Rest of World					
Energy consumption							
Coal	Percent and trillion Btu	39.9%	50,841	20.4%	50,996	11.5%	73,560
Oil	Percent and trillion Btu	42.7	54,360	52.3	130,371	47.8	306,613
Natural gas	Percent and trillion Btu	9.6	12,246	16.0	39,879	16.0	102,521
Hydro	Percent and trillion Btu	7.4	9,484	6.6	16,479	6.0	38,332
Nuclear	Percent and trillion Btu	0.3	374	4.7	11,787	18.7	120,169
Total	Percent and trillion Btu	100.0	127,305	100.0	249,512	100.0	641,195
Population	Million	3,283.3		4,175.6		6,104.6	
Energy consumption per capita	Million Btu	38.8		59.8		105.0	
Electric generating capacity	Mw	662,166		1,520,000		5,520,600	
Of which: nuclear	Percent and Mw	1.4%	9,223	12.0%	183,000	40.3%	2,227,450
Electric generation	Billion Kwh	2,768.9		6,790.8		26,802.9	
Of which: nuclear	Percent and billion Kwh	1.4%	37.4	16.5%	1,122.9	50.9%	13,655.6
Electric generation per capita	Kwh	842		1,629		4,382	
Resource input equivalent of electric generation	Trillion Btu	27,969		67,888		232,265	
Share of energy consumption	Percent	22.0%		27.2%		36.2%	

Table 16. (Continued)

C. World

	Unit	1968		1980		2000	
Energy consumption							
Coal	Percent and trillion Btu	33.8%	64,170	20.0%	68,931	12.0%	99,745
Oil	Percent and trillion Btu	42.9	81,412	48.6	167,637	44.1	366,284
Natural gas	Percent and trillion Btu	16.8	31,810	19.5	67,208	18.0	149,618
Hydro	Percent and trillion Btu	6.2	11,841	5.7	19,624	5.3	43,830
Nuclear	Percent and trillion Btu	0.3	504	6.2	21,257	20.7	171,732
Total	Percent and trillion Btu	100.0	189,737	100.0	344,657	100.0	831,209
Population	Million	3,484.5		4,419.0		6,439.0	
Energy consumption per capita	Million Btu	54.5		78.0		129.1	
Electric generating capacity	Mw	972,291		2,188,000		7,749,000	
Of which: nuclear	Percent and Mw	1.2%	12,040	15.1%	330,000	41.1%	3,183,000
Electric generation	Billion Kwh	4,203.8		9,901.2		37,605.4	
Of which: nuclear	Percent and billion Kwh	1.2%	49.9	20.5%	2,024.9	51.9%	19,515.0
Electric generation per capita	Kwh	1,207		2,238		5,840	
Resource input equivalent of electric generation	Trillion Btu	42,463		99,217		325,971	
Share of energy consumption	Percent	22.4%		28.8%		39.2%	

NOTES AND SOURCES: Data for 1968 from tables 9 and 12, supplemented by statistics on electric generation and capacity from U.N., *Statistical Yearbook, 1969*, and *World Energy Supplies*, Series J, no. 13 (1970); FPC, *World Power Data*, selected issues; and Joel Darmstadter and associates, *Energy in the World Economy: A Statistical Review of Trends in Output, Trade, and Consumption Since 1925* (Johns Hopkins Press for Resources for the Future, 1971). World nuclear generation excludes Soviet data. Soviet nuclear generation *is* included in total electric generation, and Soviet nuclear *capacity* is included in worldwide nuclear capacity.

U.S. projections are from tables 13 and 14.

World projections were constructed on the basis of estimates and analyses contained in a number of studies—modified where considered appropriate. The principal sources and considerations in deriving the worldwide projections are itemized below:

1. World population growth is assumed at 2 percent annually through 1980 and at 1.9 percent during 1980–2000. These rates are slightly below recent U.N. estimates shown in U.N. Economic and Social Council, *Demographic Aspects of Economic Development*, E/CN.9/AC.11/11.3 (June 1, 1970).

2. World energy consumption to 1980 is projected at 5.1 percent per annum. A similar rate was built up on the basis of specific region-by-region energy-GNP analysis in Sam H. Schurr, Paul T. Homan, and associates, *Middle Eastern Oil and the Western World: Prospects and Problems* (New York: American Elsevier, 1971). This is also the approximate rate of growth expected by U.N. experts in U.N., *Symposium on the Future Role of Coal in the National and World Economies*, Warsaw, September 1969, ST/ECE/COAL/47 (March 9, 1970), pp. 18–19. A 4.5 percent rate of growth is postulated for the period after 1980.

3. World coal consumption to 1980 follows the projected trends suggested by the Warsaw symposium (pp. 19–21), though adjusted somewhat and shifted to a slightly different conceptual base in the present paper. Beyond 1980, the judgment has been made that coal's loss of markets will be approaching a floor determined by diminishing opportunities for substitution by other fuels. Essentially, this means growth conforming to the demand for coking coal by the steel industry. Hence, the share of coal in energy consumption after 1980, though continuing to decline, will do so at a somewhat slower pace; and its absolute rate of increase, though markedly below that of total energy, will register reasonable gains after 1980.

4. World electricity consumption is assumed to grow at 7.4 percent per annum during 1968–1980; 7 percent, 1980–1990; and 6.8 percent, 1990–2000. These progressively decelerating rates are judgmentally arrived at. Generating capacity conforming to those projected levels of consumption is computed using U.S. plant factors assumed for those years.

5. World nuclear capacity is derived from International Atomic Energy Agency projections, cited in IAEA's *Bulletin*, vol. 12, no. 5 (1970), p. 12. There it is estimated that nuclear generating capacity will reach 350,000 mw in 1980 and thereafter grow at 13 percent per annum, reaching 4.3 million mw by 2000. Considering the many imponderables involved—especially the widespread adoption of nuclear electricity by developing economies, which is assumed in the IAEA forecast—the author is inclined to be more conservative in his expectations, though still perhaps highly optimistic. It is assumed that there will be 330,000 mw of capacity by 1980 and a capacity growth rate of 12 percent per annum. Projected U.S. nuclear plant factors are assumed.

6. The resource-input equivalents of total and nuclear generation use the same factors as the U.S. projections—i.e., the same efficiency improvements (heat rate declines) are assumed. (This calculation also enables the filling in of the projected nuclear share of total primary energy consumption: 6 percent in 1980 and 12 percent by 2000.)

7. In the projected hydro share of primary energy consumption, the assumption is 4.3 percent per annum growth to 1980—as adopted from Schurr, Homan, and associates (with allowance for recent trends and adjusted for the somewhat different definitions employed in the present paper). The oil and gas shares in 2000 are judgmental, the assumption being that both shares would fall (along with coal) as offsets to the rising nuclear proportion, but that less relative decline would be experienced by gas, given its as yet unexploited potential in numerous areas and its environmental attractions. The resulting shares agree in general with those in K. D. Fischer (head, Economic Research Division, Esso A.G.), "Energie für das 3 Jahrtausend—Prognosen und Aussichten" (paper presented at a conference of journalists, Hamburg, Germany, October 12–14, 1969, mimeo.).

8. The rest-of-world data represent subtraction of the U.S. figure from worldwide totals.

Table 17. Distribution of World Energy Consumption, by Major Regions, 1968, and Projected, 1980

	1968		1980	
	Trillion Btu	Percent	Trillion Btu	Percent
North America	68,594	36.2	106,124	30.8
Canada	6,162	3.2	10,979	3.2
United States	62,432	32.9	95,145	27.6
Western Europe	41,584	21.9	64,354	18.7
Oceania	2,240	1.2	3,743	1.1
Latin America	8,034	4.2	18,771	5.4
Asia (excl. Communist)	16,757	8.8	38,666	11.2
Japan	8,691	4.6	17,715	5.1
Other Asia	8,066	4.3	20,951	6.1
Africa	3,343	1.8	7,236	2.1
U.S.S.R. and Communist Eastern Europe	39,843	21.0	80,073	23.2
U.S.S.R.	28,628	15.1	60,611	17.6
Communist Eastern Europe	11,215	5.9	19,462	5.6
Communist Asia	9,342	4.9	25,690	7.5
World	189,737	100.0	344,657	100.0

SOURCES: Data for 1968 are from tables 9 and 10. Projections for 1980: United States, from table 12; world total from table 16. Regional distribution adapted from Sam H. Schurr, Paul T. Homan, and associates, *Middle Eastern Oil and the Western World*: *Prospects and Problems* (New York: American Elsevier, 1971)—with allowance for recent trends and adjusted for the somewhat different definitions employed in the present paper.

The most dramatically increasing share of projected world energy consumption to 1980 is taken by nuclear energy—rising from a mere three-tenths of 1 percent in 1968 to over 6 percent in 1980. The underlying 330,000 megawatts (mw) of 1980 nuclear capacity (about 15 percent of worldwide electric-generating capacity) on which this figure is based is a conservative version of the International Atomic Energy Agency (IAEA) forecast of 350,000 mw of capacity;[39] and even so, at this point in time it rests a good deal more on informed speculation and faith than on firmly anchored judgments. It goes without saying that the further projected rise of nuclear energy to 20 percent of world energy consumption (representing an installed capacity of over 3 million mw—or 52 percent of estimated total electric generating capacity) by the end of the century is compounded of still greater uncertainty. The IAEA's underlying assumption is that "nuclear power would dominate the market for new power plants in advanced countries by 1980 and almost everywhere else by 1990."[40]

[39] See IAEA *Bulletin*, vol. 12, no. 5 (1970), p. 12.

[40] Ibid. Elsewhere, however, Sigvard Eklund, director general of IAEA, has underscored the uncertainty in such estimates by indicating that even a "modest" nuclear target of

No attempt will be made here to question the reasonableness of this judgment or to try and spin out the implications of the assumption for different parts of the world. Acceptance of the assumptions for the projected role of coal and nuclear in total energy consumption, however, is consistent with shares for oil and natural gas that do not appear to be unreasonable in the light of past trends and of industrial and governmental assessments of the future outlook. To 1980 (table 16), oil and gas are both projected to increase their shares of world energy consumption. Oil is estimated to rise from 43 percent in 1968 to 49 percent in 1980, or from 81 quadrillion Btu (approximately 2 billion metric tons or nearly 40 million barrels per day) to a level of 168 quadrillion Btu (4 billion tons or 80 million barrels per day)—representing an average annual rate of increase of 6 percent. Oil consumption growth may be expected to reflect a persistent substitution for coal in uses and areas where, until recently, coal has continued to figure significantly. In addition, as suggested earlier, the potential market for automotive transport outside the United States remains enormous, with the impact of motorization—particularly in the less-urbanized portions of developing areas—scarcely having been felt as yet.[41]

The share of natural gas in world energy consumption is projected to grow from 17 percent in 1968 (32 quadrillion Btu, or 875 billion cubic meters) to about 20 percent in 1980 (67 quadrillion Btu, or 1.8 trillion cubic meters)—a yearly growth rate of close to 6.5 percent. The attractiveness of natural gas as a "clean" energy source, coupled with the growth of new supplies, in such disparate areas as the North Sea, Australia, and Siberia, and the feasibility (only now beginning to be realized) of transporting liquefied natural gas by specially designed tankers, with subsequent reformation to the gaseous state, should ensure this growing market.

Beyond 1980 both oil and gas (see table 16) are projected as slightly falling shares of total energy consumption, since it is assumed that nuclear power will have taken strong hold by then. Nevertheless, consumption of both fuels may be expected to record significant absolute growth in the closing decades of the century.

SOME ENVIRONMENTAL CONCERNS

The prospect of a world that may well contain 6.5 billion people by the year 2000, that is apt to consume about 4.5 times its present level of basic energy

---

330,000 mw by 1980 would imply, for developing countries, the outlay of foreign exchange resources of $3 billion to $4 billion during 1970-80. "It is clear that unless adequate capital is available from the industrial countries and international financing organizations, even this modest target will not be achieved." (From a speech to the U.N. Economic and Social Council, quoted in IAEA *Bulletin*, vol. 12, no. 4 [1970], p. 3.)

[41] See "Motorization of the Developing World," *Petroleum Press Service*, June 1970, pp. 215-16.

resources, that may register a rise in total electric-generating capacity by a factor of eight (with the portion represented by nuclear facilities increasing by a far greater multiple), and that may be forced to handle the traffic of over 1 billion automobiles[42] raises sober questions about the assimilative capacity of water, land, atmosphere, and other fixed, or at least relatively inelastic, endowments to cope with the environmental consequences posed by such trends. Whether human institutions will evolve the necessary flexibility to deal with these problems is an additional and major element. The fact—perhaps paradoxical—that our ability to deal with numerous *other* environmental problems (e.g., recycling and waste disposal) may hinge to an increasing extent on the very use of energy only makes the question more complex. Yet it is a sign of progress that the question is now at last being addressed. Looking back at energy projections efforts of only a few years ago, one realizes the extent to which environmental issues were then at best a subordinate component of the projections exercise, but these issues have become urgent within a few years. This recognition means that henceforth man's harnessing and use of energy resources must be judged not merely in terms of the support these resources give to higher real income and increased population, as has traditionally been the case; it must be demonstrated as well that the environmental consequences of energy use are susceptible of being managed within socially defined tolerances.

The following pages contain a highly abbreviated checklist of some of the environmental concerns that, as a minimum, deserve consideration in any balanced perspective on likely or desirable trends and patterns in energy use. Only within a broad context can the trade-offs and the costs and benefits of alternative approaches to energy problems be wisely perceived and policy be rationally formulated. As it is, all too often a restricted viewpoint highlights a particular form of environmental damage only to ignore the consequences of the implied alternative: an electric car may minimize gasoline engine emissions only to compound the problem of central electric generating plants. The fact is that, as noted at the outset of this paper, virtually every facet of energy production, conversion, delivery, and use has some significant environmental ramification that must be brought into account. It is this pervasive presence of environmental implications that will be highlighted in what follows. The treatment will be brief and is intended to call attention to problems rather than to detail their essence.

Primary Energy Production

Fossil Fuels. As estimated in table 16, fossil fuels will continue to account for the preponderant share of energy consumption in the United States and throughout the world for the remainder of this century, despite the rapidly rising share of nuclear energy. Certain aspects of coal and petroleum production

[42] In recent years, there have been less than 200 million automobiles.

cause special environmental concern. Coal mining continues to be an occupation that leaves the worker disproportionately susceptible to bodily injury, accidental death, and health hazards. Although productivity has advanced in U.S. mines, there has not been a significant reduction in injury rates.[43]

Coal mining exacts its toll on land and water as well. Over one-third of U.S. coal production in recent years has been mined by stripping; the proportion has, if anything, been rising. In the absence of land reclamation, which is slowly beginning to be practiced under rising pressure from conservationists, public authorities, and citizens, the effects of surface mining are accumulated overburden, a scarred landscape, and water pollution from both acid mine drainage and erosion.

In addition, underground coal mining "can cause subsidence unless the mining systems are designed to prevent deterioration and failure of abandoned mine pillars. Underground fires may weaken or destroy coal pillars that support the surface, causing subsidence with consequent damage to surface structures. An additional threat is the possible collapse of buildings and opening of surface fissures and potholes."[44]

Irrespective of mining method, coal preparation (applicable to 62 percent of the coal mined in the United States and undertaken to improve the quality of the coal) produces large quantities of wastes that, if not returned to the mine, pile up in open slag heaps. At times these may ignite. They may also contaminate nearby streams.[45]

In recent years, oil pollution of the seas has become a serious aspect of crude oil production. The Santa Barbara offshore oil leak in 1969 and the more recent blowouts in the Gulf of Mexico are among the more dramatic oil spills.[46] Less publicized are the seepages and the hundreds of thousands of small leaks with unknown consequences over time. Scientists appear to be uncertain about the long-term and low-level effects of crude oil pollution on aquatic ecology and on human and animal health. There is uncertainty also about the most effective way to accelerate the dissipation or recovery of oil spillage. Concern over the dangers and potential environmental effects of oil spillage are bound to increase as more oil originates in offshore fields, as more of it is transported across the oceans,

[43] Compare, for example, the record of growth in output per man-day with that in injury per man-hour, shown in U.S. Bureau of Mines, *Minerals Yearbook, 1968* (1970), vol. I–II, pp. 137, 301.

[44] G. Alex Mills, Harry Perry, and Harry Johnson, "Management of Fuels to Satisfy Environmental Criteria," in *Problems and Issues of a National Materials Policy*, Senate Committee on Public Works, 91 Cong. 2 sess. (1970), p. 144.

[45] Ibid.

[46] In 1969 over 1,000 oil spills of more than 100 barrels each were reported in U.S. waters, over one-half coming from vessels and about one-third involving pipelines, oil terminals, and bulk storage facilities. (Council on Environmental Quality, *Environmental Quality*, First Annual Report [August 1970], p. 38.)

and as the tankers carrying it grow to enormous size with diminished maneuverability. (See "Energy Transport" section below.)

A few statistics illustrate the dimension of these trends. It is estimated that, at the beginning of 1970, 7 million barrels of oil a day, or 17 percent of the world's output, came from offshore wells. This represented an increase of 175 percent over a period of only four years.[47] Projections of future trends vary, but, on the basis of a range of estimates,[48] one might reasonably—perhaps even conservatively—expect that about 30 percent of world oil output might be from offshore sources in 1980, with the proportion rising to at least 40 percent by the year 2000. If worldwide oil production rose to 80 million barrels per day in 1980 and to about 180 million barrels per day in 2000 (converted from the Btu estimates in table 16), this would mean 25 million barrels per day of worldwide offshore production in 1980 and about 70 million barrels per day in 2000. In other words, *offshore* production in 2000 might be 75 percent higher than the 40 million barrels per day of *total* world oil output in recent years.

Oil production operations on land also have environmental effects, although here the control of damage is comparatively well in hand. The environmental aspects of land operations include the effects of blowouts or other accidents in oil well drilling and production, as well as the disposal of waste water contaminated, for example, by the discharge of oilfield brines. At the petroleum-processing stage, the problems are somewhat more severe, for refinery operations involve considerable combustion and, therefore, the emission of pollutants, including sulfur oxides, hydrocarbons, particulates, and waste heat. In addition, waste water treatment is generally only partially complete, leading to at least some discharge of various detrimental substances into water courses. As pressure mounts for more jet fuel and higher-octane gasoline from each barrel of crude oil, more refining processes are added and more residual wastes are generated.

If and when conventional fossil fuels begin to be supplanted by synthetic liquid fuels from the vast store of U.S. oil shale, significant environmental problems will have to be dealt with, for the production process makes a large claim on water and generates enormous wastes. Underground fracturing by nuclear explosions presents a possible environmental problem of its own. That would also be true of nuclear-assisted freeing and extraction of trapped natural gas formations.

Hydroelectricity. Hydroelectricity is a quantitatively minor source of primary energy in the United States and in most industrially advanced countries, and the outlook is for its relative importance to decline, even allowing for the growing relative importance of pumped storage. Its potentiality is greater in the less-developed regions.

[47] *Oil and Gas Journal*, March 16, 1970, p. 123.
[48] Ibid., pp. 126-27.

From an environmental standpoint, hydro offers the virtues of emitting no waste heat or contaminants. But the installations and the impounded water may intrude into natural, often spectacular, scenery. In addition, the modification of streamflow characteristics and other changes that accompany a major hydro project may be a cause of significant disruption of aquatic ecology and possibly even a threat to human health in some instances. Finally, the remoteness of hydro sites from load centers entails the presence of electric transmission lines cutting a long-distance swath across an otherwise unspoiled terrain.

Nuclear Fuels. Open-pit and underground uranium mining creates problems of waste accumulation and injury to the landface that are similar to those of coal mining. But the quantities of uranium involved at present are slight by coal-mining standards and will be slight even with the increase of nuclear capacity over the next several decades.

More important are the problems of radioactive contamination during the mining and processing of uranium ores. The uranium ore found in nature is slightly radioactive, emitting a radioactive gas (radon) from exposed rock surfaces. The gas can be ingested by the lungs of underground miners whose "excess incidence of lung cancer . . . is believed to be induced by their exposure to radiation from the radioactive decay of the radon daughters in their lungs."[49]

In the milling process for the recovery of uranium oxide there is some risk of pollution of water supplies by radioactive constituents in liquid effluents. Safeguards are provided by impounding such effluents or by discharging them into streams at controlled rates.[50] The production of uranium concentrates also results in accumulated piles of uranium mill tailings whose finer radium-containing particles can be carried away by wind and rain.

Energy Transport

Tankers. The delivery of energy to ultimate users and its shipment at intermediate stages of the production-consumption chain poses numerous environmental hazards. The possible magnitude of the environmental threat from ocean transport oil spillage is dramatized by such events as the grounding of the *Torrey Canyon* in 1967. In recent years some 60 percent of the oil consumed in the world has involved ocean transport among major producing-consuming regions.[51] About 24 million barrels per day represented interarea ocean movement in 1968; and the amounts for 1980 and 2000 may rise to 48 million barrels per day and 105 million barrels per day respectively.

---

[49]*Economy, Energy, and the Environment*, p. 67.

[50]Mills, Perry, and Johnson, "Management of Fuels," p. 145.

[51]U.S. Department of the Interior, Office of Oil and Gas, *1968 Petroleum Supply and Demand* (1970), pp. 10–11.

The prospect is for this volume of oil to be moved in tankers of ever-increasing size. In 1968 the worldwide average size of oil tankers was 35,000 deadweight tons (dwt); oil tankers under construction in 1969 averaged 145,000 dwt per ship, and 80 percent of the tonnage was for ships of 205,000 dwt and over.[52] With the increased size of tankers, the expanding volume of oil consumption is likely to be achieved with a smaller number of ships in service. Yet much remains to be learned about the structural and operating properties of these huge ships; for example, how maneuverability (vital in collision avoidance) may have decreased as the size of oil tankers has increased.[53]

Although now a minor factor in international energy flows, liquefied natural gas (LNG) shipments promise to expand significantly in the years ahead. LNG tankers, which carry gas refrigerated at a temperature of -161°C. and compressed into a liquid at one-six-hundredths of its normal volume, have had operating experience for less than a decade. The economics of LNG, heavily influenced by liquefaction and re-gasification costs, are such that there are strong pressures to minimize transport costs. The search for optimum design characteristics of LNG tankers is still very much under way. It is thus too early to assess the hazards of this essentially novel form of energy transport. Recent experimentation by the Bureau of Mines on behalf of the U.S. Coast Guard has disclosed the possibility that sudden contact between water and supercold LNG during spillage may produce explosions. During a test, "rapid spillage of 70 pounds LNG onto water produced an explosion comparable to the blast from a stick of dynamite."[54] No definite conclusions have been drawn except the recognition of need for greater knowledge.

Pipelines. Oil and gas pipelines, by contrast, have had a long record of successful experience. In the United States there are over 165,000 miles of oil pipelines and 850,000 miles of natural gas lines. Breaks, explosions, and seepage do occur, of course; and there are efforts by various groups to secure tighter standards and enforcement authority. But as far as one can judge, the safety record seems by and large to have been reasonably good. The intense debate over the proposed trans-Alaska oil pipeline is a special case, for it poses a combination of safety and esthetic issues not encountered previously: permafrost subsidence, a scarred landscape, earthquake risks, and intrusion into a "pure" ecological habitat. On the other hand, as the problem of securing energy supplies compels

[52] The figures are from various issues of British Petroleum Company, Ltd., *Statistical Review of the World Oil Industry* (annual).

[53] Philip Mandel, "Mammoth Tankers," *Technology Review*, February 1971, p. 13.

[54] U.S. Department of the Interior, Bureau of Mines press release, January 10, 1971; a subsequent study by the Shell Pipe Line Corp. discounts this danger (*Oil and Gas Journal*, Feb. 28, 1972, p. 24).

the extension of pipelines into other remote and hitherto unspoiled regions, the recent debate may simply be a foreshadowing of things to come.

Electric Transmission. Problems associated with the transport of electrical energy are almost entirely esthetic. Even if electricity generation entailed no environmental problems, the trend toward ever-larger generating facilities and a cross-country network of multiple-strand transmission lines offers anything but a cheerful visual prospect. Power plants situated closer to load centers might reduce transmission requirements in many cases, but the trend is now toward more remote siting. This trend—dictated by the cost of urban real estate, objections to fossil fuel combustion emissions, and anxiety over the location of nuclear plants in heavily populated areas—is facilitated by long-distance high-voltage technologies.

Of course, remote siting also presents emission problems, and it does mean somewhat more energy required per unit of load center demand met. One should note, however, that increased size of power plants in the United States[55] not only achieves increased scale economies in operation but also will greatly reduce the absolute number of plants required and lower the required space per unit of power production capacity.

Many feel that the problems of public acceptance of larger station size and more extensive transmission lines can be minimized by long advance planning, by public participation in the decision, and perhaps by innovations in industrial design and landscaping. Efforts might also be made to integrate such facilities within broader industrial complexes. It has also been suggested that stations may be located offshore on man-made islands or underwater in coastal locations or underground on inland locations. Transmission line rights-of-way could be shared with pipelines or other carriers and more effectively blended into the landscape. Already 300,000 miles of such lines occupy 4 million acres in the United States; by 1990, the 500,000 miles projected are expected to require 7 million acres.[56] It may prove possible with advances in technology to achieve economic means of placing lines underground. Because of the various governmental agencies and jurisdictions involved in siting, it has been suggested that the companies need a "one-step" process and a single public authority that, while protecting the public interest, can nevertheless give a positive response to a siting proposal instead of forcing the company to deal with those who can only veto it.

Nuclear Fuels. As table 16 shows, over one-half of worldwide electric power output may be atomic by the year 2000. According to U.S. government esti-

[55]It is estimated that of the 255 new stations in the United States required by 1990, 27 of 91 fossil-fueled facilities and 78 of 164 nuclear plants will be of 2,000 mw size and over. (Office of Science and Technology, *Electric Power and the Environment [1970]*, p. 5.)

[56]Ibid., pp. 21–22.

mates, by just 1990, the United States will have to locate sites for about 165 new nuclear plants, all of them over 500 mw capacity, with a significant portion exceeding 3,000 mw.[57] If the projection of worldwide nuclear generating capacity by the end of the century of 3.2 million mw is reasonable, it is equally reasonable to expect the presence by that time of some 3,200 large nuclear power stations (assuming average capacity of 1,000 mw) around the globe. Numerous environmental problems are implied by these developments quite apart from any persistent problems regarding radiation emissions to air and water resulting from routine power-generating operations (see "Nuclear Power Plants" section below).

As for transport, if approximately one-third of the nuclear plants are to undergo annual reloading of their fuel cores,[58] the volume of nuclear fuel handling and management would be very great, with a particularly critical part of the process centering on transportation, reprocessing, and disposal of radioactive materials. In the recent report of the Study of Critical Environmental Problems (SCEP) group, it is noted that "probably the major potential for nuclear contamination of the environment will occur at the site of the fuel-reprocessing plants. Here, as the protective claddings and shields are removed to enable fuel recovery, fission and activation products are exposed and the potential for escape into the environment is increased."[59] The SCEP group cited one estimate that 99.9 percent of all radionuclides entering the environment are released from fuel reprocessing plants. Where nuclear fuel management occurs in countries with political instability or less-sophisticated technological traditions, the normal problems of nuclear fuel handling may be compounded. The assumption behind these quantitative estimates is that breeder reactors will take on an important role; thus the monitoring and containment of plutonium will become an enormous responsibility. Finally, irrespective of reactor technology, durable and technically feasible institutional approaches will have to be devised for the burial of long-lived radioactive wastes.

Energy Conversion and Utilization

Energy conversion is the transformation from one energy form to another (as in fossil fuel combustion to generate electricity). Utilization is the ultimate

[57]Office of Science and Technology, *Considerations Affecting Steam Power Plant Site Selection* (1968), p. 5.

[58]"From a 1,000 MW station, the fission product quantity after three years of steady operation is of the order of 4 tons, and can be physically confined in a single (albeit red-hot) carload." (B. I. Spinrad, "The Role of Nuclear Power in Meeting World Energy Needs," in *Environmental Aspects of Nuclear Power Stations*, Proceedings of a Symposium, UN, New York, August 1970 [Vienna: International Atomic Energy Agency, 1971], p. 70.)

[59]*Man's Impact on the Global Environment: Assessment and Recommendations for Action*, Report of the Study of Critical Environmental Problems sponsored by the Massachusetts Institute of Technology (MIT Press, 1970), p. 290.

consumption of energy to produce useful work (as in the consumption of fuels in driving automobiles). Ultimate consumption, however, does not necessarily refer to "final demand," as that term is used in economic accounting. This is because consumption, say, in the combustion of fuels to produce process heat used in glassmaking, satisfies our use of the term "consumption," since what is involved is the utilization of energy in the production of goods and services rather than in its own further transformation. This explains why it is appropriate to consider energy conversion and utilization jointly; in many cases, combustion—and hence the emission of pollutants—is the same no matter whether conversion or utilization is taking place.

Here, the points to be made will be organized around the environmental implications of three categories: fossil fuel combustion in stationary sources; nuclear power plants; and, finally, energy consumption in mobile sources. In some cases the environmental residuals are common to several categories (e.g., heat emissions from fossil-fueled plants and nuclear plants or nitrogen oxides from fossil-fueled stationary combustion or from automobiles).

Combustion in Stationary Sources: Fossil Fuels. The stationary sources burning coal, oil, and gas comprise power stations; coke ovens; blast furnaces, as well as combustion associated with other iron- and steel-making operations; other manufacturing activities; refinery operations; and domestic and commercial establishments (the latter largely involving combustion for space heating). The major pollutants emitted from stationary fossil fuel combustion (along with industrial processes), are seen in lines 2 and 3 in table 18 to be sulfur oxides, nitrogen oxides, and particulates, with the industrial process category contributing a sizable quantity of hydrocarbons and carbon monoxide (which will be taken up in connection with transport, where they loom much larger).

Along with transportation, items 2 and 3 in table 18 are clearly major sources of air pollution in the United States. In addition to the pollutants indicated in the table, fossil fuel combustion releases waste heat and carbon dioxide. Waste heat is significant primarily because of the increased temperature produced in water adjacent to power plants (and other stationary heat converters), while increased carbon dioxide in the atmosphere is of some concern to scientists because of uncertainty about its long-term climatological consequences via the "greenhouse" effect. (This refers to the heating up of the earth's atmosphere when ultraviolet rays from the sun penetrate the overhanging blanket of carbon dioxide, while infrared rays from the earth are blocked by it. There may be some compensation, however, because particulates may reflect ultraviolet rays.)

Within the stationary fossil fuel combusion and industrial process categories shown in table 18, power stations are the most important in terms of the quantities of fuels consumed. Power stations account for about one-third of the

Table 18. Estimated Nationwide Emissions, United States, 1968

(*million short tons*)

Source	Carbon monoxide	Particulates	Sulfur oxides	Hydro-carbons	Nitrogen oxides
1. Transportation	63.8	1.2	0.8	16.6	8.1
2. Fuel combustion[a] (stationary)	1.9	8.9	24.4	0.7	10.0
3. Industrial processes[b]	9.7	7.5	7.3	4.6	0.2
4. Solid waste disposal	7.8	1.1	0.1	1.6	0.6
5. Miscellaneous[c]	16.9	9.6	0.6	8.5	1.7
Total	100.1	28.3	33.2	32.0	20.6

[a] Largely power plants, but including residential-commercial heating and minor items.
[b] Major components are primary metal manufacturing, chemicals, and oil refining.
[c] Including, as major items, forest fires and agricultural burning.

SOURCE: Council on Environmental Quality, *Environmental Quality*, First Annual Report (August 1970), p. 63.

total stationary combustion energy consumption in the United States and a roughly similar proportion in numerous other advanced countries. Because of their disproportionately high requirements for water for cooling purposes (under prevailing "once-through" cooling methods), power stations are the major source of thermal effluents. Waste heat release is the principal environmental effect common to both fossil-fueled and nuclear power stations; in fact, since the latter currently operate at substantially lower efficiencies than fossil-fueled generating plants, they produce relatively higher amounts of heat per kilowatt-hour of power generated. Power plants also account for a preponderant share of the sulfur oxide emissions, though in certain metropolitan areas, residential space heating is an important contributor to sulfur oxides in the area.

The effect of stationary combustion emissions varies with the type of pollutant, as does the technology and understanding necessary to deal with these effects. While the exact biological consequences of sulfur dioxide are not completely understood (complicating the specification of air quality standards), it is widely recognized that sulfur dioxide can be harmful to persons suffering from lung ailments and other diseases.

Of the three fossil fuels, natural gas, as delivered to the user, has the least sulfur content, which explains why it might be viewed as an ideal fuel for steam electric plants. But natural gas is now in short supply in the United States, a stringency that is likely to endure for some time. By contrast, many types of coal and oil are by nature excessively high in sulfur. The principal solution to the problem is believed to lie in technologies (now in various stages of research) for the removal of sulfur dioxide from the furnace gases produced during combustion—for example, removal by stack scrubbing. Additional alternatives involve the removal of sulfur from fuels beforehand or the dispersion and dilution of

sulfur in the air following combustion. But an adequate amount of prior sulfur removal is believed to be quite costly, while post-combustion dispersal may not be sufficiently effective to meet stringent anti-pollution standards, particularly as the volume of emissions increases over time. In practice, a mix of these different methods may be appropriate, depending on particular circumstances. Although, for the moment, the feasibility of various measures is limited by technology, cost factors may in time constitute the major uncertainty.

Major components of particulate discharges are the fly ash and furnace ash from oil- and coal-burning power plants. The principal environmental impact of these discharges is that they are emitted into the atmosphere and to surrounding property, which is dirtied and otherwise harmed in the process. The 297 million tons of coal burned for electric power in the United States in 1968 produced roughly 30 million tons of these wastes—a ten-to-one ratio,[60] though of these 30 million tons, only a fractional (if not negligible) portion is actually emitted, the preponderant share being gathered by dust collectors. Different types of control equipment have been developed to combat particulate discharges, e.g., electrostatic precipitators, scrubbers, and mechanical separators. There is a promise of steady improvement in the efficiency of these devices.

In emissions of nitrogen oxides, which are common to both stationary and automotive combustion, natural gas is again the least offensive fuel. Nitrogen oxides are the chemicals incriminated in the formation of eye-irritating photochemical smog. They are also believed to be harmful to cell tissues, especially lungs. Research into means to control nitrogen oxides is not at all well advanced, and there is little promise of an early solution to the problem.

Heat emissions are particularly a problem of electric generating plants; and it is this concentrated dosage of heat rejection in certain areas, such as densely populated metropolitan centers, that some authorities believe may cause serious localized climatic perturbations long before the heat rejection that necessarily accompanies *all* energy use becomes a general problem to be reckoned with. Fossil-fueled power plants convert only about 35–40 percent of heat input into electric energy (with nuclear plants, the proportion is still lower). Most of the balance of the heat is discharged into the air or water in the vicinity of the plant. The resulting thermal pollution is not at all well understood with respect to its ecological effects. Possibly the presence of waste heat in waters is beneficial to some forms of water life in certain stages of their life cycle and detrimental to others.[61] Also, its effects will vary greatly from place to place, depending on the original temperature of the waters and the season of the year.

Given the projected U.S. demand for electricity and the greatly increased use of nuclear plants for generation (see table 16), it is possible that "more than 10

[60]*Economy, Energy, and the Environment*, p. 109.

[61]Ibid., p. 95.

times as much heat will be rejected to cooling water in 2000 as is being rejected now. Even with greatly increased use of brines and sea water for cooling, the demands for fresh cooling water [i.e., with once-through cooling] would be larger than could be supplied."[62] However, with sufficient investment in recirculation systems that are needed to avoid heat rejection into water bodies by steam electric power plants—and such expenditures may constitute a significant share of future stream-quality maintenance costs—a more sanguine outlook may be warranted.

Successfully coping with the thermal pollution problem appears to depend on the use of cooling ponds and evaporative cooling towers (the latter are standard in Great Britain). There would an incremental cost, which has been estimated at 0.4 mills per kwh.[63] Dry cooling towers, which are considerably more costly, produce no evaporative water loss and give off only dry heat to the atmosphere. In time, more efficient electric-generating modes (e.g., magnetohydrodynamics) and more productive uses of waste heat (e.g., dual-purpose electric power-process steam plants) would serve to mitigate thermal pollution.

Carbon dioxide emissions are directly related to the combustion of fossil fuels, varying somewhat with the respective carbon content of coal, oil, and gas and the completeness of the combustion achieved. As with nitrogen oxides, carbon dioxide emissions are common to both stationary and automotive energy consumption, except that in the latter case release prior to absorption in the atmosphere is in the form of dangerous carbon monoxide gases. As pointed out earlier, carbon dioxide emissions are of concern because of their uncertain, long-range climatological impact. It is feared that, via the greenhouse effect, eventual overheating of the earth's atmosphere may occur. The SCEP group was sanguine about the absence of global climatic problems for the remainder of this century, even though fossil fuel combustion is projected to increase (see table 16), and hence carbon dioxide emissions may rise by roughly 3.5–4 percent yearly. The SCEP group did view with some apprehension the cumulative release of carbon dioxide implicit in the combustion of world fossil fuel resources beyond the year 2000 and therefore urged that we undertake to learn more about this problem.[64]

Concern over the environmental aspects of nuclear power plant operation[65] arises from two factors: (1) the risk of a major catastrophe involving accidental rupture of the reactor and its containment sphere and the dispersal of its radio-

[62]Mills, Perry, and Johnson, "Management of Fuels," p. 146.

[63]Ibid., p. 133.

[64]*Man's Impact on the Global Environment*, p. 54.

[65]The interested reader will find an enormous amount of factual information as well as the representation of different viewpoints in *Environmental Effects of Producing Electric Power*, Hearings before the Joint Committee on Atomic Energy, pt. 1, 91 Cong. 1 sess. (1969), and pt. 2, 91 Cong. 2 sess. (1970).

active contents to the surroundings; and (2) anxiety over low-level, though persistent, radioactive emissions. While it is possible to conceive of accidents of catastrophic dimensions (in which case no one disputes the fact that there might be widespread exposure to large doses of radiation, with all its well-publicized hazards), the probability of such accidents is said to be tiny by most of the experts on the subject. But not all are convinced of Atomic Energy Commission and other scientific assurances on this score. The debate therefore is over probabilities of major accidents and whether even apparently negligible risks of catastrophic accident should be accepted by society.

In the case of low-level radioactive emissions during routine reactor operation, what is involved is the collection and venting to the outside air—generally from stacks or blowers on top of the power station—of radioactive gases, especially krypton and xenon. Small amounts of other radioactive wastes may also escape and be mixed in with cooling water leaving the station. These emissions are regarded as routine discharges and are well within the radiation limits specified by present U.S. standards. Though some scientists continue to argue that all radiation, including natural radiation in the environment, is dangerous to life and that the increase in radiation incidental to the proliferation of nuclear power plants should not be tolerated, many people now believe this aspect of nuclear power to have achieved a safe and manageable status.

Combustion in Mobile Sources. Motor vehicles are the overwhelming source of the pollution ascribed to the transportation sector in table 18. Of the total 90 million tons of emissions for that sector in the United States in 1968, 83 million tons came from motor vehicle operation.[66] Aircraft, railroads, ships, and other nonhighway motor fuel uses account for the small remainder.

The principal emissions are nitrogen oxides, hydrocarbons, and carbon monoxide. To these should be added emissions of lead compounds, included under particulates in the table. (Automobile exhausts are the principal source of lead emissions in the country.)

Hydrocarbons, the result of incomplete combustion of gasoline, are for the most part believed to be nonpoisonous in present atmospheric concentrations, although questions have been raised about the health hazards of the aromatic constituents of certain specific types of hydrocarbons, particularly where aromatics are used to preserve the octane rating of low-lead gasolines. Hydrocarbons also contribute to smog. Carbon monoxide, under conditions of sufficiently high concentration (e.g., inside closed, idling cars having exhaust leaks), is potentially deadly. But even short of fatal concentrations of carbon monoxide, those amounts encountered in congested areas are believed possibly sufficient to cause cardiovascular changes, dizziness, and headaches. The quantity of

[66] A more detailed breakdown appears in *Man's Impact on the Global Environment,* p. 296.

atmospheric lead compound concentrations has not yet been incriminated as a demonstrable threat to health, since there is no scientific agreement on the exact danger point of such concentrations. But lead, which is added to gasoline to raise the octane rating for high-compression engines, is known to be highly poisonous, and with the steadily increasing volume of automotive traffic there is great apprehension about the possible effects of lead. Moreover, compliance with U.S. government standards for 1975 emissions of carbon dioxide and hydrocarbons will most probably compel the elimination or severe reduction of gasoline lead content, for lead has been found to impair the efficiency of the catalytic converters designed to lower emissions of these pollutants.

The automobile has shaped the U.S. style of life and the structure of metropolitan areas; and, with a lag, it is imposing similar effects on the rest of the world. Even though the increase of automotive transport in the United States and elsewhere is assumed to fall below recent growth rates, the projections imply that without a change in fundamental patterns the world of the year 2000 will contain over 1 billion conventionally fueled cars. If that were the case, emissions per car equal to only 16 percent of those in 1968 would be necessary just to hold the total volume of emissions unchanged. It is impossible to say what cost the automobile imposes on society, or what the value is of the flexibility and convenience it also brings, although its incremental value will no doubt for years to come be regarded more highly in the rest of the world than in the United States.[67]

In the future, there is also the possibility of developing alternatives to the internal combustion engine. Other forms of propulsion receiving attention (each no doubt having at least some adverse characteristics) include steam engines, gas turbines, and battery-powered motors. More dependent on public policy and attitudes than on technological breakthroughs, a major increase in the uses of mass transit would have proportionally beneficial effects on emissions and energy resource savings, e.g., a bus may provide 120 passenger miles per gallon, a car only 30.[68]

Conclusion

The purpose of this very brief run-through has been to identify a variety of environmental effects associated with the use of energy in a modern economy. The focus has been on prevailing or prospective circumstances, without consid-

---

[67]Under the assumptions employed here—a per annum increase of automotive transport of 3 percent in the United States and 7.5 percent elsewhere—by the year 2000 car ownership in the United States would reach 65 cars per 100 persons, whereas in the rest of the world it would be less than 15 per 100.

[68]Estimate of Professor Richard Rice, Carnegie-Mellon University, cited in *Technology Review*, February 1971, p. 53. This is probably a minimum estimate of the efficiency advantages of buses over cars.

eration, for the most part, of the possible effects of major changes in the economic or technological conditions of energy use. An attempt has been made to show that, under these circumstances, no matter what energy source is used and no matter how energy is delivered, converted, and utilized, some adverse environmental consequences occur. Although certain of these effects are, of course, potentially much more damaging or socially unacceptable than others, no effort has been made here to provide any such identification or ranking. That step—which should be as rigorous and comprehensive a quantification of the environmental dangers as present scientific knowledge permits—is necessary to clarify the nature of the alternatives that society faces. It is also basic to the process of exercising choice, a process that compels us to specify the desirable objectives; to determine the costs that must be paid if the objectives are to be achieved; to spell out the means of ensuring the widest possible public participation in decision making; and to devise the institutions and laws necessary for the enforcement of public policy and for adaptation to change as improved knowledge and new technology appear.

Index

225

Living standards, 8, 128–29, 131, 138, 181, 184
London, England, 90
Los Angeles, Calif., 57, 60
Lucas, D.H., 75–76

MacDonald, Gordon J., 100
Machinery and equipment, 7, 157n
Magnetohydrodynamics (MHD), 79–80, 137, 220
Malthus, T.R., 141, 153
Mandel, Philip, 214n
Manhattan, New York, 104–05
Maoist economics, 150
Marginalism, 5, 16–17
Market system. *See* Price system
Marx, Karl, 140, 145–46
Mason, Edward S., 113
Mass transit, need for, 62, 109, 137, 222
Massachusetts, fuel oil regulations in, 122–23
Materials-use fees, 24, 26
Matter, changing of, 126
"Means" and "ends," 141–42
Mercury, 5, 9n, 17, 40, 52–53, 58–61, 63–64
Merriman, Daniel, 130n
Military enterprises, 21
Miller, Herman B., 7n
Mills, Edwin, 24, 25n
Mills, G. Alex, 211n, 213n, 220n
Mineral resources, 6, 9, 17, 26, 31; possible reconstitution of, 18
Mines, Bureau of, 163, 192, 197, 214
Mishan, E.J., 19n, 118
Mississippi River, 130
Missouri River, 60
Molten Salt Reactor, 134
Morrison, Warren E., 201n
Morton, Rogers, 93

Nader, Ralph, 122, 143
National Environmental Policy Act (*1969*), 95–96, 121
National Goals, Commission on, 141
National Petroleum Council, 94
National security, and energy sources, 113–15
Natural resources, use of, 3, 17, 20–21, 26–27, 31, 100, 113, 118
Navy, U.S., 94
Net national product (NNP), 13–15, 27n
Netherlands (Holland), 185, 189
Netschert, Bruce C., 169n
New York, N.Y., 104–05

Nitrite, danger of, 43
Nitrogen fertilizer, 34, 41–45, 60, 62–63, 133
Nitrogen oxides, as pollutants, 4n, 55–62, 97, 100, 106, 217–19, 221
Noise pollution, 5
Nordhaus, William, 9, 14–15
North America, energy consumption in, 178–81, 186–87, 208
North Sea, 209
Northeast Utilities, 130
Norway, energy consumption in, 184–85
Nuclear combat, 114, 150
Nuclear power, 101, 109; breeder reactors, 131, 133–35, 137, 216; consumption of, 156, 159–60, 164–67, 188–95, 204–09, 212; environmental impact of, 64, 78–81, 119, 220–21; generating costs of, 84; heat waste from, 76–77, 130, 218–19; safe management of, 135; uranium for, 113–14, 213
Nuclear power plants, 121, 215–17
Nutrient run-offs, 8, 17
Nylon production, 46, 52

Oak Ridge National Laboratory, 134
Oceania, 178–80, 186–87, 208
Ohio River, 130
Oil, 4n, 5, 76, 89–99, 113–15; combustion effects of, 107, 217–20; consumption of, 156, 159–61, 163–68, 171, 176, 188–90, 195, 204–09; price of, 79; production of, 118, 210–12; as raw material, 47, 201n; subsidies on production of, 26–27; sulfur in, 73, 122–23; transport of, 6, 64, 213–14
Oil spills, 90–91, 97, 108, 211
Okun, Arthur, 13–14
Organization of Petroleum Exporting Countries, 79
Oxford University, 150
Oxygen, atmospheric, 9n, 31
Oyster Creek (N.J.) power plant, 78

Paper and pulp production, 59–60
Park space, need for, 21
Particulates, emission of, 97, 100, 106, 118, 212, 217–19, 221
Patterson, Clair C., 60n
Pecora, William, 93n
Perry, Harry, 211n, 213n, 220n
Pesticides (insecticides), 8, 16n, 64; environmental impact of, 32, 35, 45–46, 52, 62; need for taxes on, 26. *See also* DDT
Petit-Senn, J., 13